Lessons

Crime, Games & Pain

Scott Magri

Scott Magri-Publisher

Lessons

Crime, Games & Pain

Printed in the United States of America

First Printing, 2012

Published by: Scott Magri
Pitt Meadows, BC

Cover art design by Scott Magri;

Cover photos and artwork by Bill Fowle. www.FowleFoto.com

ISBN-13: 978-1-48106-663-1

ISBN-10: 1-48106-663-3

AUTHOR'S NOTE

I would like to thank everyone, good or bad, who was put in place to help me learn all the lessons I have learned throughout my life, because without them my tasks would not have been possible.

I have learned a lot in forty-four years, and all the good and bad that I have done during that time has given me the character that I need to carry on in my journey.

All the headaches I have given everyone over the years when dealing with me have all paid off, and I hope they can see it the way I do. You never know what a person can turn out to be once he or she finally realizes what life is all about.

I still work for the railroad, thankfully, and I have a lot of bridges to mend with the people I care for. It will take time, but that's pretty much all I have these days. Please don't take that to sound like I'm complaining; it's just the way it is. I have a life to rebuild.

Just recently I adopted the Katzie Slough. This means I hope to start a restoration project for the place I used to fish as a kid. I am doing my part, and now you have to do yours. I am going to face huge roadblocks in this task, but I refuse to let anyone push me around, so why should you?

Anything you take from this world you are meant to put back. We, as a society, have taken a lot from Mother Nature and I firmly belicvc I am here to give a small portion back.

I wish you all the best, so bring your fishing rod.

FORWARD

For many people this book will not be an easy book to read, but it's not meant to be. The author has lived the hard life of crime, drug use and violence, and there is no way to make that kind of life easy to read about.

The story is an autobiography with a purpose. The author wants others to learn from his mistakes, and he's hoping that someone just starting down the same path he trod for so many years will read this and think twice about the journey. He's also hoping that those who haven't been down that path will take a good, hard look around them and realize that things need to change if the problems society faces with regard to education, the environment, bullying, crime, drugs and the like are to be dealt with proactively.

In many places this book is brutally ugly, but it is also brutally honest. No punches are pulled, and no attempt has been made to whitewash the truth. Most of the names of those refered to in the story have been changed for privacy reasons, but other than that the story is revealed as it happened.

The language in this book is not beautiful. The book has been edited, but a lot of the author's original word use, phrasing, and even punctuation were left intact. The author wrote this book from the heart, and while it has been cleaned up to make it more readable, every effort has been made to maintain the authenticity of the original manuscript.

In the end, this book could easily be labeled a form of catharsis. The author wrote the book as a means of dealing with the demons in his soul that were brought on by years of drug abuse, criminal activity, poor relationships and over-the-top aggression, and if in the end it serves no other purpose, it was at least a relief to him to finally tell his story instead of continuing to bottle it up.

LESSONS

I have a message for you. They knew the world would be so out of control and full of greed that they had to make someone to pass on a message. You will know who THEY are at the end of the book. Apparently I am an old soul who has lived many lives starting back before the birth of Christ. Every life taught me LESSONS that I would need to learn in order to handle everything they would throw at me in this lifetime so I could write this book – lives that go back to the Egyptian era, fighting as a Roman gladiator, and working in the criminal underground back between 1890 and 1910.

These lives taught me respect, how to wheel and deal, and how to fight. There are so many personalities in me that you will just have to read to find them all. I mention a lot of vehicles and I hope it isn't confusing, but I tried my best to keep them in order. You will have to read the whole book, even if it may get difficult at times, to understand what I'm talking about, but when you finally get to the end, it will all make sense.

I am not a religious man, but I do believe in God. I don't know if he is a guy with a white beard and a staff in his hand… I think he's bigger than that. I come across in this book as having a big ego in the way I tell my stories, but how else could I do it. It's the only way I know to tell my stories. You will see the change in me as the tale progresses. There may be a few people unhappy with the things that I have written about, but it is the truth, and sometimes the truth hurts.

Most of this book was written under the influence of Oxycontin, and was typed using just two fingers. This book was designed so that when you have a bad day you can open the book to any page and find something happening to me; it will remind you that you are not alone. The cover should remind you as well.

Everything I have learned and experienced in this life, as well as in my past lives, I did for you. **PAY ATTENTION!** This is a special, and very spiritual book. If you don't want to change your life for the better then I suggest you don't read this book for it can't help but do just that.

They say you can't judge a book by its cover, but in this case you can. You are about to read a story about the unusual life of an ordinary man. You might find some of the stories in this book disturbing, emotional, or even humorous, but they are likely things to which you can relate. I apologize for some of the language I use in this book but that is just me.

NOW GET COMFORTABLE AND HANG ON FOR THE RIDE OF YOUR LIFE.

1968

I wasn't event born yet when I was involved in the first of the thirty car accidents that have afflicted my life. My Mom was pregnant with me, and my Dad was driving toward downtown Vancouver. When we reached Main Street and Hastings my Dad drove through the green light but a bus t-boned us on the passenger side where my Mom sat. The damage to the car was so bad that it was written off because it couldn't be repaired. We were all deemed okay by the doctors, but I don't think I was.

I was born on September 20, 1968 at Vancouver General Hospital. I now know I was born with ADHD, although they didn't call it that back then, and a lazy right eye. My Dad worked for the railway as a carman in downtown Vancouver, and also drove a cab in the city. We lived in Port Coquitlam at the time of my birth, and my Mom wrote in my baby book that at three months I sat up in my buggy and watched everyone open their Christmas presents. I was baptized on Easter Sunday 1969. My Mom also wrote that at eleven months I said, "Mama, Dada, Bad boy." I also said, "Bye" – and would wave at the person leaving. My Dad wrote in my baby book that I cried like a chainsaw, which is funny because later I would be known as "The Human Chainsaw" and end up on the radio, but you will hear about that a little later. My Mom also wrote in the book that my favourite toy was my hands, and that I couldn't take my hands off of them.

Eventually my Dad was promoted by the railway. This meant we had to pack up our things and move to a small town called Field, which is nestled in the middle of the Canadian Rockies with a population of only 350. The railroad owned a couple of houses there, and we had one of these homes to live in. My Dad was already there when we arrived by train. As my mother debarked, with me in her arms and my older brother, Darin at her side, she asked my Dad, "Where's the town?" and he replied, "You're in it, turn around." There it was, on the side of the Kicking Horse River. My Mom said, "Wow, is this really all there is?"

My Dad's new job was car foreman of the repair track, and head of the wrecking crew, which cleaned up train derailments in the area. I remember Mom telling me, years later, that we had to use powdered milk to mix with the milk we had frozen, to make it stretch longer, as sometimes we could not get to the next town, which was Golden, due to the weather. We rarely had fresh eggs because it was winter six months of the year. When we shopped in Golden we bought a lot of eggs before the winter arrived, and Mom would beat them and put them in the freezer. My Dad would also go hunting and we would eat elk, moose and deer meat all winter.

In Field there was only a small corner store, a small hotel, post office/ gift shop and a school. For television there were three channels and they all came a day late. The antenna was at the top of a big mountain behind us, so when the weather was bad we could not get TV.

Field, B.C. from Burgess Mountain

1969

Dad told me a few years ago that because we lived so close to Calgary, where all the big shots worked, they would show up at the wreck sites just to get out of the office. When they showed up at the site they would line up on the hillside in their black suits with white shirts, looking like penguins.

My Dad was at a wreck site in August and trouble was coming his way. The crane operator was preparing to do a lift on a locomotive that was on its side down the bank. One of the big bosses came up to my Dad and said he wanted it lifted a certain way. My Dad had worked on more than a few derailments, and he knew the right way to do the lifting. Dad told him that if you lifted at the angle demanded there was a chance you'd bend the boom. The big shot (who did not have any experience in the use of a crane) told my Dad to do it his way or be fired. My Dad gave the signal to do the lift, and sure enough the boom bent. My Dad then said to him, "See, what did I tell you?" and called him every name in the book. Demotion didn't happen at that time; it would come two years later when he got into another war with the same big shot.

The train derailment near Field in 1969.

Now Christmas, my Mom had put me in my playpen in one corner of the family room, and the Christmas tree was in the opposite corner. This was on December 29, 1969, and even at fifteen months of age it didn't take long to figure out that if I shook the playpen hard enough it would move across the floor. So that's what I did… I moved the playpen across the vinyl floor until I was up against the Christmas tree, then I grabbed a Christmas ornament off the tree and smashed it with the rubber hammer I had in my playpen.

With the bulb in smaller pieces I was able to eat a piece, so I did. My brother went into the kitchen to tell my Mom that I sounded like a bear. Mom came to help me but she didn't know what I had swallowed. The piece of ornament had cut my gullet, which is in the back of the throat. My Mom went back into the kitchen to get a bottle of warm milk, as she thought the milk would wash down whatever I had eaten. Unfortunately, the milk only infected the cut and made matters worse. Dad was contacted at work and we all went to Golden, an hour's drive away. The doctor there said he didn't have the facilities to handle that type of surgery, so I was sent to Calgary.

The doctor told us to go home, pack a bag and meet him at the gas station across the Kicking Horse River near where we lived. One hour later Mom and I were picked up in an ambulance (a blue station wagon with a stretcher and medical emergency supplies), and off we drove to Calgary, to the Holy Cross Hospital. The doctor rode with me in the back because he thought he might have to do a tracheotomy on me. When we arrived at the hospital after a drive of two and a half hours, the nurses and surgeons were waiting for me at the emergency entrance. There was no time for Mom to give me a kiss before they took me away. Into the ER I went, where they started to operate. The surgeon told my Mom, "You got him here just in time, ten or fifteen minutes longer and he would have died because of the infection." They never did find the piece of glass; I guess I had swallowed it. They had to put me in one of those isolation bubbles so there was no chance of getting another infection while I was recovering.

Mom told me that while I was in the bubble, if I gently leaned forward to bump foreheads with anybody, it meant I liked them – and apparently there were some people who didn't get bumped. Since my parents didn't have a lot of money at the time, Mom spent the night at the YMCA. She said it was the worst night of her life. Dad had a boss friend of his who lived in Calgary, and Mom stayed with them until I was in the clear. I was in the hospital for a week and a half, and then it was time to leave.

Dad had stayed at home to look after my brother, Darin, while we were in Calgary. On New Year's Eve Dad left Field to go and get Mom from the hospital. When Mom got home she took down the Christmas tree and made a couple of dinners before she headed back to the hospital to bring me home. We left Calgary to come home on a day that started out beautiful, but took a turn for the worse. Once we hit the mountains, a storm blew in and there was a white out. It was a good thing that my Dad had ordered two of the meanest snow tires he could find when we first moved to Field. He knew the winters there were long, cold, and featured large accumulations of snow.

During that white out, Mom told me later, she couldn't see ten feet in front of her, and she couldn't stop because of the semi-trucks behind her. She could only keep driving by following the guard rail that was to her right. I was lying down on a mattress in the back when I got sick; I was throwing up and there was nothing my Mom could do because there wasn't any place to pull over. She stopped in the middle of the road, and hoped that a semi didn't hit us while she attended to me. Normally the trip would have taken two and a half hours to drive that distance, but it took my Mom six hours. Dad had sent one of his workers with a work truck to go find us because we hadn't arrived yet. We ended up making it to Field in one piece. I think that one night and that one day were Mom's absolute worst, and both occurred within a two-week period of time. You can only imagine what my Mom went through during that drive, it being the worst trip of her life, but it was a good thing my Dad had purchased those tires or we wouldn't have made it. I firmly believe those tires were bought because whoever is running the show here on Earth knew that my Mom would have that ugly trip to make, and would need those tires to get us home safety.

1970

My Dad was Santa Claus for the town of Field one year, and one year only. All the kids turned up in the school gym over several days to see Santa and sit on his knee. However, he showed up drunk one afternoon and told all the kids that they would get everything they asked for. This one kid asked for a bike, and Dad told him that he would bring him two. One mother was just livid about this and that was the end of his Santa Claus career.

1971

One day Mom noticed that my lazy eye was getting worse, so we hopped on the train to go to Vancouver to see an eye specialist there. When we finally got to the specialist, he told my Mom that I would have to wear glasses to force my right eye to work. In this way, the muscles would get strong by themselves. He said I would have to wear glasses until I was about twelve years old, and by then my eye should be strong enough that I wouldn't need to wear them anymore. He was right, because in grade seven I was thirteen years old, and my glasses broke while I was playing basketball, and I never had them fixed after that. We went to see the eye doctor after the glasses broke, and I had perfect vision and didn't need them anymore. It was a relief for me as I was rough with them. As well, they were the cause of a lot of the bullying and fights I would get into later. I sometimes had white tape on the arms, and sometimes around the bridge over my nose.

Dad was at a wreck site in 1971, and got into another war with the same guy who had caused him problems a couple of years earlier. He was called into the office and told we were to pack our bags and move to the big city of Revelstoke because he was being demoted. He never did tell my Mom the reason we were moving, she just thought it was another transfer.

My parents bought a lot in Revelstoke, in a new subdivision, and had a new house built. While this was happening we rented an old house a few blocks from the downtown core. Revelstoke is an hour and a half drive from Field. They called the place "The Town of Tin Roofs "because with all the snow it got, the roofs had to be made of tin so the snow would slide to the ground instead of becoming a heavy load. I remember looking out the basement window and watching the snow fall. The flakes were the size of golf balls. When I woke up I went to the same window to see how much snow had fallen and the window was white; I couldn't see a thing. It was time to move into our new house and, as it turned out, it was quite handy that we were just a block away from the hospital.

I remember we had a Comet vacuum cleaner that I thought was a Harley Davidson. Still in diapers, I would grab a hold of the handle in the front and ride it down the stairs. My Mom would always give me shit for doing this because the wheels were being wrecked. I would drag the vacuum back up the stairs and do this over and over. My Dad eventually took the wheels off it because they didn't work anymore. I was always looking for an adventure.

1972

My Mom and I went on the train to Vancouver to see another specialist because I didn't know colours, ABCs, and couldn't tie my shoes or do buttons. My Mom took me to Vancouver Children's Hospital Diagnostic Centre to see a specialist, to find out what was wrong with me. I was about three or four at this time. She told me they had her wait in the hallway while the specialist asked me questions. I was stuttering at this time, and Mom could hear everything going on in the office. She was crying, and all she wanted to do was to come in and grab me out of there. The specialist told my mom to get books by Richard Scarry, and not to buy Dr. Seuss. The reason for this was that the animals in the Dr. Seuss books were not real, while the animals in the Richard Scarry books were, so I would be able to see what the animals actually looked like. With the Scarry books you could point to something and try to figure out what it was. Is it a cat? Is it a dog? Is it a fish? The characters in the Dr. Seuss books weren't anything that could be recognized by a child.

Once the test was over Mom took me to my favourite restaurant, the White Spot, for a Pirate Pack. She always took me there any time I had an appointment for something, and I loved every minute of it. I stuttered for about six months after that appointment, but with help from reading the books it eventually went away.

I had two pet rabbits in a cage at home, and when we returned home after the trip I went to check on them. As I approached the cage the rabbits weren't moving. I realized then that they were dead because there was a lot of blood. On the ground to the left of the cage was a stick, sharpened at one end and covered in blood. Right away, I suspected one of the kids who lived next door. I remembered that several months earlier the father had shot our dog, Charlie, with a pellet gun. So knowing that the family just wasn't right in the head, I went over to their house and rang the doorbell. One of the kids answered the door and I punched him right in the mouth even though I was just four years old. I do believe he knew why.

One afternoon Mom had me in the kitchen playing in the Tupperware cupboard, and then she went into the living room to fold the laundry. When she came back into the kitchen to see how I was making out she started to laugh, because two of the cupboard doors were sitting on an angle. I had started to take the doors off the cabinets by taking the nuts off the hinges. If she had given me just a couple of more minutes, I could have had the whole kitchen renovated. Okay, I guess that's a bit of an exaggeration.

One night, I was standing on the counter for whatever reason and jumped down onto a bag of garbage. Little did I know that there was a broken glass in there, and it ripped my heel wide open. It's a good thing the hospital was right down the road from us because I was a frequent visitor. One night at the dinner table, while not wearing a shirt, I reached over and grabbed the hot gravy to put on my food, but instead I poured it all over my chest. Why no one poured the gravy for me, I don't know.

I always liked to dig. One time Mom looked out the window to see where I was and discovered I had mined my way under the new sidewalk. The hole I had dug must have been about three feet deep. She was surprised that the sidewalk didn't cave in on me… just lucky, I guess.

1973

Mom was in the hospital giving birth to my younger brother, Jason, and my Grandmother, Mom's mom, came up from Vancouver to help her out. One afternoon Dad thought it would be a good idea to take us to the park. This park had a spiral slide which we called the "krinkity slide" because it was spiral-shaped. Whenever we went to this park I would normally head straight for that slide, but on this day I decided to play on the monkey bars. I guess these bars were about eight feet tall, and I decided it would be fun to climb to the top, which I did. When I finally made it to the summit I freed up a hand to wave to my Dad… and fell head first onto the concrete. With blood everywhere Dad carried me to the car. He opened the passenger door and put me on the seat, but being in a panic and in a hurry (only natural, of course), he slammed the door on my toes. My Dad remembers carrying me into the hospital, and it looked like we had just got back from World War II. When we finally arrived home, my Grandmother was angry about what had happened because she thought my Dad was not watching us as close as he should. She went after my Dad with a butcher knife. Thankfully he was a little too quick for Grandma.

Some time later, with my Dad out at a train wreck, Mom thought the rest of us should go to the coast and see our grandparents. It was winter, and when we approached the town of Kamloops the train came to a stop. There was a derailment up ahead, and it took a day to clean up the mess before they could open the main line. After we were given the green light to proceed, the train came to a stop again just twenty minutes later because of a landslide. As soon as they had that cleaned up they gave us the green light again, but soon there was another landslide. They were running out of food, and Mom told me later that all they had to feed us were peas because there was no way they could get any supplies to us. It took us three days to get to our destination, and my brother Darin hates peas to this day.

1974

My Dad had had enough of working in Revelstoke and having to deal with those same managers on a daily basis, so he went into the office and told them he was transferring to Coquitlam. We moved to a small farming town just east of Vancouver called Pitt Meadows, ten minutes east of Coquitlam. As it turned out, the only job my Dad could get as a supervisor was back in downtown Vancouver doing shift work. Those managers were so pissed off with my Dad that they made sure he worked shift work until they retired. After that, my Dad finally got the day shift with weekends off, eventually working in the car repair facility in Coquitlam, but that didn't happen until 1981.

We purchased a new house in a subdivision called Wildwood Park. All the neighbours got together and we put up a fence and landscaped the whole yard. I remember the turkey manure my Dad put on the lawn, there were feathers everywhere, and the smell… just imagine. When the yard was done we actually got a letter from the city about what a beautiful job we'd done.

I was always one of those kids who would just wander off. Whenever we went to a mall I always wandered off and got lost. I would regularly find myself going to administration to get them to call my parents on the loudspeaker. When we first moved to Pitt Meadows the only mall close to us was Guildford Mall in Surrey. There was a large wishing pond in the mall, where the stairs were located to get to the upper level. I had taken off, and was in the pond up to my knees picking the money from the bottom. Knowing that the quarters were worth the most, I was throwing the pennies, dimes and nickels back and keeping the quarters. I wonder where I learned this from? Could it be a past life working the criminal underground?

I think my parents knew by this time that I wasn't normal. I would run around the house smacking the side of my face, saying "boozy" repeatedly. I must have done that for at least a few years because my Dad called me the "boozy man." The closest hospital to Pitt Meadows was in Maple Ridge, which was the next town east of us. I was also a frequent visitor there. When you were admitted to Maple Ridge hospital they would write on a card the reason you were in the emergency room; I had two of them filled up before I was eight years old. The doctor reported my parents to the RCMP. Their conclusion was not that my parents were beating me, but that I was just a kid that got hurt a lot.

I remember this one Saturday my Dad and I went to see a house that was for sale because he was talking about moving. The house had a fish pond in the backyard, and I went to go check it out. Dad was talking to the realtor while I was trying to see the fish in the pond. I kept bending over closer to the water to see the fish, and SPLASH, I went in head first. It was a good thing my Dad was standing only twenty feet away and heard the splash, or it would have been curtains for me right there.

Another time, our whole family was out looking at houses. While we were driving around looking for this address, my brother Darin threw my glasses out the window. We looked for hours trying to find them in the tall grass, but with no success. Now I had to go to school for a few weeks until I got a new pair. With one eye straight, and one eye crooked, I was bullied some more. I think most of the bullying started in grade one. I mean, who didn't get picked on for wearing glasses, but because I was so hyper I stood out more than most. I remember getting thrown around a lot by the other kids, and them taking my glasses and break-

Grade one class photo. I'm the one with tape on the glasses in the 2nd row, third from left.

ing them. We lived about a mile from the school, Pitt Meadow's Elementary, and I would run home crying sometimes, and then my Mom would have to drive me back. This only happened a few times because I realized I would only be sent back anyway, so what was the point.

1975

Sometimes I would like to play down at the local dump, which was just past the cul-de-sac to the right of my house. This one time I was there with someone, don't remember who it was, but I noticed what looked like an arrow sticking out of the mud. As I started to climb over the garbage to get at this object I started to sink into the mud. I realized I was in trouble when I couldn't move anymore, and I started to panic. I told the kid I was with to go wake my Dad up and get him to me quick. By the time, my Dad got there to save the day I was already buried up to my knees. He got on his belly and grabbed me, and slowly I managed to wiggle myself out while Dad pulled on my arms.

I always liked to take things apart, and for Christmas I would get a new Meccano set every year. I spent much time in my room by myself, and I was always building something with the Meccano. The last set I got had a picture of a cattle truck on the cover advertising that this truck could be built with the new set that was coming out. Well, I was always good at figuring things out, and how they worked. Since there were no instructions on how to build this I studied it two dimensionally and figured out how it could be built in three dimensions. It took me a couple of weeks, and just about all of my Meccano sets combined, but I finished it, and mighty proud of it I was, too. Aren't pyramids three dimensional? My Dad did help me with it a couple of nights, and this was one of only two times I remember having a one-on-one with him.

"YOU MIGHT NOT REALIZE IT, BUT YOUR BRAIN IS A CODE-CRACKING MACHINE"

From: Discovery News: www.discoverynews.com, February 10, 2012 (from an article provided by Natalie Wolchover, LiveScience.com)

"For example, it doesn't maettr in waht oredr the ltteers in a wrod aepapr, the olny iprmoatnt tihng is taht the frist and lsat ltteer are in the rghit pcale. The rset can be a toatl mses and you can sitll raed it wouthit pobelrm.

"S1M1L4RLY, Y0UR M1ND 15 R34D1NG 7H15 4U70M471C4LLY W17H0U7 3V3N 7H1NK1NG 4B0U7 17."

Do you know that you don't even need to learn how to read or write to be a genius. Not saying I am, but I can sure figure things out way before they happen, and I'm a good problem solver. I'm good at these things, but put a crossword puzzle in front of me and it's like: Six down - SANTA _ _ _ _ _ , and I can't do the stupid fucking crossword puzzle. So don't ever think that someone who can't read very well is dumb, because they might be smarter than you.

The other time my Dad had one-on-one time with me was when he took me to work with him one Saturday. There were always a lot of pigeons in downtown Vancouver, and as we were driving down by the tracks we noticed about thirty of them on the road. My Dad swerved towards them and we could hear them hitting up against the floor boards of the car as they tried to fly away. We were both laughing, and I thought, then, that it was a good start to the day, but really, it was totally wrong.

There was an old clock in the house that didn't work anymore, and I asked if I could have it to take apart. My Dad said sure, so up to my room I went with the clock. After I had taken it apart I had the electrical cord with the two marettes on each end. My younger brother popped into my room to see what I was up to, and I came up with a great experiment. As I lay on the bed and put the marette ends in my ears, I asked my brother to plug in the cord. Well, talk about a recharge. Holy cow! I managed to get one of the marettes out of my ear even with my arms flailing all over the place as my brother just stood there watching me do the bacon. I had headaches for at least three days after that, and my eyes were also sore. No, I didn't say anything to my parents.

We did quite a few stupid things, but who didn't when they were kids. This one time we had a long dowel that was sharp on one end and about three feet long. We had drawn a bull's eye on this piece of cardboard. I was hiding in the closet with the doors open, holding up the cardboard in front of me. This bull's eye was three feet by three feet. I was behind the cardboard waiting for my brother Darin to throw the dowel, but it was taking a while so I decided to look around the corner to see what was taking him so long. Well, I looked around the corner just in time for the dowel to miss the target and enter the corner of my mouth. So here was this three-foot dowel hanging out of my mouth, and I had to pull it out. Once I did that, it was off to the hospital again. I think Darin actually got the belt for that one.

1976

For my brothers' birthdays Mom would make special cakes that would take the better part of the day. My brother Darin got a "baseball glove and ball cake" because he was a pitcher, and my younger brother Jason had a "Snoopy" cake. Even though Mom never singled me out, it doesn't take much for a child to feel less important. I never got one of those cakes; I got Duncan Hines. My Mom did put money wrapped in wax paper in my cake, but it still didn't match my brothers' cakes. In my eyes I was wondering why she was taking all day to make these cakes for my brothers when mine only took ten minutes to make. On my thirtieth birthday party at the Keg restaurant in Maple Ridge, Mom was there and surprised me with a Snoopy cake. She gave me this in front of the thirty people who were there, and said to me, "Remember, I used to make these for your birthday." I just said, "Sure Mom, I do. Thanks."

The Snoopy cake my little brother got for his birthday party one year.

My Mom had hung up pictures of us three boys in the family room; at least she thought that all three of us were on the wall. For about a year I never said anything, but she had hung up a picture of Darin and two pictures of Jason. I eventually asked my Mom, "Am I a part of the family?" How could she make a mistake like that? But it WAS just a mistake. Even though my Mom and I spent a lot of time together because of the problems in school and having ADHD, it doesn't take much to feel like you were kicked to the curb. But I know my Mom did not do these little things on purpose, she was just too busy. Really, I couldn't have asked for a better mother.

My Mom signed me up for Beavers, figuring it would be good for me because I didn't have many friends. She actually was one of the leaders, with the nickname "Bubbles." All the leaders had nicknames to make it easier for us to call them when needed. Beavers wasn't much fun for me because every time I went we would play a game, and every time they picked two captains who would then pick the teams. I was always the last one picked, and anybody who has had that happen to them knows what it's like to have the word "loser" screaming in their head.

Our Beavers club had a field trip to the Canada Games pool, and my Dad volunteered to be a driver. This was an Olympic-sized pool with three diving platforms set at different heights. The top one was closed because it was just too high for the public to use, and for liability issues. I decided to climb the ladder to the second highest platform. Once up there, I walked to the end of the platform. It seemed like I was standing atop the Empire State building, when really I guess it was only about forty to fifty feet. While I was standing there looking at the water my Dad shouted, "Jump!" But I dove. Being just eight years old I didn't know how to dive so I didn't bring my arms together in front of me; they stayed at my sides. When I hit the water I thought I'd hit the concrete. I couldn't see, but I knew the edge of the pool was to my right so that's where I headed. When I got there and grabbed onto the edge my eyes started to open and I could see my Dad

Me, in my Beavers uniform, with Santa in our school gym.

laughing, and heard him saying, “I said jump not dive.” As he pulled me out of the water and we headed to the showers I looked back; there was so much blood in the water you would have thought I was attacked by a great white shark.

1977

It was early December and we were heading out to cut a Christmas tree. My older brother and I were waiting beside the house with an axe, and while waiting we took turns chopping one of the big cedar trees we had. Dad came outside to get us to leave, but that didn't happen. My brother and I both got the belt for that, and had to wait a week to go tree shopping.

The problem with most of the kids these days is that their parents are told they can't discipline the kids anymore, so now when you tell them to do something they tell you to fuck off or they will call the cops. My Mom would tell me later that when we went to someone else's house, people always commented on how well behaved we were, and what good manners we had. Today, there is no such thing as Mom saying, "Wait until your Dad gets home." In today's world, it seems that the only thing parents can do is take away their shit. What else can they do?

With my Dad working shift work, any free time he had he was busy with Darin and his sports. My Mom spent a lot of time raising Jason so I would find things to do to amuse myself. I always liked to dig, and I think the reason for this was to help take out all the anger that would build up through the day, or maybe it's because of how hard I worked, thousands of years ago in other lives. I remember digging this huge hole in the backyard beside the fence. It had to be four feet deep, ten feet long and eight feet wide. It took the better part of the day to accomplish this. When my Dad came home from work he opened the back door and laughed at what I'd done. He couldn't believe that I'd dug this myself, and told me to fill it back in.

Now, I'd dug this hole in a spot that wasn't in the way of anything because the plan was to make a fort out of it. After filling in the hole, which took me til dark, I decided the next day I would dig it up again…, but I had a better plan. I got up after my Dad left for work and, with blisters on my hands, started digging the hole out again. I was never one to run into the house after I cut myself to get a bandage; I actually looked forward to the hospital. I knew that every time that needle went in it would just make me tougher. Anyway, it was easy the second time digging that hole because the soil was soft and loose. Once the hole was dug, I found some plywood at the side of the house. I used the plywood to cover up the hole and pushed the dirt over it. I cut a small piece so I had an entrance and all I had to do was remove a small bit of dirt to get in. This hole was bigger than the first so there was a lot of dirt I had to spread around the area to hide the fact there was a hole there. This was my safe place where I did a lot of thinking.

I would play with my Tonka dump truck and front end loader in there, or just sit, think and cry. I never dreamed of being a fireman or a police officer, or anything else a boy usually wanted to be, because I was too busy just trying to survive on a day-to-day basis to worry about who I was going to become.

My grandparents had a place down at Boundary Bay, and when we visited them, the first thing I would do was head for my Grandpa's storage shed, grab a big shovel, and head for the sandbars, passing all the other kids with their small shovels and buckets. I would stay out there all day and dig until my Mom would have to yell out my name when it was time to leave. Isn't it something that when they built pyramids, they built ramps with sand so they could get the rocks to each level? Once they were built, they dug all the sand out.

My bother Darin played baseball and soccer, and my Dad thought he would sign me up for tee-ball. I played for Hales Lumber and, as you can guess, I was an outfielder. I knew I wasn't good enough to play any other position so I sat in the outfield with my legs crossed for half the season and benched the rest.

My Dad tried to get me into soccer and I didn't like that either. I don't think it was because I didn't like the sports, it was because I could never fit in. I was so used to being by myself that I felt uncomfortable in a team situation. When my Dad came home from work I would ask him to play catch with me, but of course, the answer was always, "Maybe tomorrow son." I never once played catch with him, but he did try to get me into sports. Maybe if there was fighting involved in baseball or soccer I might have liked it. I don't know what it is, but there is something so far down in me that makes me feel different from everybody else. It doesn't matter what experiences I have encountered in my lifetime, to this day I feel the same. Will I ever find out who I am?

My T-ball photo. The team was sponsored by Hales Lumber.

With the early struggles I had in school it didn't take me long to meet the principal. One morning, as I entered the school, the principal, Mr. Peacock, asked me to come into his office. I sat down and thought that I was in trouble again. This time all we talked about was Egg McMuffins. I really don't know what it was all about, other than the fact that he was trying to gain some trust from me. It worked because when I was sent to his office I felt comfortable. It was as if I was going to see a friend.

If I was within a 100 yards of anything bad happening the teachers always blamed me for it. While in grade three the teacher had me go to a special learning class for math and spelling. I would always try to be the class clown because this helped hide the pain I held inside me. I still do it today. I was the only one in this class, and I don't know if they planed it that way because I was so easily distracted, or if I was the only one in grade three that needed this special treatment. I know that this class helped me because I could concentrate without any interruptions or distractions.

Mom told me later on that my grade three teacher was excellent because of the patience she had with me. I could never just cross out a word that I had misspelled and rewrite it; I always ripped the page out and started fresh. I couldn't stand any work that was messy, and because of this I could never finish anything. Well, one day Mom got a call from the teacher to tell her that I had finally been able to draw a straight line through the word that I had spelled incorrectly, and then rewrite it. It took almost a year for that teacher to accomplish the impossible. They say grade three is the hardest grade because it's the grade where you start actually learning something. Kindergarten through grade two are just a daycare for parents. With all the problems with the bullying, fighting and the learning disabilities, I had to repeat grade three all over again. I was not a happy camper by any means.

There was this one girl in my class that I would talk to sometimes. She was overweight and I could see that she wasn't popular because of it. The G&H grocery store was right beside the school, and she would walk over there sometimes to get something for her lunch. This one time she went and bought half of a chicken and sat under the big fir tree beside the school. I could see that she was sitting by herself so I went and sat with her because I could see on her face that she felt unwanted. Even though I had my own problems, it always made me feel good to cheer someone else up, almost like watching your kids open their own Christmas gifts. In 2009 that girl, all grown up, stabbed her husband thirteen times, and she now sits in prison for murder.

Mom went down to the school several times to speak to the principal about the bullying. The bullying didn't stop, so my Dad went down there to talk to the principal. I don't know what my Dad said to him, but it must not have been good, because after that visit he wasn't allowed in any school in District 42.

My Dad decided to put me in karate for the summer so I could defend myself when I returned to school in September. I already knew how to fight, but I needed the self-confidence to bring it out. I remember our karate class had to do a show in the Zellers mall in Maple Ridge. When I was getting ready to go Dad was trying to tie my belt on, but it had to go on a special way and he couldn't figure it out. He started to get frustrated and ended up ripping my suit and just tying it any old way. I do believe this all happened because he couldn't go golfing that day, as my Mom was out having a day for herself. I noticed that everyone had their eyes on me because of my ripped suit, and the embarrassment I felt was excruciating. After that summer in karate my Dad told me not to take anymore shit from anybody, and that it was okay if I got into trouble for fighting. He was only trying to protect his son, and if he hadn't done that, I wouldn't be the man I am today. Thanks Dad

The day I received my karate uniform.

He told me a story about a time he was driving cab. He drove this guy to his destination, but the guy refused to pay so my Dad drove down this alley, pulled the guy out of the cab and beat the shit out of him. The cops showed up and asked what was going on, and once he told the cops what was happening, they told him to get in his cab and get the hell out of there. Now I understood what he was talking about, at least I thought I did. My whole life after that was built on respect and principal.

I remember half of the class failed that year, and the teacher actually got in trouble because the school felt she wasn't doing her job. Repeating the grade wasn't bad because I was in there with a handful of other kids who had failed as well.

At the start of grade three for the second time, the same three kids who had picked on me the previous year went for me and threw me to the ground. When Paul, one of the three, tried to jump on me, I brought my right foot up and kicked him right in the face; I think I broke his nose. There was blood everywhere, and the sight of the blood made the other two run while Paul went crying for help. After that the whole school knew what I had done, and these bullies thought twice before messing with me again. I realized then that if I fought it would get me attention, but I know now it was the wrong kind. This, I believe, was the start of all the hell that would come my way through life, and it all came from bullying.

In our neighbourhood, there was a small stream called the Katzie Slough. The name came from the Indian reserve that was just down the road from where we lived. I would fish and play down there because there were trout, crayfish, catfish, carp and frogs in this slough. It is now just a ditch, and the government just built a huge bridge over the Fraser River that links Pitt Meadows with Langley. This bridge travels beside the Katzie slough. All the construction that happened around that slough was sad to see. I spent a lot of my time there; it was another safe place for me. I went back to find my old fishing spot in 2011, and what a spiritual experience that was, but you will read about that later.

I came home with a frog from the slough one time, and had put it in a box with some grass and water. This kid down the street, Brian, wanted to buy the frog from me for five cents, but I told him twenty-five cents. I had to go in for dinner, and when I came out to see my frog it was gone.

There was a nickel sitting on a brick where I had the box so I knew who had taken it. I got on my bike and went down to his house to get it back. When I got there he had my frog in a bucket, so I put my bike down, grabbed him and threw him down on the driveway. With him lying there on the ground crying, I grabbed my frog, got on my bike and ran right over his face. After I ran him over I looked back and, through the tear-stains on his face, you could see the tire marks I'd made. I had my frog back and was five cents richer. I don't know why I didn't feel remorse for what I did, but I had started to learn not to take shit from anyone. There was some kind of angry monster in me.

I got a new bike one year, and it came with shocks and a false gas tank, but man was that bike ever heavy. That was a special Christmas because I got a new bike and my brothers didn't, so it made me feel special. It was the only time I ever saw my Dad with his arms around my Mom, and they were standing above the stairs in the kitchen watching us open our stockings. Christmas always cheered me up with all our relatives and grandparents spoiling us.

The bike I got for Christmas in 1977. It was an Eliminator *by Norco. Very cool.*

I remember me and my brothers opening our stockings, and finding Brut cologne in there. I still keep Brut on my bathroom counter, and I put it on before I go to bed, but the funny thing is I only started doing this a few years ago. I like the smell of it, and when I put it on it immediately reminds me of that Christmas when I saw my Mom and Dad with their arms around each other, and the new bike I got.

We would go to Penticton for holidays in the summer. My brother Darin and I were allowed to buy one thing so we had something to play with. He bought a skateboard and I got a set of lawn darts. We were playing with them at the campsite when he threw one at me. It stuck in my leg and I remember my Dad chasing him all over the campground. Off to the hospital I went. On that trip we had a tent trailer we borrowed from one of our neighbours. We were on our way home and my Mom had to go to Maple Ridge hospital for something, I think she was just seeing someone there because we all waited in the car. Because I couldn't sit still for one minute I came up with a brilliant idea. There were ropes on the trailer holding the tarp down, so I crawled under them so they held me down, and told my Dad to drive around the parking lot. My Dad just said, "Okay kid, here we go." When my Mom walked out of the emergency exit she hit the roof… that was the end of that ride.

I had a habit of running across the road without looking, and this one time I turned to see a semi-truck coming towards me. The driver put on his emergency brake and the truck went into a slide and just missed me. I don't know how many lives we have, but I think I must have used quite a few of them up by this point.

We headed to Stanley Park one weekend and I took off and headed for the monkey cage. While my parents were looking for me I was getting the monkeys all excited by copying the sounds that they make. My Dad pointed to the noisy cages and told my mother I must be nearby. I had a crowd of people around me watching me with these monkeys, and when my parents got there I was standing in front of the railing putting on a show.

Dad wanted my Mom to get a job so that he could afford the golf membership at Meadow Gardens Golf Club. She found a job working for an insurance agency. My Dad's heart was a little on the cold side after the railroad screwed him over, so there wasn't much loving toward my Mother. I guess you could say he was like Fred Flintstone, Archie Bunker and Jackie Gleason all rolled into one. As time went on Mom started having feelings for someone at work. They started dating even though they were both married, but I guess he wasn't happy either.

On a happier note, my Dad took my older brother and I down to the trailer court because they had a sports day going on there. This sports day was supposed to be for the kids from the park, but they let us attend anyway. I entered the swim race, and when the whistle went I was in that water fast, and finished the two laps before anybody else had even finished one. I walked away with my blue ribbon, and my brother came in first in another competition. The guy running the event came up to my Dad and, in a joking fashion told him not to bring us down there again. I guess it was because we ruined it for the locals.

1978

Dad came home with this mini bike for my brother Darin, and we took it down to the gravel pit for a test run. The bike ran fine when my brother took it for a ride, but things changed when it was my turn. I got on it and started to give it throttle, and when it wasn't going fast enough for my liking I opened it up. As I approached the end of the road I let go of the throttle but it stuck wide open. At the end of the road, and past the loose gravel, were blackberry bushes, and that's where I ended up. Just another trip to the hospital. I should have just lived there.

I was riding my bike in front of the house one day, and I never was one to pay any attention to where I was going because I was always too busy looking at the scenery. While I was riding I was looking down at some broken glass on the curb, not paying any attention to the trailer that was parked on the street. When I looked up I smashed into the back of it, putting a gash on my forehead right between the eyes. It was just another scar to add to my collection, and it's plain as day today on my face. I didn't know about Vitamin E cream until I was in my twenties, when it was just a little too late to hide the scars. My Mom didn't know about it either.

We had this swing set in our backyard that my Dad had built at work. This swing set was fairly tall, and when we swug on it we faced the neighbours. If we swung high enough we could look over the fence into their backyard. The mother that lived there was a real dragon. One day we were swinging and she started to give me shit for looking in her yard. I got off the swing, hopped on my bike, and rode around the neighbourhood rounding up everyone I knew. We all went back to my place and lined up on our fence and looked into her yard. Well, talk about breathing fire… she got out the garden hose and tried to soak us down, but the water couldn't reach us. It was the highlight of our day. She eventually went in the house and that was the last time she said anything to me.

That same woman had called me four eyes the year before, but that was something I was used to. My Grandmother just happened to be visiting when it happened, and this was a grandmother you didn't want to mess with. She was the director of the teen volunteers at a Catholic hospital in Vancouver. These teenage girls wanted to become nurses, and man was she strict, but fair. I came inside and told her what the dragon said, and boom, out she ran to the backyard porch, and she tore a piece off her. I also remembered Grandma calling her a bitch. You've got to love those grandmas.

My older brother Darin had a paper route with the Vancouver Sun. My parents were driving my brother around one time to help him deliver his papers. My parents were in the station wagon, and my brother and I were sitting on the fold-down tailgate when my parents started to have a heated argument. With Dad behind the wheel and Mom in the passenger seat, my Dad started to drive faster the madder he got. As we approached this gradual bend in the road, I started to slide off the tailgate, and I slid so fast that I didn't have time to grab anything to stop myself from bouncing onto the pavement. I just love picking gravel out of road rash.

My brother Darin was always being shoved off his bike while delivering his papers by a bully who lived down the street. Darin had to deliver papers on that street so this was a real problem, and this bully would also steal his money at collection time. Mom finally had enough of this, so she drove down to the elementary school and waited for recess to be over. When the bell rang she slowly walked across the school ground so as not to attract attention, and ended up next to the bully. You have to picture this… here's my Mom dressed up for work, high heels and all, walking slowly through the grass of the playground. In a very quiet voice she told him, "You ever put your hands on my son again I will be waiting behind my garden shed with a two by four, and when you walk by on your way home I will knock your nose to the back of your head." At this point a teacher walked up and asked if there was something wrong but my Mom replied, "No, just having a talk with

Mark here."

The people who ran the paper shack where Darin would get his papers had three sons. They were all older than Darin, so when they heard about the bullying one of them hopped in his car and also had a chat with Mark. Darin never got harassed by him again.

My parents weren't getting along at this time. One day I watched my Dad throw my Mom around the kitchen and that was hard to swallow. I didn't know what to do so I just stood there and watched. I was the only one who saw this happen; my brothers must have been outside. That was tough, watching someone hurt the one who had been there all of my life. I will never forget the feeling that I felt that day, EVER. On another occasion I saw my Mom and Dad arguing and it turned into a war. My Dad was sitting in his chair in the rec room, and my Mom was in the kitchen. I don't remember what started it, but my Mom finally lost it. She started throwing everything from the cupboards in the kitchen at my Dad, and he was just laughing at her while he covered up his face with the TV guide. My Mom stopped when she got to the good china, and by this time the whole rec room was covered in broken dishes. I helped clean it up, and again my brothers were nowhere around.

1979

One Friday my Mom said to us we didn't have to go to school because we were going to Grandma's for the weekend. We packed our bags and headed out. Mom was good at hiding the fact that there were problems with her and my Dad. She did it to protect us from witnessing the abuse, but when she couldn't do it any more she had my Dad removed from the house while we were at our grandparents' place.

My Dad was home when the sheriff came to the door and told my Dad he had twenty-four hours to leave the house. Dad told him to go fuck himself, at which point the sheriff told him that if he wasn't out in twenty-four he would be forcibly removed. When we got home on the Sunday we noticed a few things missing. Dad wasn't home, and then my Mom told us. To tell you the truth I wasn't upset at all, I tried to get a few more days off school instead. I didn't have many feelings for him because he didn't spend much time with me, but I know my Dad loved us kids in his own way. Only once, however, do I remember my Dad telling me he loved me. I was around twenty years old when he told me he loved me, and that was after he screwed up Christmas one year.

One time we were waiting for him to pick us up for Father's Day, and my little brother Jason made him a card. He never came that day, nor did he even give us a phone call to say he wasn't coming. I remember looking over at my younger brother and he was sitting on the couch holding the card in his hands. When my Mom finally told us that she didn't think he was coming, Jason said, "I hate that Dad." He went up to his room and ripped the card in two.

We pretty much went to my Dad's apartment every second weekend, and we would pick up fish and chips on the way home. We always called it the "fish and chip joint." My Dad didn't have much in his apartment so it was easier to have takeout. As we got older I ended up being the only one going to my Dad's for the weekend.

This one weekend I went there and he had a friend of his with him. We were going to a shopping mall for something, and we were waiting for this car to pull out of a spot so we could pull in. As we were just about to enter the spot, another car pulled in instead. I was in the back seat and telling my Dad to get out and rip his head off. I'm going, "Come on Dad, don't let that guy take your parking spot, come on." We never got that spot, but my Dad and his friend were laughing at me because of how wild I was that this person had taken our parking spot.

After we'd found a spot, and walked to the front entrance, I noticed that there were two doors. You would walk through one door and then through another. I asked my Dad why there were two doors? He said it was so that, "If you hold the first door for someone, and they don't say thank you, you can slam the other door in their face." I think he had a good point because there are a lot of ignorant people in this world.

Mom took me to Vancouver to see this specialist about being so hyperactive. There was no such thing as ADD or ADHD back then, so the doctors would prescribe Ritalin to calm me down. Mom and I hid the fact that I was taking this medication from my brothers because she knew they would ask too many questions. We managed to hide it for quite some time, until my older brother walked into my Mom's washroom and saw me taking it. Mom told him then what it was for, and why I was taking it. Once he knew what I was taking he told my younger brother, and from that time on they always teased me about taking my "crazy pills" – that's what they called them.

I only took this medication for about a year, and then I asked my Mom if I could stop taking it. It did calm me down, but I decided that I was ready to try life on my own. Besides, I was tired of my brothers every morning asking if I had taken my crazy pill.

I was in grade four at this point, and because of the problems I had, and the separation of my parents, the school thought that it would be a good idea to talk to a counsellor. The school called up my Mom and asked if it would be okay. Mom thought that this would be a good idea so they hooked me up with a counsellor that the school board used.

Finally, I thought, I had someone to talk to about everything I'd locked up inside me, but I never did open up. I didn't want to worry my Mom any more than she already was, so I never said too much to the counsellor; I always told her everything was fine.

On my way down to the Katzie slough one day there was a deer on someone's front lawn. I noticed that one of his rear legs was badly bleeding; it looked like he had been attacked by a coyote. I road my bike home as fast as I could, and grabbed some rope and a few apples. I went back down to where the deer was, and she was still there - it was a doe. I had to get her trust, and I could tell she was hungry; she was looking a little thin in the hips. I just about had her eating out of my hand she was so close; she was only about an inch away from taking the apple from the palm of my hand. I'd made a lasso out of the rope. I placed it on the ground and put the apple in the middle. Now, I was only ten years old, but I had the idea that once I'd captured her I was going to bring her home and put her in the backyard until the SPCA came to get her. Unfortunately, I was at the wrong angle to get the lasso around her head. As the deer bent down to get the apple I pulled on the rope and just missed her, but the SPCA eventually got her and fixed her up. I had tried my best.

I seemed to be the only one in the class who was always getting lines for misbehaving. The teacher didn't like the words "shut up," and I managed to slip that saying out of my mouth regularly. I received lines quite often for this, and eventually came up with a system. I spent most of my free time in my room playing with my Meccano set or my wood burning kit. Because I always had to write lines, I decided to pre-write some and put them in my book. The teacher would always make me write out, "I will not say shut up in class." I wrote this sentence a few hundred times one night and took them to school the next day. I made a point of deliberately saying shut up that day because I knew the teacher would give me lines to do for homework. When it happened he told me to write out that sentence 100 times for homework. I opened up my book, went to his desk and said, "There, how about 300? Is that good?" He just looked at me, ripped them up and put them in the garbage. That was the last time he gave me any lines to do.

With my parents separated, and Mom only making a minimum salary a month, money was tight. When the divorce was settled my Dad was ordered to pay $87 per child, and he was paying the mortgage ($250) on the house we were living in. Mom had credit at one of the corner stores called Food Mart, as she only made $800 per month. She also shopped at the local grocery store where she had credit. The owner of the grocery store was really kind towards my Mom. The store is no longer there, just three ten-storey highrises now.

This one time I had a cramp in my stomach and wanted to relieve the pain. I found this bottle of stuff called "Heat" sitting on the counter in the bathroom and thought that it would be a good idea to put this on my cramp. I opened it up and swabbed it on with the applicator it came with. As I was applying it, it ran down into my underwear and onto my penis. It felt like someone had doused me with gasoline and lit me on fire. I jumped into the bathtub and turned the cold water on to put out the fire. I must have laid in there for an hour before I felt relieved enough to put on a clean pair of underwear. I found out later that "Heat" was to be used for muscle pain in the arms and legs, not on sensitive areas.

All through those elementary school years Mom would wrap my sandwiches in wax paper. Knowing how money was tight, I could never throw the wax paper or the baggies my cookies came in on the ground because I knew how hard my Mom had to work to buy that wax paper. I felt that it was disrespectful to just throw it on the ground. I always put it in the garbage can. Anything I didn't eat, it always came home with me.

Back in 1978, there was a house fire down the road. My parents didn't know the people at all, but offered to bring the two boys to our house for a couple days until their dad got thing's worked out. Their mother had taken her own life a few years before the fire. Mom donated clothing and other stuff as the house was a total loss. The one boy, David, who was my age, later became my friend.

There was a cow field a few blocks from us where people would party and ride dirt bikes. David and I became little pyros after we saw how amazing his house fire was. This cow field was made up of three parcels of land, and we burnt all three down. The first parcel we lit on fire, we just stood there and watched it burn. The fire trucks rolled in and the chief went right for me. He was right in my face blaming us for this fire because not only were we standing there, but also our hands were dirty. I told him he was full of shit, and that we had been playing down at the train tracks and that was why our hands were dirty. And besides, did he think that we were so stupid we would have just stood there if we had started the fire. He just turned his back and walked away. I was good at reverse psychology at a young age; I had to be for all the shit that I did, and would do.

I remember the feeling, the rush I had in starting that fire, so it didn't stop there. However, we decided that when we lit the other two parcels we wouldn't stick around.

We also took a can of gas and headed to Pitt Meadows high school. At the back of the high school there was a corridor where the smoking pit was. That was our target because it was well hidden. We threw the whole can of gas all over the wood siding of the school and lit it on fire. After we'd done this, we ran and jumped over the chain link fence at the back of the school and watched. Lucky for us the fire went out and we had no more gas to reignite it.

David's grandmother lived in the local trailer park. Down by the storage parking area there was a paper shed where people put their old newspapers. As you might guess, we lit that on fire and burnt it to the ground. When we would visit his Grandmother, we always had a plan. I was to keep her busy while David went into her purse to grab money. We would then go to the local pizza joint or the local diner, The Suzie Q, with the money we stole.

We would also write notes for permission to get cigarettes at the cornerstore, but I stayed away from the cornerstore where my Mom had credit. We would hang out close to the railroad tracks and throw rocks at trains when they would come by. This one time there was another couple of guys hanging out there. When this train was heading down the track, one of those guys threw a boulder at the head locomotive. He had perfect timing because this boulder went right into the windshield. The whole windshield shattered, and the engineer put the train brakes into emergency to stop the train. We didn't stick around to see the aftermath as that was a little too scary, but I loved the adrenalin rush.

This other time another friend, Tom, and I put tie plates and railroad spikes on the tracks. I took a tie plate and used it to pound the spikes into the rail joints. After I'd pounded about six spikes in we laid the tie plates on the top of the rail. We didn't stick around for the train derailment we thought would happen, but as we were walking back along the trail to the trailer park we were stopped by undercover police officers. They showed us their badges and told us to get in the car. Someone had seen us and called the cops. They stopped all rail traffic until the track was cleared. All these police officers did was tell us that what we had done was wrong, and we seriously could have killed someone. They took us home so they could talk to our parents, but neither of our parents were at home. They dropped us off and that was the last time we hung around the tracks.

In this trailer court, there was this single guy named Joe who worked for the Post Office. David and I went to his place a few times and it wasn't good. The first time I met him he seemed like the nicest man I'd ever met. Little did I know it at the time, but he was a child molester This guy was so smooth. The second time we went there he showed us his bedroom. It didn't take him long to get our pants off after he showed us the Playboys he had. He was so patient that I felt like I could trust him, and that I wasn't doing anything wrong. With our pants off, he started to jerk me off, and then grabbed my hand and put it on his penis. He had David and I jerk him off until he came. This happened again, and the third time we were there folding his mailbags, he was giving David shit for something. I asked David, after Joe went inside, who had pissed in his cornflakes, but he wouldn't tell me what was wrong. I now knew this man wasn't the nice guy I thought he was. I never went there again and cut David out of my life. I think that Joe had been molesting David before me. I ran into David a few years later and he said that this Joe had moved to Ontario and ended up in prison for child molesting.

Mom had trouble holding on to babysitters for us because I was such a pain in the ass. One of our first sitters, Maria, had a large set of breasts on her. I went up to her with my hands behind my back and asked her to pick a hand. She picked the left, and I said no, and when she picked the right I grabbed her breast. She didn't give me hell, all she did was giggle, as if she thought it was funny. One day we made up some small, individual fruit pies. I'm not so sure what kind they were, but it didn't matter. Again I walked up to her and asked her to pick a hand. She picked the left and I said no, and when she picked the right I threw one of the pies in her face. My friend and I were laughing our heads off, but this time she got up, grabbed her purse and headed out the door. I went to the kitchen to grab another and ran out the carport door. By this time she was at the end of the driveway, so I ran and threw the other pie, hitting her in the back of the head. That was the end of her.

Our new sitter wasn't too bad, until one day she came over drunk. It was graduation time for her so I don't really blame her for it. When her Mom came to pick her up my friend and I jumped out my bedroom window and onto the roof. Once on the roof I yelled out, "She's drunk!" and the car stopped. All I saw was our sitter's mother looking into the back seat where our sitter was, and then she gave her a backhand slap. That was the end of her.

The next contestant was a girl who was smoking hot. It was October, and my friend Shane and I staged a bike accident. We took our bikes and piled them up on me in the carport with my head resting against the brick pillar. Once we had it just right I had my friend put fake blood all over me (which we bought at the local drug store). With me lying there looking all smashed up I told him to go inside and get the babysitter. When she came outside and saw me, she looked like she was going to have a seizure. I only let her freak out for about thirty seconds before I let her off the hook, but that was enough for her.

I think my Mom got a little smarter hiring these sitters because the next one was like Hitler. It wasn't that bad after I realized there was no pushing this one around. I actually had respect for her, and we would sit and talk while she helped me with my homework. We had her to the end... until we were old enough to look after ourselves. Her boyfriend at the time, who she later married, strangely enough became one of my supervisors at the railroad I would later work for.

That October, my friend and I raided this guy's garden for his pumpkins and I hid them under the couch in the family room. When my older brother went to sit on the couch the next day he could feel something was under there. I came home later that day, and there my brother was with Mom's big stewing pot, cooking my pumpkins for pumpkin pie. He loved pumpkin pie. I can remember the counters full of pies, and there were only two pumpkins left... what a prick.

We always had a nice Christmas tree in our family room every year.

One time Mom wanted a small tree for the living room in addition to the one in our family room. I told her I would go down to the gravel pit and find one.

I went looking for just the right tree. This adventure took hours but met with no success. On my way back home I glanced over at the silver spruce trees that were in our backyard. What I realized was that the tops of these spruce trees would make the perfect short tree. I got out the ladder and headed for the one in the corner of the yard. I climbed the ladder and lopped three feet off the top. When I brought it in the house my Mom was amazed that I had found such a perfect tree. She said to me "You found this down at the pit?" and I said, "Yeah, isn't it a beauty?" Those silver spruce trees were tall enough that you couldn't really tell anything was missing. Mom never did notice what I had done, but I told her many years later and we both had a good laugh over that one.

When Darin would come home, he would grab me and hold me in a tight ball only because he knew I was a little claustrophobic. He did this for a few years until I was about twelve years old, and then one day I picked him up and put him in the kitchen sink, and that was the last time he tried anything with me again. I have to admit that what my brother did to me just made me stronger, all to prepare me for the wars I would face on my journey.

He held me down one time and made me eat Husky dog food. At least now, when I taste something horrible, I can honestly say that it tastes like dog food.

My Dad had made a toybox for my room that fit in my closet. I took it out and brought it downstairs to the family room. Once downstairs, I put the toybox upside down and crawled inside it. I told my brother that once I was in there, no matter what I said or did, he wasn't to let me out. As you might guess, I was going bananas in this thing and wanted out. When my brother let me out, and once I had calmed down, I gave him shit for letting me out. I got back under there and told him again not to let me out no matter what. This time I was in there even longer and started to hyperventilate, and once he realized that I couldn't breathe he let me out. I rationalized that what I was trying to accomplish was that because I liked to fight, I figured this would help me on the ground, but really I was trying to overcome the fear of being in a tight spot. It did help me fight because never in my life did anyone ever get the best of me while I fought on the ground, but rarely did I have to anyway. If you think this is fucked, when we would go over to my Mom's friend's house for a swim, I would pull the cover over the pool and do laps from one end to the other. I managed to do up to four laps under water because it's amazing how you push yourself when you don't have a choice.

This one time I walked into my Mom's room and saw her sitting on the end of the bed crying. I sat down beside her and put my arm around her and asked her what the problem was. She wouldn't tell me but I knew that it was all because of the struggles she faced every day raising us, and trying to keep food on the table. I told her that it would be all right, and that I was there to help if she needed me. Definitely, watching my Mom struggle raising three monsters gave me the strength to get through the tough times I would soon experience.

With my parents separated, Mom thought it would be a good idea to put us in a Bible camp on weekends for the summer. There was this blind kid in the group, and when we had field trips everyone would bolt out the door and leave him behind to fend for himself. I saw this happen the first trip we had, so after that I would sit with him on these trips and take him by the hand to escort him on and off the bus. Even with him blind, I was amazed that he had just as good a time as I was having. You wouldn't even think that he was blind. People who had heard of me, but didn't know me, would think that I was this mean guy, and not to mess with me, but in fact I never wanted to hurt anybody, I just wanted to fit in.

I was hanging out at the pit one day and came across this caterpillar nest. I decided I would take it home so I went and got a box that I could put the nest in. I took it home and showed my Mom, and it didn't seem to bother her, so I put it on the chair in the family room. Mom was cooking dinner at the time and we sat down to eat. While we were eating dinner Mom looked to her left and there was a caterpillar crawling up the wall. Because this creeped her out I looked in the box and every caterpillar had crawled out. There were hundreds of them, climbing all over the family room walls and ceiling. It took all of us about an hour to get them back in the box and outside. What were the odds of bringing that nest in the house and them hatching? That was the end of me bringing wild critters into the house.

It was the first Saturday in June, and it was Pitt Meadows Day. This was a celebration the town put on every year to celebrate the town's birthday. It had a parade, as well as lots of activities for the kids, a barbecue with salmon and chicken, and the day would end with fireworks at night.

After the parade they would park all the floats behind the city hall out in the soccer field. This guy and I decided to try and hotwire a float that the Lion's Club had put together. It was a train they had made, and it had a car up front that looked like an old steam locomotive and about four cars with cages around them so the kids wouldn't fall out, as well as a caboose. This guy was trying everything to get this thing going so I told him to twist the red and green wires together and away we went. As we were driving this float around in the field a parent came running towards us and I bailed out, running into the woods. Couldn't I have any fun?

1980

One weekend my Dad took me to Buntzen Lake. There was a swing on the right side of the lake and I waited my turn to try it out. When it was finally my turn I climbed the rope as high as I could so that when I swung out I would have a high drop to the water. What I didn't realize was there was at least six feet of rope below me, so when I swung out and let go of the rope it wrapped around my leg. The huge knot that was at the bottom of the rope came up and smashed me in the face.

It almost knocked me out but I managed to find my way to the shore. By the time I climbed my way back up the bank and went to the beach where my Dad was, the right side of my face was swollen and my right eye was closed. My Dad laughed at me and asked if I had been in a fight? I told him what happened. My Dad was a tough guy himself so when something happened to me he always laughed because it was like, "What happened now kid." Something bad happened involving a swing a friend of mine, Dan, and I put up at the same spot several years later, but that's another story which we'll get to eventually.

Another time my Dad said he was taking us to Stanley Park. There was a wishing well there, so I rigged up a magnet to retrieve the change before we left his place. I tied a string to the magnet and lowered it into the well while I was standing on the bridge. I only managed to get a few coins before they kicked me out of that area. My Dad and his friend thought that it was hilarious, and so did I.

We had this neighbour who lived two doors down from us who drove this old truck that he had fixed up. He would always rev his motor up as he went down the street, and it was getting on my nerves. As he drove past our house one day, revving his motor, I waited until he was in his house and then gave him a phone call. I told him to stop being an idiot and the conversation got a little worse. He told me in this calm voice to wait right where I was because he was on his way over. I told him to come on over because I wasn't going anywhere. I went into the kitchen and grabbed the big butcher's knife out of the drawer, and went to stand in front of the big living room window. I watched him get in his truck – why, I don't know because we only lived two doors down – and pull out of his driveway. He rolled up in front of our house and I could see that he was looking right at me holding the knife. I just said to myself, "Come on you chicken shit, I'm here to do battle." I was only eleven years old, for Christ sake. He just backed up the truck and parked it in his driveway. Do you think I should join the Welcome Wagon committee?

We were playing European handball at school in gym class and I was right behind this kid. When he pulled back with the ball, the back of his head contacted my nose, and as my eyes watered up and I couldn't see, I knew that he had broken my nose. Back again I went to the hospital. I tell you, when it was time to pull out all that packing it felt that my brain was coming out my nose.

I can't remember what I did wrong to be grounded this time, but it would be the longest bike ride of my life. I was grounded, and sitting up in my room while the babysitter was downstairs. My brother came into my room and suggested that we ride our bikes to my Dad's apartment. At this time, my bike didn't have a seat on it, but part of the framing behind the seat post was a place I could sit. My Dad's place was about thirty to forty kilometres away, but we made it. I tell you riding along the highway all that way was a challenge. My pants were torn from the bolt that was at the top of the seat post; every time my leg came up I would catch my pants on it.

Once we got to my Dad's, we knocked on his sliding glass window to wake him up. He couldn't believe that we had ridden our bikes all that way and called my Mom to come and pick us up. My Mom showed up, loaded our bikes in the back of her car, and didn't say a word to us all the way home. I'm pretty sure I got another week added to my grounding for that little escapade. Oh well, it could have been worse.

The front shocks on my bike came apart one day so Dad took it to work and had the shocks welded up. When he brought the bike back I took it for a ride to see how the bike rode with no front suspension. I drove up on the sidewalk and drove off the curb doing a catwalk. As soon as I lifted the front of the bike off the ground the shocks fell apart. Now I was doing a catwalk down the street with no front tire, wondering what to do. I leaned the bike to my left headed for a nearby front lawn, but I didn't quite make it there and the front end came down, so over the handlebars I went. No major injuries, but talk about road rash. I should have done a commercial for Johnson & Johnson Band-Aids!

I didn't have much of a relationship with my Mom's boyfriend, but neither did my other two brothers. My old bike with the shocks was scrap, and my Mom didn't have much money to replace it. She found me a bike somewhere and asked if my Dad would fix it up for me, but he told my Mom, "You wanted the kids, you fix it up!" My Mom's boyfriend took it to his house, took it all apart, painted it, and made it look like new again. They surprised me with it one day when I came home from school. I knew it wasn't new, but appreciated it all the same, knowing it was all my Mom could afford.

My Mom had brought home a Guinea pig from a friend at work. Jason and I were playing pass from the rec room to the kitchen with the Guinea pig. I yelled at him "go deep" and when I threw him for the long pass he clipped the railing in the kitchen and did a few tumbles in the air before landing on the ground. He died three days later. What did he do wrong? Nothing.

We had a cat named BJ, and this cat was born with only one testicle... the other was in his intestines somewhere. He was also born with a broken tail so you know he was a little pissed off. I had to put this cat through special training if he was going to make it. I would put him in a box and push him down twelve stairs to toughen him up, and it worked. Ike the cop across the street came over one day when I was outside and told me that my cat thought he owned the whole block. I said he did, and that it took special training to get him that way. A success.

There was one guy in the same classroom as me every year who I could ever see eye-to-eye with. He and I fought a few times through the course of grades five and six. This one particular time he and I were sitting side-by-side on a bench beside the gym wall. Why he and I were the only ones sitting on the bench while everyone else was sitting on the floor I don't know. I looked down on the floor and picked up a short pencil that was lying there. With the assembly going on, I broke the pencil in half and tossed it in the air. I had no idea that one end of the pencil had hit him just below the eye. He shoved me and asked why I'd thrown the pencil at him. I shoved him back and said that I didn't do it on purpose. He suckered me in the side on the head so I got up and threw a right hand to his face, and then grabbed him and threw him on the record player. When I went to grab him off the record player to finish him off, a teacher pulled me off and sent us to the office. It was Hallowe'en at the time, and I remember that I was not allowed to go trick or treating that year.

They had a program called "Outdoor Ed", and this program meant that we went out to the University Research Forest for a week and learned about the wilderness and Mother Nature. The guy I fought, he and I weren't allowed to participate in this because of the fight we'd had. The principal made both of us bring our desks to the front of the building so everybody who entered the school could see both of us sitting together. I think the point of this was we were supposed to feel embarrassed when people would walk by and see us sitting there. At the end of the week I asked the principal if I could sit out there longer because I got to see different people every day. He just looked at me and pointed his finger to go pick up my desk and take it back to class. I don't think I learned anything that week.

I was always a grizzly bear when I woke up in the mornings. It was Grey Cup time, and I was at my Dad's for the weekend. About two in the morning there were these two drunken people outside yelling "Go, BC, go!" which woke me up. I went out to the balcony and told them that they had better shut up or I was coming down there. I was only twelve at the time, but I would have run down there in a heartbeat if they had told me off. They didn't, and just buggered off. In the morning my Dad's friend, who lived across the way, called him up and asked if that had been him yelling at those guys the previous night. Laughing, Dad told him it was me.

My Mom surprised us with a trip to Disneyland that year for Christmas. I knew now why she was working so hard, with late hours and other jobs that she did at night. I think she felt that it was her fault the family broke up, and was rewarding us with this trip. We couldn't fly because it was too expensive, so we took the train out of New Westminster. We boarded the doubledecker Amtrak train and headed to Seattle. Once we were in Seattle we boarded the single level Amtrak train and headed to Los Angeles. One night someone put a tractor tire in a shopping cart between the rails. When the train ran over this tire it ripped out the power for the passenger cars. We were all in the dark and they handed out these glow-in-the-dark sticks so we could see where we were going. The power was out most of the night before it was repaired, and then off we went.

We met this man and his kids on the train, and it turned out we were all going to the same motel. Through the week we would meet up and go for lunch, or hang out at Disneyland together. The one kid was my age, and we were sitting on a bench in the park together when Goofy sat down between us. These characters never make a sound, so this kid and

I looked at each other, nodded our heads in agreement, and then we both started hitting Goofy on his thighs until he got up and yelled in pain. We started laughing and ran away. What a couple of cowards.

Sometime just after we got back we were having pork chops for dinner. My Mom could always cook, but this time the meat was a little tough. As I was trying to cut the pork chop on my plate I was cursing in my head because of how tough it was. I left the table and went to the back porch, knowing that the saw I used to cut the bottom off the Christmas tree I had in my bedroom was still there. I had put up this tree because we were going to Disneyland and wouldn't be home for Christmas, but I wanted to come home to one anyways. I brought the saw into the house, sat down at the table and used it for my knife. Before I did this none of us had complained about the meal, but once I sat down with the saw we all started laughing, even my Mom. With all the rough times we had, we always found time for laughter.

I remember this one time I was getting on my Mom's nerves, so she turned around and smashed a plate over my head. I laughed at her and went upstairs. Sorry Mom.

1981

The 12-foot snowman we built.

It was January again, and a few of us from the neighbourhood headed down to Bonson Park to build a snowman. When we were finished with this thing, it was twelve feet tall. We had to get a ladder and take it up piece by piece to get it built. We had the Gazette come and take a picture of it for the local newspaper, but it never did run.

I really started to get out of hand at school. This one time we had a substitute teacher who was a real bitch, and it didn't take me long to piss her off. I was rocking back in my chair and combing my hair when she walked over, grabbed the comb out of my hand, and threw it across the room. I stood up, grabbed my chair, threw it across the classroom, then told her to take it and shove it up her ass. Down to the office I went, and they kicked me out of school for a week.

Wesley was another guy I started hanging around with who went to the same school. We were at his house one day and there wasn't anybody home so we thought of something to try. We went into the tool shed and pulled out a gas can. We wanted to try sniffing gas, so my friend decided to go first. He took a couple of breaths of the fumes and then passed it over to me. I asked him if he got anything out of it and he replied not really, so I decided to show him how it was done. I put my mouth around my hand so it would form a tight fit and started inhaling. It is hard to explain what was happening while I was inhaling, but it was as if my mind took over and wouldn't let me stop inhaling although I wanted to stop. I passed out and hit my head on the sundeck, but eventually I could hear Wes's voice asking me if I was all right. He was looking me over when my eyes opened, and I thought I had died and gone to heaven, and I thought, "Holy shit, God looks like my friend." That was a really strange experience that day, and I never did that again.

I was old enough now to look after my younger brother Jason by this point. When my Mom would go out in the evening she would always put money in the ice bucket in the living room for us to order dinner. It was never a problem, and if she was going to be late she would phone and let us know. This one particular night she was out with her boyfriend and said that she wouldn't be late, that she would be home about six o'clock or so. It was midnight and I hadn't heard from my Mom yet so I started to get worried. She and her boyfriend pulled into the driveway shortly after midnight. I went storming out there and said to my Mom, "Get in here you dog." After my Mom had done so much for me that was hardly called for, but there is nothing that I could do to take that back. Her boyfriend came into the house with this angry look on his face and I knew I was in trouble then. He kicked me, and threw me around the family room, then told me to get upstairs. It was totally deserved, but once I heard his car pull out of the driveway I climbed out my window and jumped down off the roof.

I headed down the street to this kid's house, Terry, who I'd started hanging out with at school. I had his parents call my Dad. My Dad lived about a half hour drive away, but he was there in ten minutes with his girlfriend and two of his friends. Once he'd picked me up at my friend's house, he headed for my place. My Mom and Dad started to argue in the street. He wanted to know what had happened, but what he really wanted was to kick the hell out of Mom's boyfriend with the friends that he had brought with him. My Dad drove away with me, and my Mom had to file a complaint with the RCMP to have him bring me back.

Given the situation, it was a good idea that I spent a few days at my Dad's apartment. When I returned back to school, I learned that that friend of mine had told everyone that I had quit school. It was embarrassing for me and I didn't like it, so I went looking for him. I found him by the baseball diamond playing ball with some other kids. I went up to him and asked if he was telling everyone that I had quit school. He said he wasn't, but I didn't believe him, so I gave him a few light kidney shots and walked away. I guess he didn't like that because he came after me with a baseball bat. It was a good thing there was a teacher standing nearby because I didn't see him coming. When the teacher grabbed him, and threw him to the ground, the bat hit the top rail of the chainlink fence, putting a dent in it. That dent would have been my head if that teacher hadn't been standing nearby.

The cops were called and they took the kid away, and that was the end of him attending our school. He had an older brother who was already in juvenile jail when this happened. The parents were nice, and to tell you the truth his brother was a real nice guy. At least he was always nice to me when I came over.

I had the opportunity to teach some defensive skills to someone else in our class. This guy, Leonard, came to school the morning after his Dad had died. When he told everyone this, kids bugged him that day because no one believed that his Dad had died. I mean, who would send their kid to school after their Dad died. I found out later it was the biological father that he never knew. Anyway, one kid in particular, Greg, was slapping Leonard around at recess time, and all Leonard could do was cover up. This Leonard guy was strong; he had a body like the janitor from "The Simpsons" television show and I was never able to beat him in an arm wrestle. After Greg had his way I went up to Leonard and told him not to take that shit from Greg. I said, "Look at the size of you, and the size of him? You should be able to hurt that guy bad."

I went over what I wanted him to do to this guy at lunchtime. To walk up to him and put him in a head lock with his left arm, and smash his face in with his right fist. We went over this a few times until he had it right. I told Leonard that I would only be ten feet away or so in case something went wrong. I also told him he had nothing to worry about. At lunchtime, down at the bike racks, Leonard did exactly what we'd discussed, and the other kid's face looked like a can of smashed tomatoes. When Greg went running away, crying, Leonard looked at me and smiled. "See… what did I tell you, don't take shit from anyone," I said. Greg later died of an overdose, and I remember the police found tombstones in his apartment. How creepy is that?

I was out riding my bike down Ford Road just after a rain storm. I see this car coming, headed right for this huge puddle at my side. The car went right through the puddle, covering me with a wave. I turned my bike around and chased the car down until it stopped at a stop sign. I threw my bike down, and started to lay into this guy, calling him everything in the book at the top of my lungs. He got out of the car and I asked him to go. I remember the look in his eyes, he was just so blown away at the fact that this twelve-year-old was talking to him like I was, and wanted to fight him, and he stood there too stunned to do anything. Maybe he was scared; I don't know. But he just shook his head, got back in the car, and drove away.

It turned out later, when I started a hockey team, that his son and I would become friends. I went over to the friend's parents' house one day and there was his Dad. I never forget a face and he never forgot mine. I looked at him and said, "How you doing, soak anybody lately?" He got up out of his chair and said that I'd never let him explain. I said, "What is there to explain, you're ignorant." He said that he hadn't seen the puddle, so I gave him the benefit of the doubt and we shook hands. He told me that he had never seen anything like it before in his life, and he told everybody the story. Look out for puddles.

It was summer, and my Dad and his girlfriend, Mary, took us on a camping trip. We were down in Lynden across the line, and what shitty weather we had. We were at this campsite for only a few nights and then we were heading for the Grand Coulee dam. My older brother Darin got into an argument with Mary and she was really upset over it. There were these three-wheeled bikes that had two seats that you could rent. I knew they had this fight so I went down to the campsite office and rented one of these bikes. I road it back to our campsite in the pouring rain and when I pulled up to the site I could see Mary sitting at the picnic table crying. I said to her "Would you like to come for a ride, chick." She had a little chuckle and took a seat on the bike and away we went. We were both laughing because I had the bike up on two wheels as we road down the gravel path. After doing a couple laps around the park, I dropped her off at our site and said, "Thanks for the date."

I was in grade seven and my teacher had my desk at the back of the class… you would think he would have had me at the front. He was trying to teach us something on the black board, and as usual I was acting out. I was tilting my head back and swallowing, making this deep gurgling sound. The third time I did this a piece of chalk went flying past my head. He threw that chalk so hard I heard it wiz by my ear before it hit the guitars that were hanging behind me. I looked back at the guitar and could see that the chalk had made a huge dent in the face of it. I realized that it could have been my head. That was the end of pissing him off; I got the point and lesson learned.

Terry turned out to be a good friend, one I could trust. One night the two of us, and two other guys, Jordan and Mathew, decided to break into the local drugstore. The plan was, Terry and Mathew were to jump the chain link fence to the compound at the shopping center to get at the pop machines, and Jordan and I were to grab the potato chips from the drugstore through the mailslot. This was all to happen when the store was closed. I made a tool out of a coat hanger and this was going to fit through the mail slot of the drug store. We had already cased the place out and come up with this plan. When we all got into our positions we went to work. Before the drugstore closed, they would push the chip rack away from the mail slot so you couldn't grab them when they were closed, but the tool I'd created made it possible for me to pull the rack over, and then I started grabbing the chips and handing them to Jordan. However, I guess we'd set off a silent alarm because I heard something, looked up, and all I saw was this cop van getting air coming right at us with no sirens or lights on. Well I tell you, I thought it was Starsky and Hutch coming up the parking lot. Jordan bolted to the left of me. I just stood there thinking, "What is he running for? We're done."

A stranger walking down the street saw the police and Jordan running, and actually gave him the Bible he was holding, but that didn't help Jordan at all. The police dog caught Jordan, and after the dog had had his way with his leg, he ended up in the van with me.

The whole time this was going on Mathew and Terry hid in the compound and stayed silent. The police asked us if there was anyone else with our crew, and we both said no. They had Jordan in the cop car and me in the van, figuring we would tell different stories. Our parents had to come to the cop shop to get us. As you can imagine, they were not too pleased with the situation. It didn't go down too well. We both had to go to court for this incident and we had to do community hours. Jordan and I had to do our hours at the local dump, sorting out all the recycled items. It was actually fun there.

That Christmas Mom managed to save enough money to buy each of us an eleven-and-a-half-inch black and white TV. It was a big deal, and my brothers and I opened them at the same time. My friend Terry and I would watch the Vancouver Canucks in the 1982 playoff run lose four straight in the final series against the New York Islanders. We also witnessed Canucks coach Roger Neilson surrender to the referees by waving his infamous white towel on a hockey stick on that TV.

1982

The Indian reserve was just down the road from us and they had tied a king size mattress to the back of a four-wheel drive truck. There were about a dozen of us on this thing, and when the driver took a corner the mattress would swing sideways and hit the piles of snow on the sides of people's driveways, and we would go flying everywhere. I was so full of bumps and bruises it took me a week to heal from that ride, but it sure was fun.

For Christmas, my parents alternated the dinner every year. Every second year we would have Christmas with my Dad and his girlfriend, Mary. I got some electronic games from my Mom's boyfriend for Christmas this year. It was my Dad's turn to have us for Christmas dinner this year so he came and picked us up about three in the afternoon. I brought the games that I got at Mom's so I could have something to do at my Dad's place. My Dad never asked us what we wanted for Christmas, so he bought things that we never wanted. Not that there is anything wrong with that because some people in the world don't even get a dinner at Christmas.

But I had the games that I brought with me in a paper bag, and I placed them in the dining room at my Dad's. They were there when I went to sleep that night. When I woke up in the morning I went to go get them so I could play with them. They weren't in the spot where I had put them so I asked my Dad and Mary if they had moved them or knew where they were. They both looked at me and said, "We don't know where they are Scott. You must have placed them somewhere else." I looked everywhere, and I even had my Dad take me down to the garbage container thinking someone had thrown the games out by accident. While I was in the big dumpster looking for them, I looked over at my Dad and noticed that his hands were twitching down at his sides. The look on his face was like he was thinking to himself, "I hope he doesn't find them."

I could tell he was nervous so I stopped looking for them because I didn't want him to be stuck for words when I found them. I know if I had looked a little longer in that dumpster I would have found them, but I still put his feelings before mine. They were nowhere to be found. My Dad hated my Mom and her boyfriend so much he thought it would piss them off if I came home without the games.

When I came home without them my Mom called my Dad to ask for them back. He said he didn't know where they were. My Mom told him that as I had taken them to his place, he had to replace them or buy me something else. My Dad took me down to the Woodward's bargain basement at Guildford Mall and bought me a second hand, re-conditioned watch for five dollars to replace the electronic games that he or Mary had thrown out.

Now it was time for high school and it didn't get any better there either. The vice-principal was a real warden. My file went with me to that school so they already knew what a troublemaker I was. At the beginning of every year I would hear my name on the intercom "Scott Magri to the office, Scott Magri to the office." It was the vice-principal asking me if I would play rugby for him, and every time I said, "Not if you're coaching!" He would tell me that I had garbage duty for a couple of weeks, and that maybe that would change my mind. It never did, and every year was the same thing.

1983

The guys I would hang out with in the hallways at school would tell me to play rugby because that way I could get away with murder if I did. I always told them that I didn't care if it was raining or snowing outside, I would pick up garbage before I played for that asshole. I was surprised that no one made a bucket with my name on it. The VP would wait until I was done on the route he'd sent me on, and then drive it to see whether I'd done it or not, because if I hadn't he said he would double it. I never gave him the satisfaction. I always finished the route, and I guarantee that block was the cleanest block in North America.

That VP kicked me out of school about every other month, and that is why people would tell me to play rugby for him, so he wouldn't be kicking me out so often. But every time he kicked me out I hated him even more. Little did he know that doing this was only making it harder for him to get me to play for him. All he had to do was save my ass just once and I would have respected him… and I would have played rugby.

Every time the VP had to suspend me, usually for fighting, he had to contact my Mom. This one time I dropped my pencil in class but the teacher thought I'd thrown it, so he sent me down to the office and the VP kicked me out for three days. This time Mom had had enough of his bullshit; she told him he should kick me out for a week so I could watch the "Price Is Right," go to the beach, mow the lawn, and all kinds of other stuff. Apparently sarcasm was lost on him because it didn't matter what my Mom said, I was kicked out on a regular basis anyway.

My younger brother Jason would play Heavy Metal music in his bedroom. I hated this music only because everyone in school that was cool would listen to it. With me not really fitting in with everyone, and not being cool, it would piss me off anytime my brother would play it. I would storm from my room and tell him to turn it off. I guess the real reason was that I was jealous that I couldn't fit in with everyone, and I wasn't cool. I even had this jacket done by my buddy Jordan, who painted the Iron Maiden album cover "Aces High" on the back just so I would look like I fit in, but I ended up only wearing it a short while before I gave it to my little brother.

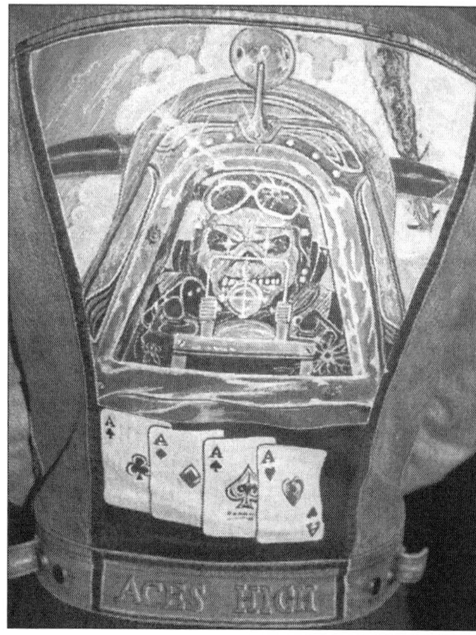

The Aces High jacket that my buddy Jordan Anderson made for me. My brother got it in the end.

I had a paper route with the Vancouver Sun, and when I was kicked out of school, I had it done before everybody got out of school. I delivered twenty-one papers five days a week, and twenty-three on Saturdays. I would flip up the handlebars on my ten-speed bicycle, and they would fit in between the grips perfectly. I only made $76 a month, but the route only took me about fifteen minutes to get it done.

I also learned how to bake because you could only watch the *Price Is Right* so many times! I baked pies, cakes, cookies and my favourite, my Grandma's recipe for "Rinkity Uncles." This was a mixture of brown sugar, butter and oatmeal that was spread on a cookie sheet and pressed down with a spoon, then baked in the oven.

I had this one customer on my paper route who told me to ride my bike across the front lawn, because if I came up the driveway the kids would open the back door to see who it was and the dog would come out after me. Well this one day the kids opened the back door anyway, and the dog came charging after me while I was on my bike. I froze as the dog jumped on me, biting me on the left arm and then biting me on the left leg.

It was a German Shepherd, an old police dog. The dog had bitten the father of the babysitter one time, when he went to check on her. My Mother, while at the police station, wanted to file a complaint. They asked if I wanted to press charges and I said no. The cop said that he could go down there and shoot the dog on the spot but I told him that I would handle it.

I went there the next night and the dog was gone, the owner had him put down. Those people were always good to me, and tipped me well… they told me I was the best paperboy they'd ever had. This one customer I had, he wanted me to put the paper in the mail slot, but the weekend paper was so large that I had to fold it and stand on it to get it to fit in the mailbox. I always got a big tip at Christmas from him. There came a time when the papers that I had put in the mailbox for that customer weren't being taken. On the third day, some guy came down the drive-way and told me not to bring the paper there anymore. The owner had just passed away.

It was spring and the blackberries were ready for picking. There just happened to be a new store that had opened up in the town just up the highway that sold everything that you needed to make your own beer and wine. Ian, from school, and I thought that it would be fun if we could make our own wine. We rode our bikes to that store and the man running the store just laughed at me, told me everything I needed to make my wine, and then sold me everything I needed. I wrote down everything this guy was telling me on how to make wine so I wouldn't forget. Ian and I went home with everything we needed but the berries.

So we went and picked two buckets of blackberries, then headed back to my house to get one of my Mom's nylons so I had something to sift all the seeds and pulp from the berries, and man, after I finished the third run through the nylon, it was clear as a bell. I had everything all done and in a one gallon glass jug that was just like the jugs you store moonshine in. I had the burper on the top, and gave my little brother clear directions on how to put water in the burper while I was at my Dad's for the weekend. What did he do? He took the burper off the jug, filled it up with water, and put it back on.

I thought that now it was ruined and dumped everything down the drain. I didn't know that it wasn't ruined, and that all that happened was that it needed to be burped all over again. Ian said that his turned out okay, and that he and his brother got drunk one afternoon. It was probably a good idea mine didn't work out because I would have had kids picking the berries, and I would have turned the shed in our backyard into a wine making shack. Then I would have gone around the neighbourhood selling it.

This one weekend my Dad picked me up, and on the way to his apartment he told me about these leather jackets that were at the Army and Navy department store. He was telling me how nice they were, and that they were only $50. I asked him if we could go look at them that night and see if they were still there. We went, and sure enough there were still some on the rack. The jackets were motorcycle jackets, and had big zippers up the front, regular $400. I asked my Dad if he could buy it for me and I would pay him back with my newspaper money after I did my collections, at the end of the month. It broke my heart when he said no, he wouldn't. The whole weekend I was trying to figure out a way that I could buy this jacket without asking my Mom. I never did get that jacket. It's not that I'm selfish or anything, I hope I don't come across that way, but I wasn't asking him to buy this for me and getting upset that he didn't. No, it was the fact that he wouldn't do me the favour. I think the thing that I learned by my Dad's rejections every time I asked him to help me out, was that now I do anything for people, but you better help me when I need it. My Dad was never an asshole to me; I just felt that he could have been there for me more often.

It was Easter and I thought it would be neat if I were the Easter Bunny for once. I got on my bike with the money I made from my newspaper route and rode up to Zellers. I had money left after collecting because my Dad had made me a wooden safe with a large lock on it for my bedroom, to keep my older brother from stealing it. I picked out some baskets and chocolate eggs, and had the store put Mom, Dad and his girlfriend's name on the outside. I set my Mom's room up before my Dad picked me up for the weekend, and had all their stuff packed with me. I had eggs on the floor leading them to their baskets, and I did the same for Mom. She was surprised the most, and that made me feel good to make her happy. I would go to the store and buy my Mom small gifts from time to time because I could see all the hard work she did for us. I bought her a coffee pot kit for the stove and would buy her Turtles chocolates, which were her favourite.

1984

Grade nine was a quiet year. I had a go-cart that I was busy with, and then I sold that and bought a Yamaha IT125 motorbike that I would ride down at the fields I had set on fire a few years back.

I wasn't interested in girls. I had fun with my hobbies and motor vehicles. While I had these recreation vehicles there were no accidents to report, luckily enough. God was saving the best for last. The main thing to report in 1984 was that I had to get my nose fixed again because the first doctor hadn't fixed it right. My nose was shifting to one side, and I could barely breathe out the left side of my nose. I love it when they pull that packing out of my nose, It feels so good – "NOT." It wouldn't be the last time.

The teacher that we had for our woodworking class was always stressed out. With Mom not having lots of money I avoided paying for my projects by taking them out the back door. I also confused him by telling him that I came into the shop while he was busy with another class, and that he was too busy to give me a receipt. I got this idea because I had seen him do this to another student while we were in class. From that time on I would pay for things for school with the money I made with my paper route, or the money I made doing jobs around the neighbourhood. I never told her this because she would insist that was her job, and if I let that happen she would have gone without more often. It was bad enough to see my Mom working two jobs and going to work with ripped nylons. My Mom's second job was cleaning offices at night, and we would go with her to help. We sure ate lots of Hamburger Helper, and you would think I would be sick of it today, but I still enjoy it occasionally.

Our gym teacher was going through a divorce and you could see he wasn't having a good time with it. He wouldn't shave that often, and you could tell his mind was always somewhere else. In gym class one day we were playing European handball and just as this guy had me around the waist, the teacher yelled out, "If I don't see any blood coming from you guys, you're all running the dyke the rest of the year." I thought to myself, "Okay" and smashed this guy in the mouth with my right elbow. He hit the floor holding his mouth, bleeding all over the place, and the teacher said, "That's more like it, way to go." The teacher told us that we were going to play football the next class, so on that day I packed my brother's steel baseball cleats. As soon as our class was out on the field I pulled the cleats out of my bag to put them on. The teacher looked at me with a smile on his face and said, "You can't wear those" and I said, "You said you wanted to see blood." He told me that my shoes were overkill as one of my classmates shook his head. Wimps.

1985

I would normally go fishing under the Pitt River Bridge on weekends with a friend of mine, Kevin, or I would go by myself if he couldn't come. Fishing was a good time that I always enjoyed. I could sit there all day on my tackle box and watch the tip of my rod. How I could have the patience to do this when I had no patience for so many other things, I don't know, other than that it was something that I enjoyed. This river had a crazy current and I was always afraid of falling in.

One time I ventured out onto this old log that was covered in algae, slipped, and into the river I went. I could barely hang onto the log. I was yelling for Kevin to help me out. As he was trying to help me out of the water I could see out the corner of my eye that his fishing rod was bouncing up and down. He was grabbing hold of my shirt, but I pointed to his rod and told him to leave me and get that fish. Kevin started laughing at me because of how I put his fish priority before myself; you never want the fish to get away no matter what. He grabbed his rod a little too late because the fish was gone, and I eventually swam to shore.

My Dad bought five acres of property out at Webster's Corners in Maple Ridge to build a home on. I was out there every weekend working my ass off, clearing land and chopping firewood to help out my Dad. I only went with him and Mary to spend time with him. I remember watching all the money exchanges from all the firewood sales, and this one time he handed me a $20 dollar bill. Three years of hard labour for $20. I wasn't there for the money, like I said, but I wish that he hadn't given me that $20 because it made me feel like that was all I was worth. It would have been better if he hadn't given me anything.

My Dad hired a high hoe excavator to clear the land and put the stumps in a pile so we could burn them. The trees were knocked down, and I was running up and down the trees limbing them with a chainsaw, when the operator asked my Dad who I was because I was so fast. Dad told him not to worry about me, because I was staying right there. He actually told me this. Hell, I could have worked for that guy for a wage, but that would have undermined the whole purpose of me being there. Mary and my Dad both said that because I was the only one of the three boys who helped, they would later help me buy a trailer or a condo when the time came.

The first time I got drunk was with my Dad. We were working one day on his acreage when a friend of his from work dropped by with a mickey of rye. My Dad took the cap off the bottle and downed the whole thing, and then my Dad told him to go bring us a twenty-sixer. When he got back to the property my Dad and I drank the whole bottle. We were rolling around in the mud together, and his girlfriend attempted to drive us home. My Dad had a 1976 Ford Super cab with four on the floor, and Mary had a tough time driving it. We got about six miles down the road and she pulled over because she'd had enough and couldn't drive the truck any further.

With me in the back puking my guts out, my Dad got in the driver's seat and took over, leaving Mary standing at the roadside. He told her we were going to McDonald's, and away we went. We didn't get too far because we made such a disturbance on the road that the people living in a nearby store called the police. When the cops pulled us over my Dad threw the keys in the ditch so that if the cops asked who was driving, he could say he wasn't. I guess the keys have to be in the ignition to get an impaired charge. The cop called us a cab and we went home while the cop went and collected Mary to take her to the cop shop. My Dad knew the cab driver, so when we got to his apartment he told him to wait right there because he was going to go get his shotgun, and then go find Mary. He didn't even own one at that time, but the cabbie didn't stick around for the woman hunt.

My brother Darin, who lived across the hall from my Dad, let us in the apartment because we didn't have any keys. They were then able to get me in the tub to sober me up, and Mary eventually took a cab home.

One night I was with my friend Terry, and he had borrowed his stepdad's Datsun pickup. We'd picked up Terry's little brother, Bart, and my friend from up the street, Shane. We were driving down the high school road at night with Bart and Shane in the back of the box. Terry started to swerve back and forth, the tires grabbed the road and the truck flipped over and did a complete 360 back onto the tires. I remember my life flashing in front of me as the windshield smashed when we rolled over. When the truck came to a stop, Terry said to me, "I just wrecked my Dad's truck."

We pushed the doors open and got out to see if everyone was alright. Bart and Shane were thrown from the box of the truck and, remarkably, had landed on someone's lawn. Terry's little brother was crying, but Shane seemed to be alright. The reason Bart was crying was because he had transmission fluid in his hair, and he thought he was bleeding. Once we noticed what it was, and told him, he calmed down and stopped crying. Bart was only four at the time and no one was hurt in the incident. The truck was a write-off, but luckily it was only a work truck and wasn't worth a lot. I do believe that Terry did pay his Dad back the cost of the truck over the course of a year.

Terry worked for a friend of his stepdad making bark mulch near the Fraser River in Port Coquitlam. Terry and a friend of his, Greg, had gotten into stealing car stereos and tires. This one time they broke into the BC Tel impound in Pitt Meadows and cleaned a whole truck out. I was over at Terry's house a few days after the theft, and had seen all the equipment in his bedroom. We took the phone that they use up the pole to see if we could get it to work on the neighbour's house line. It worked like a charm, so we could have talked to China at no charge and nobody would have figured that one out. I was at Greg's house when two undercover cops approached us. They asked which one of us was Greg. Greg told them who he was, and then they asked me to stay right where I was, and not to move because they wanted to talk to me. They took Greg inside his house, and once they were inside I bolted. When I arrived home the phone rang and it was Greg. He was talking in a quiet voice because he was in the bathroom of his house. He told me to go to Terry's house, and to break in and hide everything. I stormed out of the house and headed for Terry's. There was no one home, and all the doors were locked, but I managed to find a side window that was unlocked.

We'd played hide and go seek in their house when we were younger so I knew all the hiding places. There was an attic access in his sister's bedroom closet, and that's where I threw all the phone equipment as well as the car stereos. I hid the set of tires he had in the laundry hamper and covered them up with blankets. I didn't know how much time I had to do this so it was done quickly. I went back out the window, and was back on my bike and headed down the streetjust as the cops were heading to Terry's.

There were about four undercover cop cars, including one with Terry in the back seat. They had gone to Terry's work to arrest him, but he didn't know that I'd been at his house to hide everything. I went home to see if I might get a call. The phone rang and it was Terry, asking me if I had been at his house sometime during the day. When I told him I would be right there, he was trying to make it sound like I didn't know anything so I wouldn't be involved. However, when I arrived at his house the place was full of cops so I told them where I'd hidden everything. Terry was no dummy; he told the cops that he would go up into the attic and pass everything down. Every second item Terry hid under the insulation; he knew that the charges would be reduced if he did this. Terry and Greg were under eighteen years old so all they got was a shit load of community hours. I didn't receive any charges.

Terry and I were hanging out at my place after school and this guy we knew was walking by. Terry and I approached him near the mailboxes and told him to get on top of the boxes and cluck like a chicken before we would let him go home. He got up there, and with his hands on his hips he started clucking like a chicken. We were laughing our heads off. I gave him a piledrive in the hallway at school another time, and was kicked out for three days for doing this. It was all good in the end. That guy ended up playing on the hockey team I would later start up.

Terry offered me his job making bark mulch. It was only one day a week, but it was better than the paper route. The owner would always call the night before and tell me to come in. I never told him I couldn't make it; I always showed up. One time I didn't have a ride home at the end of the day. My Mom would normally drop me off and pick me up at the end of the day, but this time she couldn't. Standing there at the end of the day in hiking boots that were too small for me, I told Derek, the owner, that I didn't have a ride home; I was hoping that he would offer me a ride. When I told him this he just went, "Hmmm…" and walked away, saying, "See you next week." By the time I got home I had blisters on my feet. That was okay because I would come up with a small plan to get even with him in 1987.

One day, after working in the pouring rain all day at the bark mulch plant, I walked over to where these guys were chopping firewood. These guys looked pretty rough, like ex-cons or something, but grown men just the same. I was fifteen years old and asked the boss for a job. As he looked at me, with the cons staring in my direction while eating their lunch under this plastic lean-to, he paused. He looked like he couldn't believe this kid wanted to work there, and neither could the other guys. He told me that they weren't hiring right then, but to check in from time to time. I thanked him for his time and walked away. I never did go back.

At school they had a ski program that I was able to sign up for thanks to my Mom. I was surprised that my Dad actually bought me a ski jacket for the trip. He figured that if he bought us kids anything it would look like he was helping out my Mom, and he never wanted to do that. I mean, was it my fault that he treated my Mom like shit, and that she ended up in the arms of someone who appreciated her.

That's the problem in today's society? The kids are stuck in the middle of the war when their parents separate. Little do they know that using the kids as tools is damaging to them. Look at me now, telling you about it now that I'm older and understand. I have negative feelings for my Dad so learn from this. After all, that's what this book is about.

The school had something called work experience. They had a list of places that you could go and work for a week with no pay, just for the experience. I chose to work for this grocery store called Overwaitea Foods, and I was put in the produce department. I was to warehouse the produce and prepare the lettuce. I wasn't allowed to go out on the floor and help stock the shelves for whatever reason. This one day in particular, it must have been zero degrees in the back room. There wasn't anybody back there but me. Talk about cheap labour. I thought to myself, "Fuck this, they are just using me." So I put a note on the boss's desk and told him there was no one around to tell, but that I was sick and leaving the note to let him know.

The next day he started in with me, and I said to him that I was the only one back there doing everything, and that I didn't show up to be his slave. The boss said to me that he saw my point, and that he needed four boxes of lettuce right away.

To process the lettuce you had to put the butt end of the head into this electric machine that had a razor blade that rotated at high speed, and this would give the lettuce a clean cut and then you would remove any old leaves. I was doing this at a fast rate of speed and ended up shoving my finger in this machine.

I shut the machine down and went to go get some help. I walked up to these two suits who were chatting by the lunchroom, and stood there holding my hand with blood everywhere, waiting to get their attention. Once they noticed my condition you could see the panic of their faces because I was just a student with no compensation. I definitely needed stitches, but I knew that if I went to the hospital that would be the end of any other student working there.

They asked me if I was going to be alright and I told them not to worry about a thing, I would be fine and I wouldn't say a word. The boss patted me on the back, said, "Good man," and walked away. Other workers saw the bandages and asked what had happened? I just told them not to worry about it. Those two managers took a liking to me because I kept my word.

At the end of the week they did an evaluation for the school; it was outstanding, and they also offered the possibility of future employment. However, after I worked there the store decided to cancel the program for the students anyway. It all had to do with the liability situation, and I don't blame them at all.

I was in a special class in grade ten called ISP – Individual School Program. There were other kids in this class with problems besides myself. Mr. Wong was one of the teachers. I interrupted him one day while he was talking to another teacher, so he grabbed a pressure point that was up in my trapezoid area. I froze and couldn't move at all, and he told me not to interrupt him when he was talking.

Another time I interrupted him he threw a karate chop, hitting me in the throat. I couldn't breathe for a bit and he asked me, "When are you going to stop interrupting me?" That was the last time I interrupted him. I learned my lesson. He was a black belt in karate, in addition to teaching the wrestling team.

He and I every so often would move the desks away and wrestle on the floor. This one time he had me in a choke hold and I couldn't breathe, it felt like the time in the toy box. I snapped and flipped him over, and within a tenth of a second I was out of the hold and had him in one. I remember saying to him while I had him in this hold, "How do you like it, does it feel good?" He held up his hands to show me that he had given up. We both stood up and he was looking at me like, "That happened so fast, how did he do this to me?" That was the last time we wrestled.

Mr. Wong was weightlifting in the weight room at school one day; he blacked out and the bar landed on him. He went and got himself checked out at the hospital, and they found the reason for his blackout. He had cancer and died three months later. May he rest in peace. I love you buddy.

One teacher that I got along with really well was my math teacher, Mr. O'Mally. He was a rugby teacher as well, and if I had known how nice of a guy he was I probably would have played for him, but by this time I was a senior and he taught the juniors. He was a short, stocky guy who looked fairly tough himself. He jokingly told us at the beginning of the year that it would be okay if we drank pop and chewed gum in his class as long as we supplied him with a twenty-sixer.

Every Monday he would make me wait outside in the hallway before I entered the class so he could examine me for any bruises or scars. If I didn't have any, he would ask me if I'd had a quiet weekend. I remember this one time I had a detention with him after school. If you spoke out without permission while you were in detention it would start all over. He was marking my paper and I asked if I could come up front to see how I did on it. While I was waiting for him to mark my work I told him that I'd better have passed or somebody was going to be on the floor crying and it wasn't going to be me. He looked up at me and smiled while he chewed his gum. That's why we always got along with one another, we were both rough and tough and had respect for one another.

One guy from our school, not in my class, left him a twenty-sixer on the front seat of his car just because he was a cool dude and all of us tough guys liked him. I mean, he was just joking about the twenty-sixer, but giving him the bottle had to be done. He later wasn't allowed to teach rugby, and soon he couldn't even teach math anymore because he had a concussion that was interfering with his teaching. I heard he ended up living in his mom's basement. It's always the good ones that seem to get the shit end of the stick.

My gym teacher and I didn't get along so good. This one time he called me into his office and told me to close the door. He said to me, "You know what Scott, I don't like you one bit" - and I said, "You know what Mr. Durrand, I hate your guts too." We shook hands, and we got along good after that; later on in life we would sit together in the local pub.

I failed grade ten that year and asked the teacher in the special ISP class if they could recommend me for grade eleven because I could do the work but had chosen to goof off instead. They disagreed with me, therefore I had to repeat grade ten. Great, more garbage duty.

1986

The dump that was near our house was now a park. Everybody who had a beef with someone would meet at this park and fight. Our gym class was playing football down there one day, and I guess I tackled this guy, Jamie, a little too hard for his liking. When he got up he told me to meet him there after school. I laughed and said, "Okay buddy." He was a little slow for some reason so I didn't take him seriously and didn't show. The next day he walked up to me and said, "Where were you yesterday? Are you scared?"

I said, "You showed up?" and he said, "Yeah, how about today?"

I knew that I was going to mutilate this guy so I told him to meet me at my house and we would fight in my backyard because I didn't want anyone to see the mutilation. I never fought at the park because I always finished the guy off quickly and then, no matter where I was, I couldn't wait until later to smash someone else's face in because of the adrenalin rush. The word got out and the fence along my backyard was full of kids from school. I told them all to fuck off and get out of there, which they did. I mean everybody new how tough I was so they listened, but they didn't go too far because once the fight started they came back to watch..

The fight started, I threw two punches and dropped him to the ground. I pinned his shoulders with my knees and started smashing his face in. Once he wasn't moving I got off of him and helped him up. I took him inside my house and brought him to the laundry tub to clean him up.

It was a lesson to be learned for him because I told him that he could have been killed, and he agreed with me.

Afterwards, while I was feeling a little guilty for what I'd done to this guy, the phone rang. I answered and it was a teacher from school all in tears. She asked me why I'd beaten this kid up? I told her that he'd wanted to fight me, and that I hadn't asked him. She told me about his mental problem, and that his parents considered him as a mistake, and that they had put him in a high chair in a bedroom in front of a TV until he was ten. Well, talk about feeling like a piece of shit. We were friends after that, but I think he learned something from that beating.

In 2011 I was driving through Maple Ridge and picked up Leonard as he was walking down the highway. (He was the guy who came to school after his father died). He worked with Jamie at the recycling depot and I asked him how Jamie was doing? He told me that I'd taught him well because some worker was getting under his skin one day, and so Jamie followed him home and went into his house and kicked the shit out of the guy. Jamie later got fired for this because they said it was work related. I've always said to myself that if I ever got rich I would buy a company and hire those two guys just to help them out. Life isn't that simple, but maybe someday… you never know what can fall in your lap when you're down.

This guy I knew in school got his head slammed into the concrete wall one day as I came down the stairs. I never hung out with him, but we would talk to one another in the hallways at school from time to time. I noticed Mike crying, holding his head and leaning up against the concrete wall. Apparently this guy Brian had just had a fight with his girlfriend, and as he walked by Mike, he slammed his head into the wall. Mike was a guy who wouldn't hurt a fly, so when he told me what had happened I didn't need to know whether he'd done anything to piss this guy off. I asked Mike which way Brian had gone, and he pointed towards the side door to the building. I knew the guy Mike was talking about, so I went to find him. Brian was over by the front of the school right in plain view of the office. I took off my jacket and said, "How about picking on me? Come on, let's go you piece of shit." He didn't want to fight me because he knew I would have ripped his head off, but that was okay because I embarrassed him in front of everybody when I told him that he was nothing but a fucking wimp who only picked on the weak, and that next time he wanted to hurt someone he should come and see me. I went back to see if Mike was okay; he sucked it up and I told him not to worry about Brian as he wasn't going to bother him anymore.

We've been friends ever since.

My first car, a Toyota Corolla.

My Mom had a friend from work who had these two older Toyotas for sale. My friend Jake and I wanted to buy these cars. My Mom made a deal with her friend, and we paid my Mom back for them. I believe they were around $375 for the two of them. With the money I made making bark mulch, I managed to fix one of the cars up. My friend Jake took the other car and he managed to get it running. I painted mine pumpkin orange in my driveway with a Wagner power painter. It looked pretty good except for a little orange peel.

I needed a front brake calliper, and a guy I knew had a brother who was a tow truck driver, and he had some cars in his yard. I went to see him, and bought a calliper for $20 and went home to put it in. As I was trying to bleed the brakes I realized I needed the one for the other side. I went back the next day and the guy wasn't home, so I gave another $20 to his roommate. As it turned out that roommate never gave the $20 to the guy, so now he thought that I had stolen from him. One day I drove out behind the 7-11 store where we would hang out. I parked the car and this guy that thought I had ripped him off was heading right for me. He had to be in his mid-twenties, and was twice the size I was. He was demanding his $20 and I tried to tell him that I had given it to his roommate. Naturally he didn't believe me. It would have been easier to just give him another $20, but that would mean throwing away everything I lived my life for. I took off my jacket and told him that I wasn't giving him another $20, and that he should take it up with his roommate. He totally changed his tune, shook my hand, and walked away. I don't know if he was scared, or if it was because I was only sixteen and sticking up for myself. He had respect for that, I think, and must have decided I'd paid the $20.

A guy who I went to school with was having a party that I attended. He had this German shepherd that was chained up near a tree in his backyard. I had a couple of drinks in me at this point, and thought it would be a good idea to go meet this dog. Raymond, the dog's owner, told me to be careful, but I told him not to worry because I could handle him. Raymond laughed at me, shook his head, and said, "Don't say I didn't tell you so." The dog looked harmless. As I approached him he attacked me, ripped my new Levi's jeans and sank his teeth into my leg. I looked at Raymond and he was laughing, saying, "I told you so." I had to leave that party and get home to patch up my wounds and change my pants. Attacked by two shepherds in my life, and to think later I would buy one for myself. After all, I figured it wasn't the dogs' fault; that's how they were trained. Even the shepherd I bought in 2009 attacked a friend of mine, and I had to bring him back to the breeders. That was it for German shepherds, I had seen enough.

I was kicked out of school for something I don't remember and managed to con a few guys from school into skipping out the rest of the day to go pick magic mushrooms. We took my car and headed down to the cow fields by the dyke. Once we were there, we headed to the field and managed to pick enough for that night, which we'd planned earlier. When we got back to the car we noticed a car coming up the Dyke. It looked like a ghost car to me so I put my mushrooms up on the sun visor. At the last minute that was all I could come up with. My guess was right, and he stopped us before we could even drive away.

The cop came up to my window and asked us what we were up to, and naturally we said nothing. He told us to get out of the car and searched us, and when he didn't find anything on us he started to search the car. He was looking all over in there, and just as he swung his legs around to leave the car, he looked up and pulled down the visor. The bag of mushrooms fell right on his lap and he said, "Well, well, well… I came down here hoping to catch poachers and instead caught myself some mushroom pickers."

Luckily, when he'd searched us, he didn't find the mushrooms that were hidden in Dan's jacket. This cop would soon be the biggest pain in my ass. While he was doing the paper work in his car I walked up to him and asked him what was the worst thing that could happen to me if I was charged? He said, "That depends if they are real or not after we get them tested." I told him that I knew what I was picking. He told me I would just have to wait and see."

I got a call a while later to come and meet with Constable Stephens down at the local detachment. This was the cop that arrested me down at the dyke that day. Once I was in one of the rooms Stephens came in with this other big, burly cop. Stephens told me that I was being charged for the offence, but that he could make it all go away if I gave him some information. He wanted to know who was stealing all the car stereos locally, and any other information he thought I knew about. I knew everything but told him nothing. This other cop started to yell at me, told me that I was full of shit, and that if I didn't tell him something he would pull me over every time I hopped into my car. I said that he wasn't scaring me, to charge me and let me the fuck out of there. That's what they did, and one of them said to me, "It's your life." Sure enough, that Stephens pulled me over for my tinted windows. He got on the speaker and called for me to come into the cop van. Once inside he gave me a whole list of fines, and handed them to me with a smile on his face, telling me I could play high or I could play low. As much as I wanted to smash his face in, I just grabbed them and said that I would play high.

Across the street from me lived a police officer named Ike who I would talk to from time to time, and he worked for another police department. I think it made him feel good to talk to me because he didn't have kids of his own, and he knew that there was no man in our house. He didn't have people over that often. I think he pretty much kept to himself.

I remember watching him through my bedroom window as he shot a crow out of the trees with his .22 handgun. At night you could look over and just see the cherry at the end of his cigarette light up as he took a drag. One night when I got home I heard him call me over to see him. As he butted out his cigarette he told me that if that fucking Stephens ever pulled me over again to come and tell him right away. I said to him, "You know about that?" and he said, "I know everything." I was surprised that he knew, seeing as he and Stephens worked at different departments in different cities.

The harassment came to an end and I didn't see Stephens til 1988 when I had my Buick and he pulled me over for not having my exhaust right to the back of the car. He didn't know it was me until he ran my plate, and was he ever the nice guy that day. I went and ran the exhaust to the end of the car because I didn't want Ike to think that now that I had him on my side I could do anything I wanted.

One of the few times I fought down at the crossroads I finally lost a fight. This was where we would drink on the weekends and have fires. I was down at the crossroads drunk, and when I went to grab another beer out of the trunk of my car all the beer was gone. I started blaming everybody for taking my beer, and I guess one guy had had enough. As I could barely stand I was easy to take on, and this guy knew this. He threw me to the ground and started hitting me in the face. My friends broke up the fight, carried me to my car, and Brad started up the car to get us out of there. I remember my car being a tight fit where it was, and Brad had to bump bumpers to get us out. I woke up in the front seat of my car in a vacant lot that was adjacent to Brad's house. I looked in the mirror and noticed that my nose was swollen so I went and knocked on Brad's door to ask him what had happened. He told me that I was blaming everybody for taking my beer until someone had had enough and taken me down. I don't really blame the guy for it; I probably would have done the same. I don't think anybody actually took my beer; I just think that I lost track of how many I was actually drinking.

They had what they called intramural sports that the school offered at lunchtime. They would play sports like floor hockey, European handball, volleyball etc. With me always in trouble at school they didn't allow me to play in any of these activities. This one lunchtime I was sitting in the bleachers watching our grade ten class play this grade eleven class in floor hockey. There was a guy named Larry, who was playing for the Grade eleven class, and he was throwing his weight around while wearing hockey gloves and elbow pads, which nobody else had. Scott (the son of the man who drove through the puddle) came up to me and asked if I wanted to play because of this asshole. I told him that if I played they would kick me out for a week but I could see that the teams weren't fair, so I ran up the road to my house and grabbed a stick. I was back in ten minutes and on the playing floor. The first minute on I rubbed this Larry guy up against the wall and he dropped his stick right away. I looked at him and said that if he wanted to go he should drop his gloves, but he shook his head no, which meant he wasn't going to take his gloves off. I just shrugged my shoulders like, "Oh well" and punched him over the left eye, knocking him out and to the ground.

This all happened so fast the teacher didn't know that I was out on the floor. Mr. Williams yelled at me to get out of there, and go to the office. I first went into the change room to get changed and he followed me in there with the gym teacher I'd had the year before. This Mr. Williams was giving me the gears. With me already pissed off I threw down my gym bag and asked him if he wanted to go. Mr. Shivey, last year's gym teacher, stood there looking at each of us waiting to see if Mr. Williams was going to challenge me or not. After about ten seconds or so Mr. Shivey smiled and told me to get down to the office. The word around school, while I was kicked out, was that they were calling me 'One-punch Magri.'

After a week of suspension I returned to school and the first minute in the hallway this guy walks up to me and says, "One-punch Magri. Yeah right!" As you can probably guess I smashed him in the face and down he went, and I was gone for another week.

It was the end of the year and Dan and I went to Buntzen Lake, the same lake where I got hit in the face by the rope swing. When we got there we decided to set up a larger swing than what was there. It took us the better part of the day to clear out the brush on the bank so that we were able to walk up further with the rope. When we were finally finished, and swung out over the lake, it must have been about a twenty-five foot drop. It was a little scary the first time, but it was a rush with the momentum you picked up coming from so far up the bank. Dan and I went back to the lake a couple of days later to use the swing, but when we got back there we saw that the rope had been cut. We didn't have any idea what had happened until we started to ask people at the beach if they knew what had happened to the swing. After asking a few people we found out. The day after Dan and I put up the swing a young kid had tried it out. The kid grabbed the rope and started on the journey down the bank and over the water, but he got scared and didn't let go of the rope. When he swung back to the bank a stick went through his chest. He was taken away in an ambulance and then the rope was cut. I don't know if the boy survived or not, but I felt like this was entirely my fault.

While I was working for the bark mulch plant company, part of my job was to fuel the mulcher before I went home. I would go back at night and siphon the tank for my car; this was my way of getting even for the owner not having given me a ride that day. This one night I went to get some fuel from that truck with two friends of mine, Doctor Dave and Joe. Actually, I gave Dave this name later because he would introduce steroids to me, and would give me all my shots.

Anyway, while Joe and I were in the process of getting the fuel we were surprised by the cops. Joe and I ran our separate ways and I found myself hiding in some willows. As I was hiding I had time to think up a plan to get me out of the small charge that would come. I decided to find my way back to my car, were the cop car was, and tell the cop that I was looking for a bucket to get water out of the ditch because my car was overheating. The cop already had Dave in the back of the car, and didn't believe my story. He asked me to get in the back with Dave until they could find the other guy, Joe. When they caught up with Joe he told them what we were doing there. The cop that lived across the street from me showed up at the scene and told me that we were right in the middle of a large drug bust going on at the house that was just across the street from my work. There were cops all over the place at this time.

I guess we cost them a lot of money burning off their sting with our little stunt. Oh well, I can't remember what I got charged with, but my neighbour, Ike, made sure that I was taken care of.

The next job that I landed was working for a bottle making company. They asked if I was still in school – I lied and told them I wasn't because they wouldn't have hired me. I was working swing shift, so being off at eight a.m. didn't leave me much time to get to school in the morning. An afternoon shift started at four p.m. so I had enough time to get home, make a lunch, and get to work.

I was scheduled for nose surgery, for the second time, so I gave them two weeks' notice. When I was okay to return I went to see the boss to let them know and she told me that I was bumped. I said to her, "How did I get bumped if you didn't hire anybody?" So then she said, "You were away." I told her, "I gave you guys two weeks' notice, and you knew that." It didn't matter… they let me go but I would get even soon enough.

One night some friends of mine and I were out driving around and we just happened to be travelling past the plastic plant. I told my friend Matt to pull up close to a Lincoln Continental. This car was flawless, and the owner's pride and joy. As we pulled up close to it I rolled down my window, grabbed my keys, set them against the front fender and told Matt to drive forward. I dug those keys in as hard as I could and when I brought my hand back into the car, my hand was covered in paint. Karma's a real bitch.

I started hanging around one of the old bike thieves in town for a while, and he ended up getting me some work with him at Yellow Jacket farms. This farm was located in Pitt Polder at the north end of town close to Pitt Lake. Our job there was to grab the bales of hay from the field and stack them in the barn. We had a good crew. Everyone got along, and when the day was done the owner treated us to hamburgers and beer. Working like men for twelve hours a day in the heat, the cold beer was well-deserved. This job was only for a couple of weeks until we had the third crop cut and in the barn. The owner told us that we were the best crew ever because he'd never before managed to get three crops off his fields and stacked in the barn before the Pacific National Exhibition (PNE) started at the end of August.

In grade nine we had a class that we had to take, Consumer Education,. I failed the class that year and had to do it all over in the first year of grade ten, but I failed again. Mrs. Lambert was teaching it this year, my second time in grade ten, and my third time taking the course. She and I didn't get along too well. Not that I got along with any teacher other than Mr. O'Mally , but I went to see her at the end of the school year to see if I had passed or not. As I walked into the classroom I noticed that she was marking our papers and totalling up our marks. I asked her if I had passed or not and she replied, "I don't think so." I then looked at her sideways and asked, You don't really want me in here for a fourth time, do you?" She looked at me, grabbed my paper, and with a smirk on her face wrote down 51 percent. I think we were both relieved.

We were getting some special guests at the school one night from All-Star Wrestling. I was sitting up front and took a dislike to a wrestler named "Spider. He gave me a look that I didn't like so I jumped up on the ropes and asked him if he wanted to go. We got into an argument, and I was throwing every word I could at him trying to get him to throw the first punch. The wrestler jumped down from the ring and went over to one of the teachers to try to get me thrown out of the gym, but nothing happened. When I left after the matches were over I noticed there was just one bus outside for all the wrestlers. From all the smack they were talking when in the ring you would have thought they hated each other, and here they were, all in one bus. They must have learned to forgive and forget quickly.

Jason, Dan, Jordan and I went downtown to PlayLand, which is an amusement park at the PNE. It opened in the early months of spring, and the exhibition opened at the end of August ending on Labour Day. It was free to get in the gates, and you would have to buy a pass once you were inside for the rides. The problem with this was that all the gangs would hang out there through the day. As we were walking around we passed this group of guys sitting at a picnic bench. As we walked by one of them spit at my buddy Jason, who was a boxer. As the situation worsened, we all decided to take this down to where they have the lumber show when the PNE is taking place. It was early in the season so no one would be there at this time. These guys were pretty smooth, and one of them smoked a joint with me as we were walking to the lumber area. Once we were there Jason took off his jacket to fight this guy, and one of the other guys started throwing all these kicks to warm up, and Jason looked at me and said, "I thought I was fighting that guy." The fight was only supposed to be between the guy that spit at us and Jason.

As I was sitting on the bleachers with all those other guys I got kicked in the face. I stood up and raised my fists to defend myself, and now there were three of them in front of me, plus another guy in the distance holding a knife. At this point the other guys we were with took off and left Jason and I for the wolves. With my nose gashed open and being outnumbered, Jason and I walked away, and I went to first aid to get cleaned up. After getting patched up we walked back to the car, figuring the other guys we were with would be there waiting for us, but they were nowhere to be seen. We decided to go back into the park to find them, and if you can believe it we found them on the log ride. After giving them shit we started walking out, but we were spotted by the gang and now there was about twenty of them. We ran to the car and managed to get there in time to get it started and drive away before they got to us.

I had blacked out windows in the car so they couldn't see us until Dan rolled down the window to look at them, then they realized where we were. All they could do at this point though was throw rocks at my car. There was some damage, but nothing compared what would have happened if we hadn't gotten out of there.

The weird thing about this was that a year before this incident my Mom had gone to see a psychic. She told my Mom that she could see me bleeding from the head, and she could see a knife, and that I would be close to death. Gee, what else is new? That was the only time I ever walked away from a fight, but I think it was the right decision. All things in life happen for a reason, and this was one lesson learned.

I had traded my Toyota for Jason's 1970 Nova. It needed the motor rebuilt, so while I was working on it in mechanics class I bought a Vega station wagon to get me around. I landed this job delivering pizza and that ended quickly. The second week working there they sent me on a wild goose chase. They wrote down avenue instead of street on the invoice so I ended up in the middle of nowhere. I knocked on a door and the guy said that he didn't order anything, so off I went to look for a payphone to call the restaurant. They told me they'd made a mistake, and when I finally delivered it to the right house after about an hour, I knocked on the door and this single mom answered. I told her how sorry I was, and explained what had happened. She was so nice about the whole thing that I told her not to worry about paying for it because I QUIT. She said, "Why are you going to quit?" I said, "When I called to find out your right address they never apologized for their mistake, so now all their orders are going to pile up." She laughed, I smiled, and off I went.

I had to stop and get gas before I headed back to the restaurant to tell them I was quitting. At the gas station the guy working there had his car for sale. It was a Ford Pinto with a 351 Cleveland, and a posi-track rear end from a Cougar. I asked if I could take the car for a test drive and he threw me the keys. I fired it up and off down Dewdney Trunk Road I went. As I was testing the car out I came up behind this IROC Z28. Now this road only has one lane each way, so I pulled beside him in the oncoming lane and the race was on. Holy fuck did this car go. It scared the fuck out of me. That IROC didn't have a chance, and all I saw in the rear-view mirror was his front end disappearing in the distance. I took the car back, put gas in my car and told the guy that I would think about it. I went back to the restaurant, told them I quit, and they said, "What about these orders." I said, "You deliver them."

1987

Kevin and I were always pretty desperate to try different fishing spots. We drove to the Capilano River to try our luck one Saturday morning. We parked Kevin's truck and walked down to the river to give it a shot. After several hours of no luck we decided to climb our way across a cliffside to get to a pool of water that caught our eye.

With a fishing rod in one hand and the tackle box in the other, it was sure difficult to make this journey. As I reached out and grabbed a root from a tree to help me across it gave way, and backwards I went into the river. Trying to swim with all my gear to the shore, and listening to Kevin laughing his head off, you could guess I wasn't very happy once I got to shore. I started yelling at Kevin, "You think that was funny you fucking prick, you try to make your way across now." As he started across he grabbed the same root and ended up in the river with me. Now I was laughing at him, and at the same time this couple that was out sitting on a rock together having a romantic day got a comedy show instead. I think they got their money's worth.

As we were now on the other side of the river there was no turning back. To get back to the truck we had to climb a cliffside to get to the road. While attempting this I lost my tackle box and it went rolling down the cliff. I was so pissed off at this point that I told Kevin, "Forget it, let's get out of here." He again started laughing and said, "You can't leave without your box." So he climbed down and grabbed it for me. That was enough fishing for a while, the Safeway was much easier and safer.

Dan had met this guy through his job at the bottle plant; his name was Joe. The three of us took Joe's twelve-foot aluminum boat to the Georgia Strait off of Vancouver where all the ocean freighters anchor, to do some crabbing at night. What we were going to do was rob all the commercial guy's nets, and with Joe having done this before he knew exactly where to go. We put the boat in the ocean and off we went. Joe took us right to the lead crab trap and got me to start pulling it up. Now these commercial nets put weights in the trap's, so people like us can't rob them. As I was trying to pull up the net it started to get heavier. What was happening was once the first net was off the bottom I started to pull up the next one. The commercial guys use a winch to pull up their nets, so they connect them all together, and man was it getting heavy. The side of the boat started to get closer to the water because I was using it for leverage, and after twenty minutes Joe cut the rope and left all the nets at the bottom. With him cutting the rope there was no way the commercial guys could retrieve their nets so all the crabs went to waste. Another thing I feel remorse for.

Now in grade eleven, I had that teacher Williams for English, and my desk was always out in the hall. One time, when he sent me out there, he asked me if I knew why I was always in trouble with him, and I replied, "No, I don't" and he told me that I was the only one he heard. I have a loud, deep voice, and I said to him, "Well is it my fault I have a loud voice?"

I quit school a month later when a few of us were out of class at the pop machine, and the principal walked up to us. Like always I was his main priority, so he told the other two to get back to class, and that I had to go to the office with him. In the office I told him it wasn't fair that I was the only one he dragged in there, then I grabbed my pop off his desk, gave him the middle finger, told him to go fuck himself, and I quit. That prick had the biggest smile on his face because he'd finally won. I was pissed off, and when I walked outside to go to my car and saw everyone in my metalwork class looking at me, I threw my pop through the open garage door. It hit a vice and exploded everywhere. I then walked into the mechanics shop, grabbed my bare small block, walked out the door with it, put it in the back of my Vega and drove away.

I couldn't rebuild that motor because I wasn't at school anymore, so

I found a 327 small block for it, and man, did that car haul. I bought it off this guy who had it stored in his carport. He told me that all he knew about the motor was that it had had a lot of work done to it. I got into one accident with it while racing someone, but nothing major.

I was working at the Chevron gas station at this time, but a week later my Dad called to tell me that the railway was hiring. I started working for the railroad April 13, 1987 as a carman's apprentice.

I would still help my Dad from time to time with the firewood, and this one particular day, on the way back to drop me off at home, I saw this car for sale. I asked my Dad to turn around so I could look at it. The car turned out to be a 1970 Buick Skylark custom two-door. The car was in beautiful shape and the guy wanted $1200 for it. On the way home I asked if my Dad would co-sign for it, thinking he would have no problem doing this for me since I had done all the work for him, and that I was working full time with no problem making the payment. I couldn't believe that he said no to me. This was hard to swallow because my life was based on respect and doing favours for people cause you never know when you might need one. I then gathered enough guts to ask my Mom if she could help me, and without hesitation she replied, "I will do anything to help you out, honey." I phoned the owner up and in three days I was driving it. They say that your parents are already picked for you before you are born. If my Dad had helped me out when I asked him to, I wouldn't have learned the things I have learned today, even though my Mom was always there for me. Thank you both.

I blew the motor up in the Nova and was using a four-door nova my Dad bought off this guy from work until I found that Buick. With the Vega sold, and the Nova just sitting in the carport at home, I decided to sell it to this guy from our school. He only had half of the money on him but I let him tow it home. I was to sign over the papers to him once he gave me the rest of my money. He had put another motor in the Nova and I heard that he was now driving the car around without paying me even though it was still in my name. I went to look for him in his neighbourhood and found him outside this corner store with my car. I walked up to the car, pulled out the keys and told him that he would get them back once he paid me.

I would always pull over and help anybody when they were broken down. I helped this guy one day who had to be six foot nine and about 350 pounds. We were at the side of the road for about an hour. It turned out that the guy who had bought the Nova knew this guy, and not long afterwards I heard this knock at the door. When I opened it, this monster was standing on my mat with Eddie, the guy who had welched on the deal. We both looked at each other and said, "Hey, how you doing buddy?" Then he looked at Eddie and said, "Pay the man." Do you see what I mean about helping people? Good things happen; I got my money and signed the papers.

Ike (the cop that lived across the street from my home) did ask me for a favour, but it wasn't for him. We had an elderly couple that lived next door to us, and the husband had a stroke. He was in pretty rough shape, so the wife was the one who had to mow the lawn. They were both in their late sixties so it was a lot of work for her to accomplish. Ike asked if I could start mowing their lawn for them and, of course without hesitation, I said to him, "Consider it done." The lady asked if seven dollars would be enough to mow the lawn and do the edging. I told her that it would be fine, considering that the money wasn't the issue. With me now working for the railroad and making good money, I still took care of their lawn right up until my Mom sold our house.

Whenever someone does you a favour, you have to pay that back when asked, with no excuses. The problem with most people is when they are asked for a favour, right away some start to think, "What do I get out of this?" and that's not the right way to look at it. You say, "Yes," and when the time comes for him or her to pay it back, and they try to come up with an excuse, you let them have it because obviously they need to learn that lesson. This way they will think the next time they need a favour, and they will appreciate it more instead of using you. I have a saying, "Look after the ones that look after you."

I remember my little brother coming home from school, and telling me that this teacher had kicked him in the ass and thrown him to the ground. I called up my friend Gus, who was built like a brick shithouse, and we drove down to the school to pay this teacher a visit. It was after school and I was lucky that he was the only one left in the staff room. I approached him about the incident and he denied all of it. I then told him he was full of shit, and that if he ever laid a hand on my brother again I would bring my Dad into it and we would beat him so bad his own mother wouldn't recognize him. My brother never had any more problems with that asshole, lucky for him. Here is the weird thing, he just happened to be the same teacher who had tackled my friend Wesley with the baseball bat that day. I heard from someone else that he was abusive to kids in another school he taught at before he came to my school.

I was at an outdoor party one Saturday night, I went to get another beer from the cooler but the cooler was gone. I asked around if anyone had seen anything and they told me that this guy Jay (from school) had taken my cooler. He was nowhere in sight, so I decided that I would take care of it on Monday. He was still in school and I knew that he was building a car in mechanics class. I drove up to the school and parked about a block away with binoculars. I could see that Jay was outside the mechanics shop working on his car.

I waited until the bell went and everybody had left the school. Our mechanics teacher would let us stay after school to work on our cars as long as we locked up before we left. Knowing this, I knew that he would be there for a while. I then drove up and he was under the hood of his car. I started kicking the shit out of him, and when he was bleeding on the ground I told him that he had until six o'clock that night to get the money for the beer that he'd taken from me.

After the beating I gave him, he went home and grabbed these two brothers who lived across the street from him. I was driving around looking for him after six, and when I saw him in his car with these two guys I pulled over, knowing that Jay had grabbed these guys to hunt me down. I walked up to the window and asked Jay for my money. As one of the brothers got out of the passenger side, Jay looked at me and said, "What money?"

These two guys were older than me and worked at the cedar mill in Hammond. I knew I couldn't take on all three of these guys myself at the time, so I just took my lumps. These two brothers were the tough guys in the school before they graduated; one had me on the ground and was kicking me in the head with his steel toed work boots. After he was tired of kicking me, I got up and smiled at him. With blood running down my face, he couldn't believe it.

A few years later I was in the Haney Hotel drinking, and came across him while I was talking to the manager. I asked him if he remembered me. He said he didn't, and I told him he was full of shit, and he walked away. I finished talking to the manager and then went looking for the guy, but he had gone. I knew then that he knew who I was. What a coward. I never did get even with him, and still think of that day every once in a while. I should have kicked the hell out of him right there. Consider yourself lucky, buddy, but now when I think of it, Jay was the one who should have just taken his lumps and paid me.

Dan and I took a drive one night to the grocery store and I got caught stealing Stetson cologne. As I walked out the door an undercover working for the store stopped me and asked if I would like to go back inside and talk about what I had stolen. I said to him no problem, telling him I didn't know what he was talking about. As we were walking to the office in the back I slipped the cologne in a garbage can. I think he must have heard it because he turned around and took it out of the trash. He called the cops who took me away for this petty theft, and I got charged with theft under $1,000.

A couple of days later, Ike the cop from across the street came over, pissed off that I was in trouble again. He told me that he was tired of bailing me out, and suggested I plead "diversion" when I went to court. Diversion means that you will agree to plead guilty if the criminal charges get dropped and you agree to work with the government on probation or community hours. As I got called into the courtroom, the judge asked me, "How do you plead?" and I told her, "Diversion." She then said that I had to appear at a later date, and when I told her I would be working and couldn't make it, she replied, with a smile on her face, "I suggest that you show up." The judge knew what was already going to happen that day because of some strings that were pulled for me.

Ike had never asked me for anything for helping me out, he just didn't want me to throw my life away and I thank him for that. Little did I know what hell I would later get myself into. I felt that I owed something to Ike for what he had done for me, so I bought him a twenty-sixer of rum. He thanked me.

After pleading diversion I was ordered by the court to serve community hours, working for this old man who looked after the garden at the Haney bypass. There were other guys working there too, but I was the only one with a car. The old guy was too old to drive and he didn't have any way to get around. He approached me about driving him around to work off some hours. I jumped all over this and we headed out on the road. I took him shopping, to the drug store, and to see his wife in the hospital. I would lie on the hood of my car at the hospital while the man saw his wife, and suntan while all the other guys were working there asses off. Whatever hours I drove him around he would give me credit for double. I think I only worked three Saturdays and I was done. I actually told the old guy that if he ever needed a ride anywhere, to give me a call at home, but I never heard from him. That was the end of the petty little things… the assault charges would come later.

I've always been the type that, if I found a wallet full of cash, I would feel so good about seeing the reaction of the owner after handing it to him that I wouldn't even think of keeping the money It would feel like when you watch your children open their birthday presents. I never did find a wallet, but I did find a binder at the high school when I was about twelve. It was thrown all over the place and, luckily, it had the kid's phone number in the back. I called the guy up and his dad came to my house to pick it up and handed me $5. It turned out that the girl I would later have a thirteen-year relationship with starting in 1995 was the sister of the kid who owned the binder, and he was always being picked on at school.

I recall being at the beach one day when I suddenly remembered that I had a court appearance for something (can't remember what it was now). After drinking all day I showed up at court but missed my appointment, and they told me if the judge can't see you today we will have to lock you up. While I was waiting in the lobby my name got called. I was wearing a Hawaiian shirt unbuttoned up the front. It was flapping in the wind and I had a dark tan, and a hairdo like Napoleon Dynamite. I was shit-faced.

As soon as I walked through the court door I started telling the Judge a bullshit story about why I had missed court. She was smiling at me, and actually thought I was funny, so I smiled back and she gave me a later court date. I wasn't in there five minutes and I was a free man.

I was eighteen years old at this time and met a really nice girl. Sheri was a few years younger than me and her parents were very protective. Her parents were alcoholics, but she seemed normal to me. I was her first lover and she was mine. Like I said, I was more interested in motorsports than girls, so I guess you could call me a late bloomer. She was my first, and we all know the first is special, and how strong the feelings we have are. Not having any experience with relationships, we would split up quite often. I think everyone can relate to this experience with their first love. I dated her on and off for a year and a half, and I would attempt my first suicide towards the end of the relationship.

Me, Sheri and my friend Chris headed to the PNE one day. We stepped up to that game that has the four concrete milk jugs that you have to knock over to win the big stuffed animals. Chris went first and with his third and final ball he knocked the jugs over. With him standing there receiving this big animal, a crowd started to form. Now it was my turn.

They gave you three balls, and with my first throw I knocked them all over. The guy running the game said it didn't count because one of the jugs was leaning up against the back tarp. I told him the rules said that in order to win the jugs had to all be off the platform they were sitting on, which they were. I told him he'd better get the manager over because I was going to grab a prize otherwise. The manager came over and verified that I had won, and I picked the big elephant for my girlfriend. Now I still had two balls left, so I told the manager I was going to try for another one but he told me that he thought Chris and I won enough, so he gave me back my $5 and off we went. It was sure funny driving home with these animals sticking out the windows of the car because they were bigger than we were. I ran into Sheri a few years ago, and she told me that she still has that elephant. Cool.

My friend Dirk and I were the last ones to leave this party down at the crossroads one night, except for one other couple. They were stranded there and asked If I could give them a ride into town. I had these large Mickey Thompson N50 tires on the back of my car, and if there was too much weight in the back the tires would rub on the fender walls. So I told them it wouldn't be a problem, but if my tires got ruined on the way there, they were buying me new ones. The guy said not a problem because they had no other way out of there. The tires rubbed all the way into town and the fender walls cut the sidewalls of the tires. We were now parked in front of the 7-11 and were standing outside. When I told him he now had to buy me tires, he said, "There's nothing wrong with them and I'm not buying you anything." Just as he said that he threw his beer bottle at me. I moved to my left and the bottle went through the window of the store. Once he did this I kicked the shit out of him and the cops showed up, taking him away. Isn't it amazing what you get for helping someone out, but you can't stop helping people out when needed, all because of one asshole.

Sheri and I had broken up for some reason, and when I found out that she was seeing someone else it just shattered my heart. I found it hard to take and decided to take my own life. I had now traded my Buick in on a 1980 Z28.

I drove my car down to the railroad crossing and parked the car about 100 yards back from the crossing. With both hands on the wheel, and tears rolling down my face, I waited for the next train. I was going to drive into the moving train, but when the train came I just didn't have the balls to go through with it. I got control of myself and realized how selfish that would have been, but I would attempt four more suicides later on.

I started to see this beautiful aerobics Instructor, Elizabeth. On our first date I took her to the movies. I had bought a bag of Twizzlers liquorice and waited for the movie to start until I opened it up. Knowing how much noise you could make opening the bag, I pretended that I was having a hard time opening it just to see how long it would take for someone to yell at me. Elizabeth didn't know I was doing this on purpose, and when someone yelled at me, "All right already," I started to laugh. The whole place was laughing, knowing that I was just putting on a show and Elizabeth loved every bit of it. I only dated her for about a month and then got back together with Sheri. Sheri and I only dated for about another month and then we broke up for good.

My friend Dan and I decided to go to Cyprus Mountain to ski for the day. I was coming down one of the hills and noticed this large sign that said, "CAUTION, slow down." I didn't pay any attention to this, and when I turned the corner, "Wham" – everybody was there taking off there skis to go and get something to eat. I was probably going seventy kilometres an hour at the time so there was no way I was going to stop. I crashed through everybody, running over their skis, and hit a snowpile created when they ploughed the main road. I flew about twenty feet in the air after hitting this and landed right in the middle of the road. While I was kissing the yellow line I was yelling at Dan to get the skis off of me. That was the end of my skiing career.

Mom was in the middle of renovating the downstairs bathroom, so she had the mirror off the wall and had it standing up against the door. I had a friend from school over, so we took the mirror outside and held it up to blind this plane in the sky. Like, holy shit, I'm surprised the cops never got called, but maybe they did because once we figured out what we'd done we hopped in the car and fucked off. I hope they were wearing their sunglasses.

1988

On another occasion three friends and I were driving my Z28, with two cases of beer in the car, and we drove past the high school at night while there was a basketball game going on. The game was over, the players were getting into their vehicles, and one of them fingered us as we drove by. I cracked a nut and the chase was on. We chased that van for about an hour until we ended up at their school. By this time there was another vehicle following us but I don't know how they were contacted because no one had cellphones back then. We all turned up this dead-end street beside the school, and when I drove to the end they pulled over and made a road block. I could see that there were about twenty players and some parents with them. We got back in the car and I told everyone to buckle up because I was going to pull a Rockford. I matted it, cracking the wheel to the left and to the right, and almost made it around the cars but hit a pole and put the car in the ditch. They all just stood there and told me that the cops were on their way. I told them all to fuck off and we started walking down the street with beer in our hands. I was walking with Dirk, and when we came to the bottom of the road he threw his bottle through the driver's window of one of the vehicles driven by one of the players. We saw the cops coming, so we started running through this cow field. One of the cops drove through the field, and by the time he caught up to me I was winded. He just reached out his window, opened the back door and told me to get in, which I did. The cops had all four of us at the cop shop and wanted to charge one of us with assault. They released us with a promise to come in at a later date to take a statement because they were understaffed that night.

My buddy James called his parents to come and pick us up, and we rode in the back of the truck under a canopy in the middle of January. As we were freezing in the back we made an agreement that nobody would talk to the police, but two of the guys didn't keep the agreement and gave statements, so I went over to Dirk's place to tell him. I told him that because the other two guys had given statements we should too, because the guys never told them who threw the bottle. I told Dirk we should go give a statement or they would charge us, thinking we were the guilty ones.

I went to my appointment the following week, but as Dirk never gave a statement they charged him. He was a stupid idiot. I told him how this was all going to work out but he wouldn't listen. I mean, they couldn't charge all four of us. That was the end of our friendship. I take some of the blame for him getting charged, but I did tell him what to do after the other guys gave their statements.

I had my car back the next day out of the tow yard. I had to pay to get it fixed myself, because the cops had given me a twenty-four hour suspension for drinking, and the insurance company wouldn't pay for the damage.

After I got that car fixed, James and I were out driving one night, turned left onto Hammond Road from Harris Road, with Def Leppard playing *Hysteria* on the stereo. I cranked it up and put the pedal to the floor. This stretch of road before I hit Hammond hill was about half a mile long. As we passed one cross street I looked at the speedometer and the needle was buried at 170 km/h. I kept the gas pedal to the floor until we reached the crest of the hill. At this point we were going about 209 km/h. I didn't see any cars until we got over the crest of the hill. We were going so fast at this point that when the car went over the crest the whole body lifted off the chassis. There was a car approaching in the oncoming lane, and a couple of cars in front of us. With the road wet I just touched the brake pedal and quickly made the decision not to brake because there was no way we were going to stop in time. Instead, I drove between the cars. This happened so fast the cars didn't have time to move out of the way, and I remember yelling to James, "This is it." It took us about quarter mile to slow the car down enough to make the corner that was up ahead. James was wedged in his seat and we didn't say anything to each other for about fifteen minutes. The adrenalin that was going through my body was something I can't explain other than my life flashed in front of my eyes once again. I sold that car and bought a 1970 Chevelle with a 307… something a little slower.

Being winter still, I came up with an idea to have some fun in the snow. I put this snow tire we had in the shed at home on my car. It was one of the ones my Dad had bought when we lived in Field. I put on my skis and boots, and tied a rope to the back of my car. I got my buddy to pull me around the streets, and then told him to go down the main road in town so we could drive past the 7-11. What a great time that was; no chair lift, and my legs were pretty sore, but fun.

We had our house robbed one day with our dog Henry inside. I knew this had to be someone who knew the dog because they wouldn't have been able to rob us otherwise. The cops were called and they finger-printed the house. They were able to get some prints lifted from a booze bottle that would later come in handy. I got a knock at the door one afternoon and it was Ike from across the street. He told me who had ripped us off, and sure enough it was a friend of my younger brother Jason. Ike told me to beat the shit out of him because he was nothing but a pain in the ass for the police, but not to kill him. I was itching to get my hands on him, and helping Ike was good too. I was driving home from work one day and turned onto Hammond Road, and who did I see working for the city but this guy Todd, who had robbed us. As I drove past I looked at him and he gave me the middle finger. I turned the car around and, when he saw me doing this, he jumped into a hole a bunch of city workers were digging nearby. With all those people watching, all I could do was tell him what a fucking little weasel he was, and that when I found him alone I was going to put him in a wheelchair. The workers were looking at me as well as him, because they didn't know what the hell was going on, and the weasel just kept his mouth shut. I never did find that punk again, but guys like that always get theirs sooner or later. Karma is a bitch.

It came time to have our dog put down. Ike across the street had told me that the dog was going crazy because she was starting to attack people on their bikes. This was hard for me to do because I had saved her life one day, and now I was going to take it. A few years earlier we had come home and found her hanging by the neck from a rope that had been strung between two trees in our yard for a swing. I looked out the window in the kitchen and she had her head in the loop, and it had twisted around and caught her. I ran out there, picked her up, and got the rope off of her neck. She was bouncing up and down to get some air, with her feet barely touching the ground. Anyway, I put her down only because I was the closest to her, and felt that I was the one to do this. What a horrible day that was.

This friend from school, Eric, had a party in the backyard at his parents' house. We had a huge bonfire going, and I had the idea to ride a bike through it while I was all liquored up. I rode through it not once, but twice. If I had wiped out, it would have been curtains for sure. The stupid things we do with liquid courage.

In October a friend of mine, Kenneth, and I were going to play some pool. It was lightly raining that night when we headed to Wayne's house. Ken owned a Mercury Bobcat that we were driving north on Harris Road. We crossed the Lougheed Highway and noticed a truck up ahead parked in the oncoming lane. With his headlights blinding us, we couldn't see that it was a semi parked across the road. Once we'd passed the glare of the tractor headlights we only had time to duck as we drove under the trailer. The trucker was trying to back into a driveway so the trailer was on an angle. The car hit the chassis before exiting through the other side, but if we hadn't hit the chassis we would have made a convertible out of the car. The truck driver didn't have flares out, or a second man, and there weren't any lights on the trailer.

I managed to crawl out of the wreckage to go get the driver, but there was nobody around. He left the truck unattended to go into the house to get someone to help him back the truck into the driveway since there was poor lighting. The cops and the news showed up with an ambulance.

They could only charge the driver with unsafe backing up, but he got that dropped in court because there was no proof that he was backing up at the time. I had an insurance claim for $4,200 because I told the insurance company I had a sore back due to the accident. This paid off the 1969 Chevelle I'd just bought after selling that 1970 Chevelle. As you can see, I went through a lot of vehicles.

Aftermath of the accident with the trailer. How we survived, I don't know.

It was Hallowe'en and I went as Jason from *Friday the Thirteenth.* I always spent a lot of time on my costumes, getting them as close as I could to the real thing. A friend of mine was at the party, and we were told he was on acid, so I jumped down off this fence and landed right in front of him. The look on his face was priceless; he probably thought he was in the movie. Dan and I walked down the street to the 7-11 to get some mix. I had an axe with me so I stayed outside and hid the axe behind the garbage can that was by the entrance door. As Dan was inside the store manager came out and told all the people hanging outside to take a hike. Then he called us all punks. I didn't like what he said to me and some words were exchanged.

The next day I went in there to buy something and he stood in front of me and told me to get out of the store. If he'd wanted me to leave he should have got out of my way. It doesn't take much for my blood to boil so I grabbed him and threw him into the chip rack. On my way out the door, he said, "I am calling the police." I said, "Great, I will wait outside for them." After the cops had shown up and finished talking to the manager, they came out and one of them told me, while rolling his eyes, that he was charging me with assault. The cops knew this was ridiculous and asked if I wanted to go with them, or could they trust me to meet them at the station. I told them no problem, I would meet them there. The manager charged me with assault and I had a court date at a later time. This time, however, I was on my own because Ike had moved to Vancouver Island and I lost contact with him. I wasn't going to ask another favour anyway; he had already done enough.

The judge that I had was African-Canadian, and what a cool guy he was. Having done my homework on assault charges, I knew that the first two were free. I told the judge my story, and when it was time for cross-examination the judge started to pour a glass of water. As he was pouring, he lifted the jug higher and higher as the prosecutor spoke so it would muffle out his voice. He just didn't want to hear their side of the story because he already knew what the case was about, and how pathetic it was. I gave a guilty plea only because they had me on video, and the judge gave me a $200 fine and three-months' probation. That was it. I was out of there in less than an hour. This was my first assault charge and two more would come.

Across from where I worked there was a bar called Frisco's. Some of us apprentices were going there one Saturday night. When I finally got there, the other apprentices pointed out a guy who had been bugging them all night. This guy came up to me, shook my hand and asked how I was doing? When I told him that I was fine, he refused to let my hand go, so I pushed him back and pulled my hand free. He then said, "How would you like it if a little guy like me kicked the fuck out of a big guy like you." I figured that he was about two steps away from me so I put my beer down and stepped right into him with a right hand. He flew back into the brick wall and slid down, just like on television. It happened so fast nobody knew what had happened. One of the apprentices gave me the guy's beer to hold as a prop. I took a sip of that beer and it was piss warm and full… he never even took a drink from it.

This apprentice's dad was a big shot for the rail company, and right away I thought that he had given his son a job there as a spy. We decided to get the hell out of there. Sure enough when we went outside there were fire trucks, an ambulance and the cops. When they got this guy in the ambulance that apprentice got in there with him. The cops weren't letting anyone leave the parking lot because they thought that this guy wasn't going to make it. We had our car parked down the street so my buddy and I got out of there in a hurry. The next week, when I drove by the place, I noticed that they had put up emergency parking only signs in front of the building. I guess the guy made it because I never heard anything about it, and as for that spy apprentice I just stayed far away from him and a year later he transferred.

A girl that I knew from school was having a house party one Saturday night. My older brother, myself, Rob from work, as well as my buddy James, showed up at this party fairly late. We had been drinking before we arrived and my brother was pretty wasted. He was standing outside by the front door while we went inside.

We weren't there half an hour when my fishing buddy, Kevin, came to get me because someone had punched out my brother. When I got outside he pointed to the guy that he thought had beat up my brother. This guy was just getting into a Chevy Blazer when I approached him, so I told him to get out. After smacking him around a bit he decided he'd had enough and gave up with his hands in the air. I told him to get in the truck and get out of there. As he closed the door and locked it with the window up, he fingered me. I put my right fist through the window at the same time my brother came running and punched out the rear side window. He put a perfect hole in it, but the window was still there. I then punched out the rest of the window and started to clear the broken glass out of the window frame with my hands. I was clearing a path so I could climb in to the vehicle to get this guy

I had torn my left wrist open as I tried to remove the glass, but with my adrenaline so high I didn't even notice. The guy managed to get the truck started just before I was going to dive into the vehicle, and took off. My brother then started walking down the street punching out car windows. He stopped when he approached Rob's car because Rob yelled out, "You punch out my window, you're walking home."

James took me to the hospital because I was losing a lot of blood from my wrist. Rob took my brother to get him patched up as well, but I had to get there first. While we were getting patched up, Rob and James were having wheelchair races in the hallways. Eventually they were kicked out, and waited in the parking lot for us. My brother got a ride home from Rob, and a cop who came to the hospital looking for me took me home. This cop just wanted to know what had happened, and was good with the whole thing. I sat in the front with him, and he didn't even make me wear my seatbelt. I had a thing about seatbelts since my older brother had held me in tight spots, and I felt constricted when wearing it. For instance, if I had been wearing my seatbelt that night of the trailer crash, I wouldn't have been able to duck down, and I might have been killed.

On the way to my place he was saying that I had really scared the hell out of those guys. I told him that Pitt Meadows was our town, and the Maple Ridge guys didn't get along with us, and they shouldn't have been there. He agreed with me, and when he dropped me off he said, "Don't be going back to that party now." I told him no problem, and when my brother, Rob and James showed up, we hopped in my brother's car and went back to the party. When we got there it had already been broken up by the riot squad. The next morning the party was on Vancouver's rock radio channel CFOX. They said that a riot had broken out at a house party Saturday night, and there was $1200 damage done to a Chevy Blazer. I did get charged for assault and was back in court again. I was getting good at representing myself so I pulled the prosecutor aside and made a deal with him. The deal was he would drop the assault and I would plead guilty to mischief and pay the guy's deductible for his insurance company, which he had to pay to get his truck fixed. I kept my mouth shut to save my brother's ass because they knew there were two of us, and even though we were in the same hospital that night they didn't know we were together because we came in at different times.

Two weeks after that court appearance I received a bill in the mail from the insurance company because now they knew who had done the damage, and they came after me for it since I had pleaded guilty. I thought that if I kept my mouth shut my brother would pay for half, but he never gave me a dime. "Brotherly love!"

I was drunk and walking down Harris Road about two in the morning one night, pissed off about something I can't remember. As I approached each road sign along the way I would jump up and punch them. The next day, as I was driving down the same road, you could see that all the signs for about half of a mile on both sides were bent over. The power that I had in that right hand was definitely not from this planet because it would go through just about anything, It's nothing to brag about now, however. I have scars on both wrists from all the cuts earned when I put my fists through glass windows. It is embarrassing when I put my hand out at a cash register to grab my change because the scars are easily visible. In the wintertime I used to have to sit on my right hand just to get it to move properly.

I was washing my '69 Chevelle one day and a friend of my little brother walked by about 4:15 p.m. I asked why he was late getting home from school. He told me that this black guy from school had put him up against the wall at the 7-11 store and tossed him around a bit. This guy was a few years younger than me, but he needed to be put in his place. I asked Sean if he knew where he lived, and he replied yes. I told him to get in the car and we headed for this guy's place. We were a few houses away and stopped him in his tracks. I got out of the car and started to call him everything under the sun. I yelled that if he ever bothered my brother or any of his friends again he would have to deal with me.

That night Mom got a phone call from the guy's mother. I hadn't realized his Mom was standing at the front door to his house and heard everything I said to her son. She called my Mom that night and told her that they had a hard enough time being the only black family in town, and didn't need anything from me to add to their problems. The conversation was calm, and when my Mom handed me the phone I apologized to her for everything I'd said. I also told her why I did such a thing, and she promised that she would talk to her son so what he'd done would never happen again.

I ran into that guy about eight years ago in a mall in Burnaby while I was buying clothes for my daughter. He was all dressed up and a totally different person. He apparently had joined the military services and become a U.S. Marine. It was good to see that he'd done something for himself, and in return he'd found himself.

I'm not a racist person by any means, but occasionally the odd wrong word slips out . I don't intend harm by it. I mean, I don't care what colour or race you are, I would still help you. My favourite actor is Denzel Washington and look how hot Halle Berry is. Denzel Washington had a good line when it comes to fighting in the movie *Remember the Titans* – "Any two-year-old can throw a punch; it's how you use it."

Some friends and I were up hanging out in the parking lot of the McDonalds in Maple Ridge. One of my friends, Bob, had just had his car painted. These other guys pulled up and we started a conversation. Everything seemed fine until we all went to leave and Bob noticed fresh scratches on his fender. One of these guys had brushed his Levi's jeans up against his fender to make all the scratches. They'd told us what party they were going to so I said we should go find the prick. We got to the house party just as they arrived. I told the guy, who just happened to be the toughest guy in the junior hockey league, that he needed to pay for another paint job. He told me to fuck off and the fight was on. He didn't land a single punch before he gave up, at which point I told him to start walking down the road to get the hell out of there. As he started on his merry way, I suddenly heard someone say, "Fuck this." and as I turned to face him again he dove on me, crashing us into a fence. Because I was at an odd angle when I hit the fence post, it knocked the wind out of me. I couldn't move, so he finally got a few shots in, and then he jumped up and down like he was the champ. Yeah, real hero, jumping me from behind, like my back wasn't screwed up enough from that car accident.

A friend was seeing this girl and she brought along her friend, Candy. We were all in his car and headed down to the airport. The two of them started to make out, so I grabbed Candy's hand and we walked towards a grassy area. Within a few minutes she was riding me and saying, "Fuck me, fuck me harder." She was only sixteen at the time and I couldn't believe what was coming out of her mouth. As soon as it was over, she jumped off "Stanley" (my penis) and started to give me head. You would think I would fall in love right there. We could have hooked up after this, but she was too young. What a piece of work, eh, but she was one hell of a screamer.

1989

It was summer and off to Penticton for Peach Fest in the Okanagan. It was like the college kids in Fort Lauderdale. Peach Fest is located where all the peaches grow in B. C. The town is in-between two lakes, Okanagan Lake and Lake Skaha. You can drive from one lake to the other in just twelve minutes. The sand can get so hot that you can't even stand on it. You have a choice: in the water, on a blanket, or sit on a chair.

Some of the people heading to Peach Fest would dress up a car to drive around, checking out the town. Three friends and I bought a 1976 Cutlass Supreme and made it into a "Batmobile" by cutting off the roof. Scooter just happened to be seeing this girl who was an artist. She drew the Batman emblems on the doors. When we arrived in Penticton we were pulled over and had to go through this roadside vehicle inspection that was there just to catch the beaters. Once we got there, all the tow-truck drivers, police and inspectors dropped everything and headed over to our car to check it out. They let us go with a whole sheet of things wrong with it, but told us that we only had to fix the front brake line that looked worn.

The 'Batmobile.' The photo was taken in Penticton at dusk outside of someone's house.

On one of our days at the beach Scooter was out on an air mattress talking to a couple of hot girls. I ran up to him in the water and told him that his girlfriend was looking for him, (she wasn't even there). Those girls paddled away on their air mattresses and boy, did I ever get a dirty look.

If that wasn't enough, he had this girl in the bedroom in our hotel room one night, so I knocked on the door and said, "Your old lady is coming up the stairs." That door flew open and she ran out of there, and man was he pissed. I guess he had every right to be pissed.

That night when he was passed out I shaved one of his eyebrows off. Man, was I ever an asshole.

That car kept dying on us so we eventually destroyed it and left it in the back of the hotel where we were staying. While we were at the festival we met up with Gus, a friend from home. We all did LSD the night before we left, so when we departed in the morning we were still high, and Gus gave us a ride home in the back of his truck. It was a about a five-hour drive, and just before we got home we pulled over to have a piss break. My back was killing me so I looked under me to see what the hell I was lying on, and realized it was the tool box that I had brought up there with us.

Once we were back home for a couple of weeks, I decided to have a party at my Mom's house, where I lived. The party was crazy, and a friend and I were up in my bedroom snorting coke. All of sudden there was a knock at my bedroom door and it opened. My buddy Jake said there was a guy in the house looking for my brother and threatening to kill him. As Jake was saying that, Scooter looked to me to see what I was going to do, but all he saw were the curtains in the window swaying in the wind. I'd gone out the window, jumped off the roof and landed in front of this guy. We started to fight and it ended up in the street. At one point the guy had pulled my sweater over my head and I couldn't see what I was hitting. We were on the ground by the back end of Terry's Honda Civic. I thought I was hitting him in the face, but when Terry pulled the sweater off my head I realized that I was punching the rear bumper of his car. Now that I could see him I started smashing his face in, and as a result split his face open from the top of his eye down to his cheekbone. The cops were called after the guy got home, and they were looking for me but had no success. They did stop a friend of mine at the 7-11 because he fit the description. Apparently the guy I beat up had come to the party because my brother, Jason, had not allowed the guy's younger brother into the party because Jason didn't know him. Seems they'd just moved into the area and I guess this guy thought that he was the boss, when in actual fact I was. I always liked to give a warm welcome.

I was still living at home, and was working afternoon shifts at this time. I had borrowed $100 off Jake, who is one of my best friends today. It's amazing how many people we call our friends, when really there are only a few of them you can count on… these are your true friends. I stopped by Jake's apartment to give him his money and he was there with a buddy of his, plus Melissa and Candy. They had been hanging out and drinking together most of the day, and Jake's friend was trying to get down Candy's pants. I walked in and opened my wallet to hand Jake his loot, when Candy grabbed it out of my hand and ran into the bathroom. I ran in there after her, and in thirty seconds, I was screwing her on the bathroom counter. When I was finished I pulled up my pants, said thanks for the screw, and thanked Jake for the loan. What a pissed off look Jake's buddy had on his face. I just laughed and left.

It was Christmas when Scooter and I went to Guildford Mall to do some Christmas shopping. There was a restaurant there called The Elephant and Castle. We sat in there from when it opened in the morning until one p.m., drinking. We did some shopping, and then went to Coquitlam Centre, where we decided to get our picture taken with Santa. We stood in line, and all I remember was talking to this little girl who was with her mother. I remember asking if she was a good girl, because Santa knows if you've been naughty or nice. Her mother was just laugh-

Scooter and me, shit-faced, with Santa at Coquitlam Centre in 1989. Scooter didn't get the blonde.

ing at us because I could barely stand, and we were waiting in line to see Santa. Scooter told me the next day that he'd asked Santa for a 20-year-old blonde, and Santa had said, "Me too, kid."

Shortly after that, I moved in with Jake, and naturally this became an animal house. I remember one time we were making strawberry margaritas. We were standing on the balcony watching these two girls on their balcony. The one was combing the other's hair and I yelled out, "What time is the dog show?" and they yelled out, "Fuck you, Magri." I didn't know who they were, but obviously they knew who I was. I then said, "Combing her hair isn't going to make her look any better." Man, do I know how to pick them up, or what? Saying this started an egg fight, and they eventually came over and partied with us.

I started seeing Tina, who was a real sweetheart, but I was just an asshole. I picked her up at school one day and she hopped into the car with this little basket. I asked what was in the basket, and she replied an egg. I said, "An egg, what for?" She said that she was supposed to look after it like a baby all weekend for an assignment. As we drove away with the basket on the seat, I hit the brakes and the egg ended up on the floor, broken. She kept saying, "My egg, My egg." I just said, "Well you should have been hanging on to that, it could have been your kid." I offered her a new egg, but she said no. She failed. Just one more lesson!

Tina and I were in the living room with Jake and his friend Daniel one day. Tina and I were playing around and I decided to let her have a free shot at hitting me in the face as I thought she couldn't even get close to hitting me. I closed my eyes and said, "Go ahead, hit me right in the face." I was waiting for a punch that took her a while to get the guts to do this, but when I opened one eye to see what was taking her so long, all I saw were her rings. That was the first time I saw stars, and it was a punch from a girl.

There are five spots on the head that enable you to knock someone out pretty easily if you hit them there. My neck was sore for a few days from that punch, and when she did it Jake and Daniel just said, "Oh no!" They thought that I was going to kill her. I will never do that again.

The next week I was cutting up some onions and noticed Jake and Daniel walking up to the front door to the building. I held the onion up to my face and forced tears to run down. When they entered the apartment I put on quite the show. They asked me what was wrong and I told them that I just got a bad phone call. They asked me if there was anything they could do and then I let the cat out of the bag. They both called me a fucking asshole and we laughed it off.

I was leaving to go out of town. I wanted to end the relationship with Tina so I told Jake to screw her while I was gone, so I would have a good reason to break up with her. What a coward I am. Jake had broken up with his girlfriend Melissa before I left, so the door was open for him to do this. When I returned from my vacation someone told me that Jake had slept with her when I was gone. I decided to play a game with him, so I told him that I hoped he hadn't slept with Tina because I had had time to think about it, and I really liked her. One week went by and Jake suffered the whole time before he finally told me what he had done. Before he could finish telling me, however, I told him that I already knew he'd slept with her. He was pretty pissed off, but eventually we had a good laugh about making him sweat for a week.

We were the talk of the apartment building, because Jake was now seeing Tina and I had started to date his ex-girlfriend, Melissa, and we could all sit in the same living room without a problem.

Jake had a friend who was in the navy. He was a little out there, but I wasn't a prize either. Jake had just picked him up at the port of Vancouver, all dressed up in his uniform. We all decided to go 4x4ing with Dan's truck up McNutt Mountain for the day, and we asked Rick if he wanted to get some other clothes to wear, but he said he would be fine. As you can guess the truck got stuck in a huge mess of mud. I found some wood to put under the rear tire to give us some traction. With Jake behind the wheel, and the rest of us pushing from the back, including Rick, we got Jake to mat it. Rick was directly behind the drive tire so he got himself all covered with mud. He had to board the boat that night, but without a clean change of clothes he decided go AWOL. He had to come up with a good excuse, so he sat on the couch with his leg extended on the coffee table and he had Jake jump on his leg in an attempt to snap it. Boy, what ideas we have when we are in these circumstances. Jake tried a couple of times but with no success. Daniel came down the hallway with a baseball bat. Rick looked up and was almost in tears when he said no fucking way to the bat. When he finally got back to the boat later that next week they threw him in jail. I didn't see that guy that often, but he would surface every once in a while. He sure loved his beer, and he looked and acted just like the bearded dude in the movie *The Hangover*. It could have been his brother.

After a while I started lifting weights and using steroids. What a downfall that turned out to be, like I wasn't nuts already. I quickly gained twenty-five pounds. I was six-foot four-inches tall with a thirty-one-inch waist, and I now weighed 235 pounds. Steroids made me feel like king of the hill, and I was very aggressive. I probably used steroids on and off for about ten years. I think I was addicted to the feeling it gave me.

I mention a lot of friends in this book, but in everyone's life there are real friends, and then there are users. I didn't know at this point whether all these guys that I mention were real friends or just people using me. It didn't matter, I had people around me and that was all that mattered.

Rick came back to town for a visit after a few months and we were sitting around talking and telling jokes and the phone rang. Ring. . .

Ring. . . Ring. . . . The ringing drove me nuts. Rick picked up the phone and handed it to me, all in a friendly manner, but I grabbed it out of his hands, head butted it and threw it into the middle of the living room floor. I then went out to the balcony to grab a screw driver out of my toolbox. I walked back in, jumped on that phone and started stabbing the phone with it. After the phone was destroyed I decided it was time to stop taking the juice, but that didn't last long. When you use steroids, it is so easy to lose your temper at the drop of a hat.

Shortly after this episode I moved out of the two-bedroom apartment and into a single apartment in the same building because Jake was moving into his mom's basement suite with Tina. This was my first time living on my own, and I developed a case of obsessive compulsive disorder (OCD). It started with how I walked into a room, I had to leave the same way I entered. Then it gradually worsened, and soon I was touching the doorknobs and things a couple of times before I could walk away. I don't know what my lesson was, except maybe how quickly I took control, because after a year, without any assistance, I eventually stopped doing these things. Like a lot of things in my life I kept this a secret, and nobody even noticed that I had this disorder.

Scooter and I went to a house party the day I got my Chevelle out of the body shop with a new paint job. When we arrived I parked the car down the road, away from everyone else. A bunch of us were standing outside when a guy came up to us and said some guy was beating up his girlfriend. I took off with this guy so he could show me where this was happening. I ran over to where this guy had his girlfriend on the ground; he was sitting on her chest with his knees pinning her shoulders. I jumped on this guy and gave him the beating of his life. While this was happening, Scooter told me his girlfriend was trying to pull me off him. I was so focused on beating this guy into the ground that I didn't notice she was trying this, nor did I know that Scooter was also trying to get me to stop. When I eventually got off the guy, Scooter and I left the party, and when we got back to the car there was a noticeable dent in the driver's door and a beer bottle through the windshield. I guess that's the thanks you get. Was this a lesson about not interfering? Just stand by and watch what was going on? No. I couldn't stand by. Just because this didn't turn out well doesn't mean you stop helping people. Sometimes you have good intentions that are not appreciated at the time, but come back to you later.

I helped again, at the local hotel, when I witnessed this guy smacking his girlfriend around while we were waiting in the bar line up. I gave him a beating on the bar floor right then and there. About a year later we were sitting in the strip joint and that same guy's girlfriend was working there. She was going around in her bikini charging the horny guys for a massage. She noticed me across the room and came over to give me one. As she was massaging me she was telling me that she remembered what I'd done for her that night and told me this one was on the house. How perfect… I'm on my day off with a couple of buddies, watching girls take their clothes off at the same time I'm getting a rub down, and I have a beer in one hand. Good things come to those who wait.

A friend of mine was having a party and he asked if another buddy and I could watch the door that night. I said no problem. Ernie had a large set of lips and people would often bug him about it. When this happened, he would normally take care of things himself, what with the boxing experience he had when he was younger. In a short time I would be boxing myself. I was in the house when Ernie came to get me because there seemed to be a problem outside. He told me there where about ten guys out there that he didn't know, and they were bugging him because of his lips and wouldn't leave. I said let's go deal with this. I had already drunk a twenty-six ouncer of rum and a case of beer, and I was in no condition to battle, so I did something I never did – I stood there with my arms crossed and told them all to get the fuck out of here.

Normally I never approached anybody without being ready, and my shoes were always tied tight before a blood bath. You lose a shoe in battle and you could lose the fight. I didn't notice, but the guy I was telling to get out, and to take his friends with him, had a beer bottle in his right hand. He told me to go fuck myself and turned like he was going to walk away, but he smashed me on the right side of my face with the bottle. I blacked out but was still standing, and he hit me in the face with his fist and down I went.

I woke up on all fours with this guy punching me in the face, and wondering why my face was warm and wet. Ernie pulled this guy off me, and when I stood up and looked at my hands I knew I was cut open. I took my shirt off to hold the right side of my face together, and I was driven to the hospital. I received 23 stitches around my eye and down my nose because the bottle broke on my face.

The guy that did this to me found out who I was and managed to find my number; this wasn't hard because everyone knew me. He called the next day to apologize. I just gave him a devil laugh, and told him that when I found him I was going to carve his face up so bad his family wouldn't recognize him, and hung up the phone.

When my Dad found out what had happened he told me to do go carve the guy up like he'd done me. My older brother said, "Don't do that, sue him and get a house out of the deal." I never wanted to be a rat, but I took my brother's advice and charged him. I already had it in my mind that after the court proceedings I was going to wait a few years and have this guy taken care of. He finally was charged with assault with a weapon, and the court proceedings would happen in 1992.

Time marches on and I still had not learned many lessons, or figured out why all this was happening to me.

James and I were hanging out at the 7-11 when this guy and three girls showed up. This guy was a lot bigger than I was, but I wanted a piece of him. I wanted to fight this guy because he was showing off by throwing some kicks and thought he was something. Pat, and a friend of his, pulled into the store parking lot, and when I approached them I said that I was going to light this guy up like a Christmas tree. Pat, looking at the guy, said to me, "Look at the size of that guy Magri, are you sure?" I looked at Pat and said, "Yeah, want to watch the show?" I turned to this guy and told him to get the fuck out of here. He looked at me with a smile, then took off his cowboy boots and walked over. I laid a licking on this guy, and when he was lying there I let James finish him off.

Just fight, fight and more fighting, just get the guy down. Don't get in my face or you will regret it. Take my revenge. I always come to the rescue. Where was all this coming from? Did I have a terrible need to right the wrongs that had been done to me over the previous years? I would find out much later, without help from my Dad, just how many lessons I was put on this Earth to learn. And I am still learning. There are a lot of beatings in this book, but they all come to an end when I end up in jail in 1997.

The only fight that I could honestly say was a draw, was one night down at the cross roads. I was good friends with these brothers in town. They were a family that farmed all the blueberries in the area, and I would work out at the weight gym they had in a barn. They had everything that you needed there. It was nice and dumpy in there, which made you feel like you were training for a *Rocky* fight.

I had just had my nose fixed for the third time, and I had a cast on it. Melissa and I were drinking down at the crossroads when five guys showed up from Maple Ridge. One guy, who was bigger than the rest, told one of the brothers to give him a beer, so the brother reached into his case to hand him one. I couldn't let that happen to the guy who let me work out at his house for free. I stepped in, ripped my cast off, and said that if he wanted a beer he'd have to go through me first. The guy looked at me, paused for a second, took off his leather jacket and the fight was on. This guy didn't know how to go toe to toe, but he was sure strong.

I'd been off the juice for a while by this time and was a lot smaller, but this guy was juiced to the max. He had a hold of my hair and was trying to slam my head into the hood of a truck without success. I was throwing what punches I could because it was an inside fight. At this point, I knew he was waiting for me to tire out, but before that happened my girlfriend showed up and got in-between us. Maybe it was a good thing because a friend of mine found a handgun on the ground after the fight.

Being a fighter your whole life, something like a draw bothers you until it is finished. I never had the opportunity. I had a reputation to protect and that bothered me for almost twenty years; it took me that long to learn this lesson. Let it go. I actually got hold of him through Facebook because I found out that his wife was a photographer, and I thought it would be cool if his wife took the photo shots for the cover of this book. He said they were interested but it never materialized. Too bad.

A bunch of us were heading to our favourite beach, White Pine. On the way home, we ran out of gas and had to walk to the station, which was about a mile or so up the road. I was trying to use my bank card and it wouldn't work. This older guy, who was paying for his gas, asked me how much I needed. I told him $10 would get me home, so he opened his wallet and handed me $10. He told me the next time I was in the area I should drop the money off with one of the workers at the station because they all knew him, and he would be sure to get it. The next day I drove out there to drop it off. It cost me that in gas to get there and back home, but I had to get that to him. Thanks.

Back on the crank, and having larger traps than Goldberg, it was off to an outdoor party. While outside talking to some people in the backyard, someone came to get me because my little brother was getting thrown around. I ran over to where this was going on, grabbed this guy and threw him into the fire. He suffered a few burns but it could have been a lot worse. Hey, it sounds like Johnny Cash's song *Burning Ring of Fire.*, It should be *Throw him in the fire.*

At this time I had my driver's licence suspended for three months due to a poor driving record. I had a co-worker pick me up for work in the morning. On the way there we stopped to let this guy merge into traffic. Because I was always on principle I snapped when this guy didn't wave his hand at us to thank us for letting him in. When the traffic came to a halt I jumped out of the car in a rage to approach this guy about his manners. It was winter, and with the road being icy I was slipping everywhere and just getting madder. When I approached the car I just about ripped the window out of the door. The driver was leaning away from me, stretched out across the passenger seat. As I was yelling at this guy, telling him that he should say "thank you" when somebody lets him merge, he was saying, "Okay, Okay" – but with a smile on his face. I think he was smiling due to the fact that I was so angry over such a small infraction, but I bet he will never do that again. So many of the severe over-reactions I've had in my life were over things that now seem so minor, and that just blows me away.

1990

I had just put my Chevelle away for the winter and bought a beater to drive . A friend, Bill, and I headed out in the beater to do some shopping at Costco in Burnaby. As we were driving along the Mary Hill Bypass I said to Bill, "Have you ever hit a cement median before?" He replied, "No I haven't." I said, "Neither have I" and started to steer the car towards the median in an attempt to sideswipe the car against the concrete while going 90 km/h. I could see in the rear view mirror the traffic starting to back off. I must have been only a centimetre away from impact but just didn't have the balls that day to go through with it. When we got to Costco we parked underground and did our shopping. When we came back to the car it still bothered me that I hadn't had the balls to wipe out the side of my car, so I steered the front clip of the car into the cement pillars holding up the building and put the pedal to the floor. It was a four door Nova, so all the door handles, moulding and the mirror were ripped off, and the side was all smashed in. What did I care? It was a winter beater. About three weeks later I received a letter in the mail from the motor vehicle branch with a warning about dangerous driving. I guess someone had taken my plate number and reported the incident on the bypass.

Another Saturday night down at the cross roads, and another fight. As this guy was walking backwards, egging everyone on in front of him, I stepped forward so he would walk into me. As he bumped into me, he spun around and shoved me. I then smiled at him, and put him to sleep. Just as he hit the ground I noticed his friend throwing his beer bottle at me. I moved to my right and the bottle went over my left shoulder. I grabbed a hold of the guy, threw him on the hood of a car, and started beating him. I was hitting this guy so hard his head was caving in the hood. After I finished him off I asked someone for a smoke so I could calm down. This guy puts a smoke in my mouth and two girls with him said it was their car that got damaged. After a couple drags I apologized for their car and offered to pay for the damages. They said, "No way, that was something else to watch, and he had it coming." The next day I was driving down River Road and there were those two girls, at Gary's Auto Wrecking getting a hood for their car. Hey girls, sorry about that. I hope you enjoyed the entertainment.

My Mom called me one afternoon and asked if I wanted to go on a cruise with her. It was a Carnival cruise that was to visit Cozumel, Mexico, the Grand Cayman Islands and Jamaica, so of course I said sure. Nothing to report about the first two places we visited, but Jamaica was a lot of fun. Just as the ship docked, and we were about to aboard for the island of Jamaica, the captain got on the intercom and told everyone to stay away from the fence that was just up the way from the boarding dock. He was telling us this because the islanders would be climbing all over it asking us if we wanted to get a ride somewhere with them. My Mom stayed on the boat that day so I joined these two other guys to seek out some adventure. As we walked up to the fence I looked to my left and here was this guy on our side of the fence, wearing all this jewellery and telling us to come follow him. Clearly this was the guy that ran the show on the island, so I looked at the guys I was with and I said, "We're going with him." We followed this guy around the fence, hopped in his car, and off we went. At least I thought it was his car until he started it with

Mom and me on the Caribbean cruise she took me on in 1990.

a screw driver. I asked him, "Where did you steal this car?" He looked at me with a smile and I said, "Get us out of here" and away we went. As we were driving, everybody would be waving at this guy, and now I knew he was the man.

I asked him, "How about taking us to the marijuana fields?" He said no problem, but it would take about four hours. I told him we had to be back at the boat in four hours so that wasn't going to happen. He told me to reach back, grab the bag he had, and hand it to him. He pulled out some pot he had in the side zipper and handed it to me to roll up. We smoked it back, then we got him to drop us off at some waterfalls, and to come back and grab us in an hour and a half. Well just over two hours later we walked back to where we were dropped off to see a line of cars up the road but no sign of our crooked driver. I asked one of the cabbies if they had seen our driver, and when I gave a description he said, "That's Jerry." This cabbie yelled out the guy's name and all the drivers started yelling for him. I looked up the road, and at the top of the hill there he was, jumping up and down. He grabbed his car, or should I say the car he had, and took us back to the dock. I remember one of the guys I was with grabbed some pot off of him before we left Jerry, and I didn't see that guy all till the next day. He said that he got so paranoid smoking all that dope that he couldn't come out of his room that night.

It was the summer of 1990 and I was off camping with a few friends at Harrison Lake. My friend Greg couldn't make it until the next day so I was going to drive back the next afternoon and bring him up to Harrison. We found this spot that was along the lake, far from everybody else. The next day I drove to get Greg but he wasn't home, so I loaded up with beer and headed back solo. My objective was to be more intoxicated than them. It was just over an hour's drive and I had already drunk eighteen beers. I was drinking them so fast I couldn't stop burping up foam. When I got to the gravel road just before the campsite this guy in a Chevy Blazer stopped me and asked if I had a light. I said I didn't, so he asked if the lighter in the dash worked and I said yeah. He held up this big ball of hash and I told him to get in. He rolled up some smaller balls and dropped them into the lighter, and after smoking that I was just about paralysed. I managed to get to the site where I made the decision to get back into the car and head down to the other campsite. I was so intoxicated I had locked the driver's door and couldn't get the key into the lock to open it. I could see that the passenger door was unlocked so I rolled my body along the side of the car until I made it to that door. I opened the door, reached over, and grabbed the steering wheel to pull myself across the seat, then started the car and drove away.

Unfortunately for me, they were just starting to pave the road so once I hit blacktop I picked up the pace a bit. The pavement ended and went to gravel again just before a corner. I didn't make the corner and clipped a pole, smashing my nose on the steering wheel before driving off a cliff. Ironically, on the drive up I had looked down the cliff as I went by and said to myself, "I would hate to end up down there." So already knowing this, I managed to dive down to the floor and hang onto the dashboard. The car was picking up speed as it headed down the mountainside bouncing off of the trees, but finally it came to a halt. It only went down about 70-100 feet before it got caught up in a tree. I could see people down below with a big fire at the beach so I pushed the door open with my feet to get out. I heard this guy tell me to stay in the car, but I told him not to worry, that this was a minor accident. I climbed down to the beach and they had the ambulance coming.

The cops showed up before the ambulance, and while I was leaning up against a car a cop came up to me and asked if I had been drinking. I said to him, "Look at me, I'm shit-faced." I remember him smiling, and he told me to wait right there because the ambulance was on its way. I told the cop, "Look what I did to my car." I told him to throw the book at me, and I asked him to give me the max. I already knew what a lesson was, and I always took my lumps. After the paramedics looked at me and said everything was fine, I was cuffed and put in the cop car. On the drive to the cop shop, the cop was telling me that I had co-operated so well with him he would really like to wash the whole thing away, but how could he explain me having driven off a cliff. He also told me that when he'd gotten out of his car and seen the size of me, he'd shaken his head and said to himself, "Not tonight."

He had a new rookie female cop with him that night so I'm glad I didn't give him a hard time. Back at the cop shop, they got a call about a fight at a party they had to attend, and being the only ones on duty they had to take me with them. I could barely fit in the back of his car as I was so cranked up on steroids. We arrived at the house party, grabbed this guy, and when they went to put him in the back, the cop said to the guy, "Now give Scott all the room he needs." I just smiled at this guy because he looked terrified. I got charged with drunk driving and the cops were nice enough to drive me to a bank machine to get money for a cab to get back to the camp. They actually came back to the bank to see if I was still there, waiting, and I was, so they called the cab company to see if they were on their way, at which point the cab rolled in. I told them thanks for everything and waved goodbye.

My friends didn't believe what had happened so I showed them the "promise to appear" court papers. I was sober by this point, and asked them how they could have let me drive away like that? James said, "Well Mag, you know what you are like," and I replied, "Yes, but you could have just pushed me over I was so drunk."

The 1969 Chevelle that I drove off a cliff at Harrison Hot Springs.

You can't blame anyone else for your own mistakes, and you're the one that makes the decisions. The funny thing about this was that when I went to see my car at the garage on the way home, that same Chevy Blazer was in their yard too because it had gone down the same cliff a little further down the road from where I went off. Boy, that cop sure had a busy night.

Everyone has a choice, and why I chose this path is anyone's guess. But at that point I wasn't thinking like that. All I could do was what I wanted to do, and to hell with anyone else. Another lesson learned.

When I got home, I grabbed the local paper and starting looking for another car. I found one in Maple Ridge. A 1968 Beaumont, and by Tuesday I had the loan and picked it up. On Friday Melissa and I were having more problems so I took my car for a drive to burn off some steam. I was doing more than a 140 km in a 50 km zone when a pickup truck decided to stop and hang a left. Going at that speed there was no way I could stop. He had stopped with his signal on to turn left, and there was a kid on his bike to my right who froze when he saw me coming. I had a split-second decision to make, and decided to drive between the truck and the boy even though I thought I would end up crashing into a heritage building after hitting the sidewalk. I slammed on the brakes and headed for the building. I hit the curb and the car bounced up into the air, spun ninety degrees, and slammed into the side of the truck before coming to a rest. I guess I made the right decision because no one was hurt, and the only damage to my car was the front left fender. I found out last year that there is a ghost story about the heritage building. The man that used to live there died in his bed upstaires many years ago and you can still hear him from time to time.

My heart was beating so fast, talk about an adrenalin rush. Thank goodness the boy on the bicycle was unharmed. I felt a great relief, and with my heart beating a mile a minute I realized I had made the right choice in handling my car as I did. Split decisions. Quick decisions are a part of my daily life, and I hoped that one day I would see the reasoning behind all of the torture I put myself through. Where is the peace? Where is the freedom? I still had much to find out about myself.

The driver and his buddy in that truck had a Harley Davidson in the box, and when I smashed into his truck the force knocked over the Harley. After smashing up two cars in less than a week you could say I wasn't in a good mood. I told the guys before the cops got there that all of this would be covered under my insurance, and that I had $3,000,000 in liability so they should tell them the frame on the bike was bent so they could get a new one. They both looked at me and smiled just as the cop showed up. This cop started in with me, and I said to him, "You came here from the doughnut shop and now you're going to tell me what happened here." He said, "Shut your mouth or we will take it downtown."

I ended up just getting a speeding ticket, which I took to court to fight. I thought, how could he give me a speeding ticket when there was no officer to see how fast I was going? Two witnesses came to court that day, one of the guys from the truck, and an off-duty cop who had been putting air in his tire at the Chevron gas station, and who had seen everything.

They put the guy from the truck up first and he was asked if he even saw me coming or if he saw anything at all. He told them he didn't see anything, just felt the impact. He was released and as he was walking out of the courtroom, he turned his eyes my way and smiled as if to say, "Thanks for the new bike." I smiled back, as if to say, "Thanks for not saying anything."

It was the off-duty cop's turn on the stand, and he told the court I was doing at least double the speed limit. Well, I was doing more than that, and now it was my turn to cross-examine him. I stood up and asked him, "If your eyesight is so good, why are we wasting taxpayer's money on radar guns if you guys are that accurate?" I asked the cop who gave me the ticket if I could borrow his pen for a minute. I held up the pen to the witness and told him not to take his eyes off it.

I said, "Okay, here we go, watch the pen." Then I threw it across the courtroom. "How fast was that going?" I asked. The judge started to smile at me. The witness looked like he was getting upset by the question. He said, "I'm not an expert on how fast pens travel across a court room." The judge told him to answer the question, then turned to me and smiled again. The cop replied, "About three miles an hour." I said, "It is impossible to know how fast that pen was travelling and not even the judge knows, so how can you know how fast I was going?"

Surprisingly enough, the judge said to me that even though I put on a good show for them that day, he still had to find me guilty as the witness had been a cop for twenty-five years, and had a reasonably good idea about how fast I was going. What a bunch of bullshit. I should have won that by a landslide, but in Provincial Court you leave your law books at the door and the judges do whatever they want. I guess the best way to describe me would be just like the guy who played "Clifford" in the movie *Dead man on Campus*... always going 100 miles an hour and hair straight back. My friends would always call me "Turbo," "Crash" or "Smash."

Marcello, a new trainee at work, calls me a "Showpiece." My favourites out of all the new kids hired in the last couple of years would have to be Anthony and Hunter, they remind me a little of myself. The guys at work call Anthony "Mini Mag" because he's just like me, but smaller, and I even had a shirt made for him that say's "Mini Mag" on the back. "Beauty!" he would say.

It was time for my court case for the impaired charge, and I knew that I was going to lose my licence for a year because it was mandatory. Prior to the court case I had sold that 1968 Beaumont and bought a winter beater, something I didn't care if someone else drove for me. Sure enough, when the case came up for my impaired charge I did lose my licence for a year, ten points and a $1,000 fine. While I was waiting in the courtroom for my case to come up, I listened to two other impaired charges. Just before the judge handed them their sentences he asked them if there was anything they wanted to add. It didn't matter what they said, they both got the same thing. Now it was my turn to tell the Judge what I wanted to add and he gave me the same thing. After he gave me my sentence I snapped at him and said, "Well, what the hell is the point of you asking us if we have something to add if you're not going to give a shit anyways." On my way to the door I turned to the judge and wished him a Merry Christmas, then kicked the court doors open. It was only early September.

Now, here was the situation: NO DAMNED CAR! Like this was a surprise to me. I was always "on the ready"' to come and go as I pleased, but now that would be curtailed big time. I now had to depend on others to get me to work, get home from work, to plan ahead for a ride for anything I wanted to do. Depend on others? What is that? I had to learn this lesson very quickly. This was, as they say, a rude awakening. Just imagine coming home from work, looking at your four walls and you need smokes. I had never relied on anyone except myself up to this point, and now I thought I could depend on the many friends that I had helped through the years. We know how that would turn out.

I only ever did something mean to one of my friends once in my whole life. This friend, Dan, was over one day years ago, and we were playing around on this pogo stick I got for Christmas in 1981. As he was jumping up and down on this thing I kicked it out from under him while he was in the air and he landed on his back on the concrete. He started to cry and ran out the basement door. I chased after him, laughing and telling him to come back because it couldn't have been that bad. Don't ever do this to your friends. Better yet, don't ever buy your kids a pogo stick for Christmas.

What we do for the ones that we think are our friends. For instance, years later in 2001, this guy from work needed a truck to finish pulling this tree out of his yard, and I said that he could borrow mine. I went to his house after work because I had a winch on my truck and he needed this tree torn out of the ground and taken to the dump. I hooked up the winch and pulled it out, and we loaded it up in my truck. He also told me that he needed to take all the junk from cleaning up his yard. I loaned him my truck for the weekend, and when he was done to bring it back. He said that he would leave a case of beer on the seat of my truck but I told him that he didn't have to do that. Now that being said, you would think he would do it anyway, but the case wasn't there. I had no idea that he was cleaning up his yard because he was having a party the next weekend. I lived about a block away, and when the day came for his party he never even gave me a call to invite me. Just another user, I guess. However, he did give me a ride to work a couple of times when I didn't have enough gas to get me there, so maybe that was his idea of payback.

Another man from work that I played golf with about a dozen times a year was having a family golf tournament. In the lunchroom at work he was telling another co-worker about the tournament. He didn't know that I was standing behind him. He quietly told this guy to keep it quiet because he didn't want me there. I put my hand on his shoulder and walked away, passing in front of him while looking right into his eyes. I hope he felt like shit.

On another occasion, I took orders from people at work for some salmon because friends I had down at the Indian reserve had an opening on the river to catch some sockeye. The same guy who didn't want me at the golf tournament was one of the guys who put an order in with me. I was just doing this as a favour for the guys on the reserve and not making a dime on it.

On the Saturday I had the fish at my place for pick up. Everybody had come and picked up their fish but the golf guy, so I gave him a call and asked when he was coming because the fish weren't on ice. He told me he was busy with something, and asked if I could put them on ice until the next day when he would come and pick them up. I said sure not a problem.

I went and bought some ice with my own money and packed them on ice in a cooler for him. I found out later that week that he couldn't come because he was having a party at his house. Why couldn't he say he was having a party, and to grab a case of beer, the fish and come over? Just another heartless, selfish user. You have to give the person another chance, but if nothing changes with them then give up on them for they have to learn more lessons in order for them to change. Then you can help them again.

I have added this poem for my Grandfather Nodge, who passed away, because he loved poetry. He would write poems on his typewriter, which I have at home. I found this poem in his wallet, which my Aunt gave me after he passed; she said it was his favourite. I don't know if he wrote this, or if he got it from somewhere, although it was typed on a small piece of paper. This poem didn't have a name but I suspect it could be called:

FRIEND

There are pioneer souls that blaze their paths, where highways never ran.
But let me live by the side of the road, and be a friend to man.
Let me live in a house by the side of the road, where the race of men go by.
The men who are good and the men who are bad, as good and as bad as I.
I would not sit in the scorner's seat, or hurl the cynic's ban.
Let me live in a house by the side of the road, and be a friend to man.

Webster's Dictionary:

FRIEND: *One who is attached to another by affection; one who has esteem and regard for another and loves his society; one not hostile; one of the same nation, party or kin; one who looks with favour upon a cause, institution, or the like; also a term of salutation or familiar address.*

I felt that I had taken responsibility, and thanked my lucky stars that I had not injured anyone while driving drunk or stoned.

1991

Once in a while lighter moments happened, but these times were far and few between. I experienced a sense of joy for a fraction of time. I now know that with all the violence I was involved in, it does take a toll. Sometimes it felt like I was standing outside of my body and watching the funny things that I did. Basically, I really am a funny guy. The joking and laughter and appearing to be so confident; sometimes this was an act to cover up the pain I felt inside. No one to talk to. No, that's not right. I could have asked for help but that would have shown I was weak, and needed a crutch to get through. It was better to keep all of my thoughts inside and try to ignore the pain.

An example of a lighter moment was the time Jake and I were hanging around the apartment, and out of the corner of my eye I noticed something floating down past the patio doors. Believe it or not, it was a hamster wearing a parachute. A what? I opened the door and looked on the ground, and who do I see running to the hamster but my younger brother Jason. He and his friend had tied a parachute to him that they'd got from a box of Crackerjack. The hamster wasn't hurt at all from this. In fact, as he went past the window it looked like he was having the time of his life.

I was having a heated argument with Melissa at a party and felt I needed to get into a fight to burn off some steam. I called my boys and headed to Frisco's. Bill was driving, and when we arrived I got him to pull up front and told him to wait right there as I'd be right out. He said, "No way man, we're coming in to watch the show." It didn't take me long to find an altercation. I cased out the joint and noticed this table of guys in the corner. I waited until one left to go to the can, and then went and sat at the table. Nobody at the table said anything to me but I knew this guy was going to be pissed off when he came back. Sure enough, when he arrived back, he said, "You're sitting in my chair." I stood up and said, "It's my chair." Then I hit him with a right. Down he went, and I jumped on him.

I got the worst of it because the bouncers grabbed me first, and that enabled this guy to use his feet to kick me in the face. They escorted me out the front door, and I said, "What about him?" They told me he would be thrown out the back door so I ran around the building but there was nobody in sight. My boys came out to find me, and we hopped back in the car and headed for home. That was enough for the night. You can always throw your right when you know your opponent doesn't know what he's doing. Why waste a left when you can put him down with a right.

I had moved into a new apartment by myself and was still seeing Melissa. I was the only one moving into the building that day on the third floor. I had moved everything to my apartment, other than one large plant. I left it in the hallway, as I was the only one on that floor, thinking it would be safe until the morning. Well, what a surprise! First thing I saw when I opened the door in the morning, was… nothing. My plant had disappeared.

A few months later, Barry dropped by for a few beers. He asked me if I wanted to go down to the first floor to visit a friend of his. I agreed. I wasn't in this friend's apartment thirty seconds when I noticed my plant in the living room. Right away I said, "That's my plant."

There were lots of knives all over the floor and I kicked them out of the way to get to my plant. Barry's friend stood up, but Barry told him it would be a good idea if he sat down. I grabbed my plant and took it up to my apartment. My plant had sentimental value to me because I had personally repotted it when I was kicked out of high school one day, and what is personal is personal, even a plant.

.

I had heard that Melissa was sleeping around with another guy and we broke up for good. Hearing this information, and knowing what she had done to me, was hard to swallow. But after a few days it was onward and upward, and off I went to the next challenge. I'd lost my licence and now my girl. I'd had enough. Now what?

I had a shoebox in my closet where I kept my steroids and needles. I went into the closet and took out a syringe. I'd heard that if you have an air block going to your heart it will stop your heart. I filled the syringe up with air and injected it into a vein in my arm… at least I thought it was a vein. I then lay on my bed waiting to go but it never happened. It wasn't because the girlfriend and I broke up. It was everything else I had gone through that led up to the decision to end my life, but the break-up was the icing on the cake. I was here for a reason, just like everybody else, but I couldn't figure out why.

I went drinking with a friend of mine at the Haney Hotel. When we left, and were heading to the car, we were approached by these three guys from Burnaby. They'd came out this way to challenge me, but unfortunately my friend couldn't beat his way out of a wet paper bag. I just stopped and looked at these guys to see who I was going to hit first. Luckily another friend, Bruce, came running to help. It was then that I said, "Now the fight is on."

I was fighting this guy who was throwing all these kicks, and just as I knocked him out I looked over and saw that Bruce had one guy out cold and the other one was ready to hit the ground. Before he hit the asphalt I ran over and kicked this guy in the face, knocking him out. One of the guys had gotten up and started their car. I walked over and started kicking the tail lights out, telling them not to come back. One of them had to pick the another guy up and put him in the car. I talked to someone later that week who happened to talk with the manager at the hotel afterwards, and the manager told him about the incident. She said it was the worst bloodbath she had ever seen in her seventeen years as the manager there.

I had moved into a townhouse with Shane, the guy I grew up with. This was a new place and they only rented it to me because the same company that owned the apartment building I was living in owned the townhouses, and they did not have any complaints while I was there. It was going to be a different story now that there were two of us. We got an eviction notice the second week of living there. We partied every night, and a neighbour walked over one night and told us to cut it out because his kid was waking up in thc middle of the night crying about monsters.

Jake and I got back to the townhouse one night after partying down at the crossroads. We had left early because my ex-girlfriend, Melissa was there and I could see that she was talking to Jake about something. Once we got back I asked him, "What did she say to you?" and he said, "You don't want to know." But he told me anyway. Turns out Melissa had said that whenever she saw me, she wanted to puke. What a horrible thing to say. I picked up the bike that was in the hallway and threw it into the living room, smashing the glass in the coffee table, and started to punch holes through the kitchen and living room walls. When I punched a hole through the den wall I forgot that the electrical panel was on the other side and the power shut down. At first it looked a mess, until we realized it was easier to ask visitors what they wanted to drink because you could look through all the holes in the place.

My buddy called me up one day to help bring his chickens in to get slaughtered. We pulled up to this guy's backyard with forty chickens in the back of a truck, and started to unload them over at this lean-to. They had these funnels nailed to six posts, with five-gallon buckets under them. My buddy said, "Come on, let's go," but I wanted to stay and watch. As my buddy walked to his truck I watched these two guys put on their plastic aprons. They each grabbed a chicken out of the cages and cut their heads off with an axe on a chopping block. Then they put the headless chickens upside down in these funnels so that as the chickens did the bacon, the blood would pour down the funnels and into the buckets. I just shook my head and walked away.

I was in traffic the other day next to a semi-truck that had all those chickens in tiny cages. Some of them were dead, probably because of the stress. I can't believe how inhumane we are when it comes to feeding ourselves. How would you like me to shove you in that small cage? It wouldn't feel good. Trust me, I know what it feels like to live in cage. Any living creature that can eat pebbles and shit them out should deserve a little respect. You have to kill them some way I guess, but some chickens are raised in small cages. Come on!

I had only been at this nightclub in Port Coquitlam, called Club Chaos, a few times. This one night, after leaving the club, Pat and I, with a few other people, headed over to McDonalds for something to eat. The drive thru was the only thing open at that time, and there was a line-up that looked about a forty-five minute wait. I was in the back seat when we approached the window, and just as we pulled up to the window they told us they were closed. Being on steroids I didn't have much patience. I lost it in that back seat. I wanted to get at the order person, but Pat wasn't letting me get out of the car. It was only a two-door, and Pat had his legs up on the dashboard, pushing back to stop the seat from coming forward and at the same time yelling to his girlfriend, "Go, go, go.," Pat knew that if he had let me out I would have smashed the drive-thru window, and would have gone inside and wrecked the joint. I guess I should thank him for that. I had been in enough trouble, and I didn't need any more, short fuse or not.

I had just come from the doctor's office, and he told me that it was time to stop fighting or I wouldn't be able to move my hands when I was older. At the time I had started to see Candy, and we were on our way to the Haney Hotel for a night out.

I didn't know that Candy was still having contact with her ex-boyfriend. She told him that we were going to the Haney that night, and he wasn't too happy about it. He knew who I was, and because he couldn't take me on himself, he brought this big juice monkey with him. I was off the juice for a while at this point so I was a little smaller. While in the bar this guy was giving me the eye and throwing ice cubes at me. I was trying so hard not to retaliate because of what the doctor had told me.

It was closing time, and when we were outside this guy started to call me "MAG FAG." The whole bar was out there, waiting to see what would happen. I guess they were wondering why I wasn't ripping his head off. I was just standing about seventy feet from him when a guy from school came up to me and asked how I was doing. I told him that I was just wondering if I was going to put this guy in the hospital or not. He asked me, "What are you going to do?" I looked at him and said, "I think I'm going to put him in the hospital." I gave him my jacket to hold. I walked up to this guy saying, "Okay, you want to go, let's go." His hands weren't up in a fighting stance so I led with a right hand, but he ducked and went to grab me around the waist to take me down. Just as this happened I thought, shit I'm done, but threw a right uppercut anyway, which landed on his chin. His eyes rolled back and he was out like a light.

I grabbed him by the hair with both fists and threw him to the ground. I jumped on him and started smashing him in the face. I was hitting this guy so hard his head was bouncing off the pavement every time I hit him. It was like bouncing a basketball. When I got off of him I heard this guy calling my name. I turned to my left to take him on and realized it was a police officer who knew me. He was trying to calm me down. When I was calm, I told the cop the other guy had started it. Two other officers came over,.who just happened to be by the Chevron gas station across the street, and who had seen everything. They put me in the back of the cop car until they figured everything out.

While I was sitting in the back of the car, Candy's ex walked in front of the car while looking through the windshield at me. I had no handcuffs on so I was able to look back at him and run my finger across my throat, giving him the sign that I was going to kill him. The police opened the door to the car, let me out, and asked if my hand was okay.

The police told me that they had seen everything, and that this guy was egging me on and had it coming. I asked if they were going to charge me with assault, and they said they wouldn't know until he woke up. I had to wait until the ambulance arrived to see if he was going to make it or not before they were going to let me leave. I heard that after a few days in the hospital he was released and there were no charges.

It's funny, months later I was at a house party in Port Coquitlam and that same guy came up to me. I didn't know this was his party. He shook my hand and said, "Man I thought that I was tough, but you sure cleaned me up." Then he told me to enjoy myself as this was his party. Those days are over, now everyone uses guns.

We left the party just after he shook my hand because we didn't know anybody there and things might have gotten ugly if we had stuck around. Who knew whether this guy was going to change his mind, and then I would have 100 guys on my ass. I didn't see Candy for very long. She was a wing nut. I know this might sound like a perfect match, but it wasn't.

Bill and I had pulled an all-nighter, and were in the parking lot of the liquor store waiting for it to open. We headed back to my apartment, and were later going to a party at my friend Bob's house, who lived on Lougheed Highway. The party was starting in the early afternoon, and we were the first ones to show up. Bill worked for a construction company and had safety vests in his truck. We put these vests on, and with drinks in our hands headed out to the highway. We stopped the traffic in the fast lane, which forced the traffic into the slow lane. We had the traffic backed up for miles until Bob's dad yelled out the window for us to get off the highway. It was dark, and after trying some moonshine it was time to get some rest.

My roommate and I finally got evicted from the townhouse we were in. I grabbed a basement suite down the road, and the day I moved in I woke up on my couch not remembering moving because I was so shit-faced. The couple that owned the house were just about to get married, and man was his wife hot. I was surprised he let me move in because they were only a few years older than me, and you'd think he would be a little worried since I was looking pretty good myself.

I was holding off on filling my waterbed because this place just didn't seem right to me, so I slept on the couch for a while. The girl would bring me down cookies that she made, and when she mowed the lawn she would wear this small skirt and only mow the sections of the lawn that she knew I could see from my window. Well, sure enough, a week later – the day after I filled my king-size waterbed up - there was a knock at the door. It was the girl telling me her husband had sent her to tell me I was to leave because one of the neighbours was complaining about me. I knew the real reason. It was only because he thought that something might happen between his wife and me. Little did he know that was something I frowned on. Now it was time to move again, and I found this house to rent with a guy that I'd met named Al.

Al was into cars and liked to party, so for a while things were going okay. I had tried cocaine a few times in the past so I thought I would try to sell it myself. I only had $750 to my name at this point, but it was enough to buy a half ounce. I had a party that night and hoped to make some money. I managed to sell everything I had, and made $800 profit. I turned into a cocaine dealer overnight. I was making $10,000 a month not including my wages at the railroad. I never saved any of it, but was able to keep up with the high rollers and never missed out on anything. I would buff my coke with glucose, and would weigh my gram's a fraction short, and just doing that I made an extra $600 an ounce.

I got this phone number from a girl who worked for the phone company to check and see if my phone was being tapped. It was something like a 15-digit number you could dial, and if it rang, your phone was tapped, and if it sounded like a fax machine you were good to go. I used that number for a few years until I was told it didn't work anymore and the whole system had changed. Damn!

I started doing another stupid stunt and that was chewing up bar glasses. I would take a bite out of a bar glass, chew it up and spit it out. I remember this one guy was eyeing me up in the Haney Hotel because I had beaten up his brother the week before. I looked at this guy and grabbed a glass and did my thing; minutes later this guy was gone. Doing this was so hard on my teeth that by the time I was in my late thirties I had had one of my molars pulled, one crown and two root canals. Now that's pretty stupid!

I always had a high tolerance for pain. There were times when not only would I chew up glasses, but I would put cigarettes out on my feet and forearms. I would be out boating and have a friend of mine put them out on my feet, and I'd just ignore any pain, not even a blink of an eye. I believe the tolerance I have for pain all came from my past lives.

I sure could be harsh towards women, and you might think I deserved everything I got, and that's okay, because so do I. I was in the Haney Hotel drinking when I spotted this good looking brunette eyeing me up. I went over to talk to her and she just laughed at me for having the nerve to talk to her, so I let her have it... the old 'Magri, make you feel you're worth nothing' talk. I had her in tears with the things I was saying to her and walked away. The next week, when I was back in there, she just happened to be there too. As soon as she spotted me she came right up to me and apologized for how horrible she must have made me feel. I apologized for the way I'd treated her too. I told her it was time someone put her in her place or she would have done that to every guy, and she thanked me again. I just talked to her the other day – she's now working at one of the town pubs – and she seems to be doing just fine.

I only ever took one strange girl home from the bar. Of course I didn't use a condom, and when we were done I got my roommate to drive her home. She was pissed off that I told her I was too drunk to drive, especially after I'd driven us to my place. The next week there she was again, so I walked up to her, flipped her a quarter, and said, "Thanks for the fuck." The next day I discovered that I'd got the dose from her. Karma! I mean, what kind of a prick does something like that when she didn't do anything wrong in the first place. I had a lot to learn, and believe me I would, when I would later meet the woman who would tear my heart apart.

It was Christmas time and I was off to the local nursery to buy a tree. I was driving a 66 Pontiac Parisienne, which had the biggest trunk I had ever seen. I was walking around looking at all the trees, and ventured back where they sprayed the trees with that white snow stuff. I spotted a tree that was so perfect it didn't look real. It had a tag on it with instructions about what to do to this tree. Whoever bought that tree had paid $1,200 to get it sprayed, decorated and delivered. I thought this guy had too much money, so I ripped off the tag and put on a red ribbon, which meant the tree was now worth $19.99. I took this huge, eight-foot tree to the front, and got one of the workers to put it in the trunk. He looked at me and thought I was kidding until I told him to put it in the Pontiac. He took off the ribbon so I could go inside and pay for it, and told me what a beautiful tree I'd found. We had that tree up in our house until the following March.

One day we were sitting in the living room and Al said, "I wonder how fast this tree would go up in flames." He took his lighter and lit one of the needles on fire, and discovered it quickly went up in flames, but he managed to put it out with his hands. It scared the shit out if him because when I came home that next morning from work the tree was in the back yard.

1992

Being the fighter in town, I was banned from most establishments so I had to venture out further. Scooter and I headed out to Club Chaos in Coquitlam. We waited in line for about half an hour until we were finally at the front of the line. It only took a minute until every bouncer, including the manager, was there to greet me. The manager said that I wasn't welcome there. I had only been in the place a few times before and had had no problems. I guess the news was getting out that if I lost it, it wasn't going to be easy getting me to leave.

The Grand Prix I decided to drive through the front door of Club Chaos. Luckily, cooler heads prevailed.

I said, "Yeah, you don't want me in here," and grabbed Scooter and headed for the car. He asked me what was I going to do? I had this nice 1980 Grand Prix that I'd bought, and I told Scooter that I was going to drive this car up those front steps, through the front doors and that's how we were getting in. He said no fucking way were we doing that, and grabbed the keys just before I put them in the ignition. It took him a few minutes to talk me into leaving before he finally handed me the keys.

My Dad and I went out one night to have a couple of drinks and ended up at the Caddyshack strip joint. We were getting pretty drunk so when they asked us to leave I threw the table over, cutting my right palm wide open on some glass. I dropped my Dad off and drove to the hospital. When I walked in the door it looked like MASH 4077; there were people everywhere but I admitted myself and took a seat. After about an hour, not one person was called so I got up and went home. In the morning, after sobering up, I realized my hand needed some serious attention. I drove back to the hospital, and man were they ever pissed that I'd left. I told them it wouldn't have mattered if I'd stayed because I probably would have still been sitting there. They called me in and the doctor said I should have stayed. He looked at the wound, and then he tore it open again because it had already started to heal. I told him I still had my left hand, but he told me he still had to look. Without any freezing he started to clean it out. At one point he reached in with some pliers and pulled out a large blood clot, and told me I could have lost my hand over this. He stitched me up, and when he walked away this guy laying in the bed across from me, who had seen the whole thing, was just shaking his head in disbelief at what the doctor had done. There was blood all over the place, so much you might have thought I'd been shot ten times, but the doctor was just teaching me a lesson and I knew that, so I took it.

I was off work for that week, and the day my doctor signed the medical forms to get me back to work I did it again. It was time to mow the lawn for the first time that year, so in my bare feet I went and got the lawn mower out of the garden shed. I tried to start the mower but was having no success. What the hell was I thinking? Then again, having been patched up so many times in my life, perhaps I'd stopped giving a shit about safety. I loved to learn the hard way. Anyway, as I started to get really pissed off I pulled on that cord harder and harder, I pulled it so hard the last time that I lifted the mower off the ground and it started. Of course, as it started in the air I pulled it towards me and as a result it landed on my foot. Well, it chewed the hell out of my right toe before I could pull it out. I started to laugh, believe it or not, because now I would have to phone work again and fill out more paper work.

I got myself another dandy of a doctor this time. This doctor comes over, has a look, and puts in some freezing. I could hear him talking to one of the nurses about how pissed off he was that he got called in from his family reunion. He came back forty-five minutes later and started to sew me up. Now freezing is only good for about 20 minutes, so needless to say when he put that curled needle through my toe nail and up to the top of my toe, it hurt. I let him do another one and then said, "That's it, you're done." He didn't give a shit either, he wanted out of there.

This one guy in particular would always come and get a front (this means getting the coke first and paying me on payday). He owed me money and he knew that I was looking for him. I saw him driving his Camaro one day in Hammond in the middle of a snowstorm. When I saw him, I cranked a nut in the middle of the road in a Ford four-wheel drive that I had just bought, and tried to chase him down. How he was able to outrun me in the snow I have no idea, other than he must have been scared shitless. This friend of mine told him to show up at my house with my money, wearing a hockey helmet, and sure as fuck, if he had I would have laughed my head off and invited him in for a drink.

I decided to take my Dad and this guy from work, Mike, fishing on the Fraser River for spring salmon. We put the boat in at the boat launch and away we went. We fished for most of the day without success, and then headed back to the launch. Now this river has a strong current and is normally murky, and that's why they call it the Muddy Fraser. As I steered the boat close to the bank I thought it was safe enough to jump in the water to pull the boat to shore, so I jumped over the side. Well I didn't hit bottom and just managed to reach up and grab the edge of the boat while I was submerged. It's a good thing I was able to grab the boat as I was wearing my neoprene hip waders and they filled up with water. I would have sunk to the bottom like a lead weight. I started paddling with one arm as I steered the boat to shore with my Dad and Mike talking to one another. They didn't even see what was happening until I stood up on the shore soaking wet. My Dad, with his usual sarcasm, said, "It's a good thing I didn't see you kid or I would have had to jump in and save you." We all laughed and loaded everything up and called it a day. Mike died about five years ago of a heart condition, and I don't think he was even thirty-five years old. I miss you buddy.

My Dad and I decided to try our luck again at the river. We took the boat to the same spot we were at a few weeks prior, and the whole island was full of fisherman. We set up our rods and cast them out, put our rods in the holders and took a seat in our lawn chairs. After a few hours of fishing we opened up the cooler and grabbed a sandwich each. Just as we did this the bell on the end of my Dad's rod started to ring. He looked at me and I said, "Grab the fucking thing." He pulled the rod out of the holder, set the hook and reeled in an eight to ten pound spring salmon. As soon as we beached it, my rod started to ring and I landed one about seven pounds. We were only allowed one each and, with our limit caught, we packed up and went home with smiles on our faces. We were the only ones to catch anything that day. Any other time I'd been there I always saw fish getting caught, but not this day… it was special.

Me with the fish my dad and I caught on the Fraser River that day in 1992.

I really think that was a spiritual moment for my Dad and I, as my Grandfather and my Dad didn't see eye-to-eye with one another. My Dad told me he didn't talk with him that often, and remembered one time when they were driving together in downtown Vancouver one afternoon. On the radio it was announced that the next vehicle to pull into the Chevron gas station on such and such a corner would win $150 worth of free groceries. My Dad told my Grandpa to pull into the gas station and they won the groceries. I also have the fishing sweater my Grandma made for my Grandpa at home in my closet. You will read how close my Grandpa and I are when I talk about the psychic later on. Crazy! He died when I was four.

It was summer and time for PeachFest again in the Okanagan. Scooter and I headed up to Penticton in my Grand Prix. The second night there we were driving around in my car with two other guys we knew. I was drinking pretty heavily, so I had one of the guys drive the car; with the cops everywhere we needed a sober driver. We had just picked up a case of twenty-four Molson Canadian, and when I lifted my hand to take a drink a cop pointed at us to pull over. Once pulled over, the cop took our beer and started to write me a ticket for open liquor in the vehicle. We just happened to get pulled over right in front of a beer and wine store. I said to the cop as he was writing the ticket, "You know what I'm going to do when we leave here, don't you?" and he said, "Yip, but don't open any." I opened my wallet, gave the driver some money, and told him to go and get another twenty-four. Just as the driver came back with the beer the cop handed me my ticket. The driver put the beer in the trunk right in front of the cop and off we went.

Starting to party every weekend at the house, which meant doing all-nighters, I didn't want anybody knocking on the door to wake me up. At work one night I made this sign of plywood, painted it black and stencilled, WAKE ME UP AND YOU WILL DIE on it. I put it on a chain so I could hang it on the front door while I was sleeping. One of the neighbours from up the street walked down one day to complain about the parties. When he got to the door he saw the sign, turned, and walked away. I think it scared everyone but the neighbour next door. He knocked one morning, and when I answered the door he tossed a beer can that had been on his lawn over his shoulder. He said he had had enough of the parties and people in the streets every weekend. I apologized and promised I would make sure everyone stayed inside so they wouldn't bother him. I kept my word and he never had to bother me again. I feel bad for him because years later, when he finally bought the Harley Davidson of his dreams, he had a stroke and was unable to ride it. You're a good shit Mike, hang in there kid.

I partied in that house for five years until I meet the heart-crusher who would change my life forever. My roommate started to get jealous because of the money I was making selling coke and wanted a piece, but that wasn't going to happen. We got into a few arguments about who was going to move out of the house. It wasn't going to be me. I put my fist through the glass coffeetable a few times during these arguments, and I still remember the size of the replacement glass after all these years – 34 1/4 by 32 1/2. He eventually moved out when I was away for the long weekend. When I came home he was gone, and so were my tools and some things from the kitchen that were mine. I put a bill together for $750 for half the rent he'd stiffed me on, plus the rest of the things he took. While I was hunting him down I had a friend of mine, Wayne, move into the house. He and I got along well with no problems.

Eric and me at a party in 1992. He would die later in a car accident.

I was out one night with my buddy Eric, just driving around doing my rounds, and later I dropped him off at his place because I had to go to work. I was working the nightshift with Thursday and Friday off. In the morning, on my way home from work, I saw a friend of ours, Chris, walking in the rain with his head down. I pulled over to ask him what was wrong, and he told me that Eric, Matt and this girl had died in a car accident. Matt had a five-litre Mustang, and the girl was apparently driving it very fast, lost control and all three died. Eric was in the back seat and died of a broken neck.

I had a dream about six months after the accident, in which I was sitting at a table in a hall with Eric and Matt and it felt so real. I think the dream happened because it was their way of telling me they were all right. This was just a dream or something similar, not like the death experience I would face later.

Working midnight shift was hard on the body because of the lack of sleep. My bedroom had black plastic on the window to help keep it dark. One day it seemed like everybody was mowing the lawn and I got very little sleep. I got up because of this and then the phone rang. It was Wade's girlfriend calling. She said to me, "Guess who's here?" and I said, "Who?" and she replied. "Al." He was down at Wade's house so I told Donna to keep him busy because I was on my way. I got into my car and, wouldn't you know it, it wouldn't start. So I got a jumpstart from my neighbour. I got the car running and headed for Wade's house. I pulled into the driveway and it sure felt good to see Al was still there in Wade's garage. I got out and closed my door, and you could see the worry on his face as I smiled and said, "Hi Al." He knew then he was in trouble. I started to beat him so bad his blood was flying all over his Dad's Chevelle, and all over the garage. He was on the concrete going into convulsions, and his eyes were rolling back in his head as I kicked him in the face. He was finished. I got back in my car to drive away but it didn't start. I yelled at Donna to drive her vehicle over so she could jumpstart me, and then I peeled out of there.

Thinking I'd killed the guy, I didn't go to my house, but headed to my Dad's house instead. I got there and knocked on the door, and with the blood on me he knew I was in trouble. I told him I thought I had just killed someone so I took my clothes and shoes and burned them out in a burn barrel in his back yard. After he gave me a change of clothes, I got him to drive me a few miles away to use a payphone. I did not want to use my Dad's phone in case the cops were at my place, and then they would know where the call was coming from.

When I phoned my place my roommate answered, and I asked if the smoke was clear. By this time Wade was already at my house, so my roommate handed him the phone. Wade told me Al had managed to drive himself to the hospital. You would think he'd have paid the debt after that but he didn't, and because of that he would get another beating.

Al would not drink anywhere around town for fear that he would run into me along the way. A friend and I decided to venture out to Coquitlam to go to the Boone County country bar. Once inside I noticed Al standing across the way. I pointed him out to one of the guys I was with. I walked over to him, approaching from behind so I could tap him on the shoulder. When I did, he turned around and noticed who it was; I just smiled and smoked him in the face and he hit the floor. You would think after having been beaten twice by me he would pay up, but that never happened. I even beat his brother up, but you will hear about that later.

Scooter and I were out driving around one day and he told me he needed a second job so he could get out of debt. Out of the blue he told me to pull over at this construction site. He got out of the car and said he would be right back. He was gone fifteen minutes, and when he got back into the car he said, "I start Monday." We both laughed because Scooter was a good bullshitter, and he'd told the site supervisor he was a framer even though he'd never framed a thing before. He would work nightshift with me at the railroad, and go work construction during the day.

When he came into work the next Wednesday I noticed all these bandages on his fingers, and so I asked what had happened. He told me he kept smashing his fingers, so his boss had called him into the office and asked whether he'd ever framed before, at which point Scott told him the truth. The only reason they kept him on was because he was a hard worker and had a good sense of humour.

It was getting so bad locally that I had to go out to New Westminster to drink. My little German friend, Flex, and I headed out to a club there called Kits Pub. We were there early, and there were only a few other people inside. Flex was playing some pool and I was leaning on the bar by myself eating peanuts. As I was cracking peanuts five doormen and the manager approached, and asked me to leave. I just kept cracking peanuts and asked them what I had done wrong, but the manager just said I had to leave. I was looking at the doormen and you could see the fear in their eyes, so I just smiled and yelled out to my buddy, "Hey Flex, these guys want us to leave." Flex looked at me like, "Oh no, here we go." But I only had one drink in me and I wasn't particularly belligerent, so I just said to them, "Yeah, I guess I'll leave" so I grabbed Flex and they escorted us down the stairs and out the front door.

All the nightclubs I would normally spend a lot of money in had time restrictions on when I was allowed back into their establishments. So I pretty much had a calendar in my head as to when I was allowed back into each place, but sometimes they would overlap each other and I would have to go to another city to have some fun. What a life! I hope you are enjoying yourself so far, but better yet, I hope you are learning something, and I hope I'm not boring you to death.

I was back on the steroids and went to this new nightclub, Rumours, in Port Coquitlam. There was an upstairs and downstairs to this place. I was upstairs and noticed Melissa in there, and after a few drinks started to get pissed off for what she had done to me. I started picking beer bottles up and tossing them in the air, and when they came down, I was punching them, shattering glass all over the place. People started moving away because I had that psycho smile on my face. The bouncers approached me and asked if I could leave, and I actually said no problem. My idea was that when they were escorting me down the stairs I was going to run to the back bar and start wrecking the place. I never made it that far because I was tackled from behind and started fighting with these guys. It took every guy they had working there to get me out.

Once outside, and with the front doors closed, I was still determined to get back in. The cops were called, and while the doormen were looking at me through the small windows in the doors I felt this hand on my shoulder. I turned around and an RCMP officer was telling me I was not going back in there. I grabbed him by his collar and belt and threw him onto his car windshield, telling him to fuck off. With one of the doormen smiling at me through the door window, I put my fist right through it. The cop knew he needed help at that point and two more cops pulled up. I beat the hell out of them, so they backed off and waited for a couple more.

Now I was starting to get a little worried. It took all five officers forty-five minutes to get the cuffs on me before they could throw me in the back of the car. I tried to kick out the door window to escape, at which point they opened the door, dragged me out, hog tied me, and threw me in the paddy wagon. Fights started all over the place outside, and a guy in the back of the van with me got his lighter out of his pocket and burned off the zap straps holding my legs to the cuffs. On the drive to the cop shop, with a full van, they sure had fun with us. They were taking sharp corners and slamming on the brakes – we were like a mixed salad back there. All of this took a few hours before we got to the cop shop.

They brought me in to the front counter, and took the cuffs off me. When I brought my hands forward and placed them on the counter the women working there almost puked. My hands were horribly mutilated, and they were all purple. I looked at all the cops who brought me in and said, "It looks like you guys were going tonight, too." They were all beat up, and replied, "Yeah, with you. Don't you remember?" I said "No."

They gave me a cell by myself and put everyone else in another cell. In the morning, a cop came down and said, "Okay, okay which one of you is Rocky." I was waiting to see the judge, and with my clothes soaked in blood I asked if I could have another shirt because I didn't want the judge to see all the blood. The cop just told me to wear my shirt inside out. A lot of good that did when it was soaked right through. I saw the judge and got a promise to appear for an assault charge. The charge wasn't because of the fight I'd had with the cops, it was because when I punched out the window a girl got glass in her face. They barred me from there until the court date.

At home a few days later I could smell something bad. I couldn't find it anywhere until I looked in the laundry room. It was the shirt from that horrible night, which was in the laundry. It was so soaked in blood it had started to rot, and now I know what a dead body smells like.

In the meantime, I was out at Frisco's one night, and the owners of Rumours were there. I went up and apologized, and they said not to worry about it because it was entertaining. One guy said, "Ever since we opened, so many people have tried to knock that window out and nobody was able to even put a scratch in it, and you put a hole in it six inches in diameter." They also said it had taken all their guys to get me out of there, and they asked whether I wanted a job. I told them I couldn't because of my shift work and days off.

The guys at work joked about making one of those boards people use to pick scores for sporting events, the ones where you pick a square and if your numbers come up you win. Only they were going to bet on what year I was going to die. I love you guys, you pricks.

It was court day, and I was sitting in the courtroom waiting for them to call me when this guy came in, walked over, and sat beside me. I looked at him and asked who he was. He said, "You don't remember me, do you?" and I said, "No, I don't." He said, "I was the cop that night. You picked me up and threw me as if I was nothing." He also told me he had been a police officer for thirty-two years, and had never seen anything like it. He asked what I was on that night, and I told him nothing, I was just having a good time. He just smiled, shook his head, and looked at the fresh scars on my fists. He said, "Looks like you've been going again" and I told him, "Yeah about twice a weekend." I told him I was sorry, and then my name was called into court. This was my second assault and, in Canada, the first two are free. I pled guilty and got a small fine with some probation. I was also ordered to pay for the window.

The cops called the house for something and left a message on my machine. There were a lot of blank messages besides the one they left, and

I didn't think anything of it. I called the cop shop and the officer asked if I was wondering why I had a lot of blank messages. The cop told me it was because the whole office had been calling my place to listen to my message. What I had done was brought the answering machine into the bathroom, and at the end of my message I started to piss in the toilet, finished off with a few dribbles, and then I flushed. They loved it.

The court date finally came up for the incident when that guy had smashed a bottle on my face. The case was at the Supreme Court in New Westminster. I was waiting for the elevator, and when the doors opened, there was the piece of shit who had done this to me. I got in with a smile on my face, and when the doors closed it took everything I had not to start beating this guy, but I never said a word, only because it would have been used against me in court.

I was on the witness stand and the prosecutor handed the jury the photos of the damage to my face. I could see that these photos sickened the jury. He got off because he had a doctor's note from a clinic which showed he had a broken nose, and he said that I had hit him first. Given my reputation he was scared and had to defend himself, is what he said. His lawyer got permission to bring in my previous charges to help back up his case. I remember the prosecutor calling for a recess. He and the lawyer went around the corner in the lobby. I could hear the prosecutor yelling and swearing at him because he had no idea that he'd received permission to do this. I later found out the guy's lawyer was his uncle. Family is family I guess.

I remember having a lunch break, and afterwards his lawyer asking me what I had had for lunch. I'd gone for lunch at a strip joint down the road from the court house. Knowing that it would be disrespectful to have a beer and head back into court, I'd had water. I knew someone would be watching me anyway. The lawyer knew that I only had water but asked me what I'd had to drink anyway, knowing that no one would believe me, and it would make me look like a liar and disrespectful. I mean I shouldn't have had lunch at a strip joint, because who goes to a strip joint and has water? That was my mistake.

I didn't remember until after the trial that when the fight happened a friend of mine punched this guy in the face through the open passenger window of the van these guys were driving, and that's how he got his nose broken. I hope the jury members were proud of themselves because I never laid a hand on anyone that night.

This story doesn't end there. One night, at home with a few friends and my Dad, there was a knock at the door. A guy I went to school with was working for this bottle plant with a cousin of the guy I'd had charged. He told me he'd overheard a conversation this cousin was having on the phone, and that it sounded like a gang from Surrey was coming to my place that night to beat the shit out of me and wreck my house. I told my Dad it would be a good time for him to leave because I had to get ready for this. I made a call to Rick, who I bought my coke from, to bring some weapons over. He was over in about fifteen minutes with some guns, including a Defender twelve-gauge shotgun. My friend Doctor Dave was at my place when I learned about the threat, so he went home and grabbed the sword his parents had on the fireplace. I called a few more guys to come over and had them all park one street over. I had Rick on call to park his semi-truck at the end of the street to block these guys in when they came so they couldn't get out. We waited until just after midnight but no one came, so I told everybody I thought they'd "wimped out" and they could go home.

After everybody left I took my stormrider jacket and cut the inside open so I could fit the box of shells in it. I laid in bed that night fully dressed, with the jacket on and twenty-five rounds of ammunition in the inside liner, and I had the shotgun on the floor loaded with the safety off. I still had Rick on call to block the road, and I was up all night peeking through the blinds every time I heard a noise.

I remember looking through those blinds and saying to myself, "Come on you motherfuckers, come on." I had already made my mind up that if they came, I was going to kill every one of them and, with Rick's truck blocking the road, I would be able to chase them down and shoot them all. Eventually daybreak rolled around and still no sign of these guys. It never materialized into anything.

My friend James asked me to be best man at his wedding and, of course, I said I would be honoured. I was up all night the night before the wedding, partying and using cocaine. Having had no sleep, I was sitting on my bed at 8:30 in the morning saying to myself there was no way I could make it to the wedding. But I got up, looked in the mirror, and told myself there was no way I could do that to my pal. I had to take control, so I hopped in the shower and it was enough to give me a second wind. I was dressed, got in my truck and headed to James' house. I was supposed to be there at 9 a.m. for the decorating of the cars. I got there in time, but when I opened the truck door I fell on the ground. His parents knew how wild I was, and when I stood up James' dad pointed to the fridge in the carport and that's where I headed. I threw down three beers in five minutes and started ordering people around about what to do with the decorations.

It was summer, about 90 degrees out, and the wedding took place in a one hundred-year-old church. The temperature in this church seemed way higher than it was outside, and standing up front through the ceremony I had sweat pouring down my face from all the booze. That was the worst hangover day of my life, but thankfully, if you look at the wedding picture, you wouldn't think I'd been up for two days. After the ceremony I took off in one of the wedding cars and headed for the liquor store. I simply couldn't wait for all of us to get to the hall, I needed liquor right now. Overall, the wedding went well, and when I did my speech I didn't have anything re-

At James' wedding after a two-day bender. I didn't look half bad considering the shape I was in. I had the hots for this bridesmaid, I'll tell ya, but who could blame me.

hearsed, but I had everybody laughing and that's all that mattered. My deed was done.

Scooter and I were out one morning having breakfast and started to get into an argument. He piped up and said, "Me and you in the ring." I said, "No problem, when do you want to do this?" and he replied, "In two months." His brother was a fighter at the Maple Ridge boxing club so Scooter was going to ask him if we could have it in there one night when the place was closed. I joined the club while Scooter sat on his ass. When the two months were up, I said to him, "Well, I'm ready for you, what night do you want to do this." Scooter had received a little information from his brother about how well I was doing so he bailed. I joined the Maple Ridge Boxing club weighing in at 235 pounds.

I asked the coach how long it usually took before he allowed someone to start sparring, and he told me about three months. After he saw my potential, he had me in the ring after the first two weeks. The third week he took me downtown to Vancouver to spar with this bronze medallist middleweight. After a round with this guy, and beating him, I can remember the coach of that club asking John, my coach, where he'd found me. I was still partying like I normally did and it took three days of working out before I was back

The boxer. A buddy stopped by while I was working out so I had him take a couple of pictures. I'm glad I did.

to the same condition as the week before. When the sparring session was over, this medallist came over to me and asked, "You've only been boxing three months?" and I said, "Three months, three weeks." He shook his head and walked away. At one time, before joining the club, I was going to start a fight pit somewhere in the Pitt Polder area, but I was too busy doing other things.

I was at the club one night and saw a couple of girls I knew. I started to date one of the girls, Maria, and everything was fine for a while. The second date we had we ended up in the bedroom. The lights were out and all of a sudden she started to hyperventilate. I got up in a panic and turned the light on because I didn't know what the hell was going on with her. It turns out I had given her her first orgasm.

After a few months of dating I got a dose of chlamydia. I hadn't slept with anyone else, but figured I just wouldn't say anything, because once I took the medication it would be gone in a week anyway. However, once I'd taken care of the problem it would just come back. I had no idea that a woman could have this disease and not know it. I would find out what was going on shortly after.

She played baseball, and it was time for their end-of-the-year party. The night before the party, Maria went to a concert with a friend of hers. When I showed up to pick her up for the party the next day, her lip was split open. I asked her what had happened and she said that she got elbowed in the face while she was on the floor of the concert. Right away I thought to myself, "Great, everybody at this party knows that I'm a boxer, and they are going to think that I did this."

The dose kept coming back. I went to Scooters house and he was washing his car with his girlfriend, who happened to be a friend of Maria's. I started telling Scooter what was going on and he looked at his girlfriend for answers. She told me that while I was at work on the weekends Maria would go over to her ex-boyfriend's and sleep with him. She also told me that the split on her lip was because of him. Maria went over to his place after the concert and he was there with another girl; when she saw this, she slapped him in the face., and when she did that he grabbed her by the hair and kneed her in the face.

We split up for a while, and I eventually caught up with this ex-boyfriend. I saw him in a pub one night, and when we made eye contact I gave him "the smile," then walked over and knocked him out. I could have beat him to a pulp, but the knockout was enough for the knee in her face. After all, he didn't rape Maria; she'd wanted the relationship to continue while seeing me. I did get even by sleeping with her best friend, but it still didn't make me feel any better because two wrongs don't make a right.

We eventually got back together, and it was time for my first boxing match. I weighed in at 191 pounds. I thought I was in shape at that weight, but man I was tired after the first round. However, I still won. That was the only trophy I ever won. Mission accomplished.

I started to train for my next fight, which was to take place at the maximum prison. While sparring, I threw a left jab and threw out my shoulder. The pain was so great I fell to the canvas. That was the end of my boxing career. I was 1 and 0. I didn't have the shoulder looked at until about fifteen years later, when I found out that I had a three-quarter tear in my labrum and two other tears. There was a reason for waiting this long to find out what had happened, but I would only find out later when I saw the psychic.

Maria and I decided to catch a movie one night mid-week. I can't remember what movie we went to see, but it turned out not to matter anyway. A few minutes into the film I realized there wasn't anybody else in the theatre but us, so I told her to take off her panties and away we went. Who said that the movie theatre was made for just watching movies?

I knew a butcher who worked for the local grocery store, and we would make a trade-off for coke. I would bring him a flap of coke and he would wrap up a $100 prime rib custom-cut roast and put a round roast sticker on it for $20. He was hilarious. Once, when I was shopping there, he put about twenty condom boxes in my cart when I wasn't looking. I went up to the cashier and started to unload my groceries. The cashier said to me, "Are all these yours?" and I said, "I'm not that busy." I looked around for my pal and there he was, laughing his head off down one of the aisles. I ate well until he was fired for stealing chocolate milk. I think he sells cars now.

A friend of mine and I were out drinking one afternoon and stopped at the Burger King for something to eat. The place was packed, and it was taking forever to take our order. I grabbed the intercom, and started talking like one of those DJs at the strip joint and had everyone laughing. They did give me some free fries. I was always looking for a laugh.

A bunch of people and I got together and rented a houseboat at Shuswap Lake for the weekend. There must have been about 12 of us, and what a rough weekend that was. A few of the guys had to take an hour-long course on how to run the boat so they could take turns driving it around. I took my twelve-foot aluminum boat with us so I could do some fishing while on the trip. This one morning three of us headed out in the twelve-footer, but before we went we told one of the guys to come over to where we were fishing to pick us up before they headed up the lake. A couple of hours went by and we headed back, but no boat. This guy had decided to take off without coming for us.

All the houseboats looked the same, so trying to find ours was like looking for a needle in a haystack on that huge lake. When we managed to find the boat I was yelling at this asshole to stop the boat, and once we were boarded, did I ever tear a strip off of him. This was a guy I'd known most of my life, but I was never good friends with him. He sat there on one of the couches all day after that and didn't say a word.

That night someone woke me up and said my boat was out in the middle of the lake ready to sink. I looked at the rope I'd used to tie the aluminum boat to the houseboat and it had been cut. I grabbed an air mattress and paddled my ass off to go and get it. I managed to get it and pull it back to the beach. When I looked inside the plug had been pulled. In another couple of minutes it would have gone down like the Titanic. I would have lost all my fishing gear, the boat and motor that night. I didn't know who'd done it for certain, but I had a pretty good idea

We'd wrecked the prop on the house boat, on some shallow water coming into the beach the night before, so I looked at the bolts holding it on, got the right size wrench and went for a swim. I managed to take someone's prop off in the middle of the night and do the old switch-a-roo. If we had brought that boat back like that we would have lost our $250 dollar deposit.

While my friend Flex and I were on the beach partying I gave him a bell I had in my tackle box to ring if someone tried to take the cooler away from him while I went for a stroll. He was a small guy, and that was the reason for me giving him this bell. He was talking to a couple of chicks and they asked what the bell was for so he told them. They didn't believe him so he rang it and I came running. I was there in a flash and the girls couldn't believe he had his own bodyguard.

There was a couple on the boat that had just married a few months earlier, and they thought it would be a good idea to do a wifeswap with this other couple I knew. Everybody was watching the performance when one of the girls realized she'd done the wrong thing. She got upset and jumped into the lake but didn't know how to swim, so I jumped in, saved her from drowning, and brought her back to the boat. I don't think she will be doing that again any time soon.

With all of us using just one toilet, towards the last day we were using the toilet plunger to pack down the shits we had to take. When we finally brought the boat back the attendant said he'd never got a boat back before with the tank that full. We were all so proud.

It was Christmas Eve and I hadn't done any shopping, so I headed to Coquitlam Centre to get all my shopping done. I was already stressed out because I always waited til the last minute to get my shopping done, and I was putting on a Christmas party on Christmas Eve, as I did every year. When I went to Zellers the tills had large line-ups, but I waited patiently while the cashier rang in this Chinese lady. When it came to the lady's last item the cashier charged her a dime too much. The lady said, "You charged me dime too much." Yes, that's exactly how she said it, so don't think I'm being racist. Anyway, in those days they had to go through all the items all over again, they just couldn't cancel the item they'd screwed up on, and this lady wanted her dime. Once the cashier knew she'd made a mistake she looked at all of us in the line-up as though to apologize. I put down all my stuff because I didn't have a shopping cart and made my way up to the front. I dug into my pocket and pulled out a quarter, threw it down on the counter and yelled out, "There's your fucking dime, keep the change and get the fuck out of here." She took the quarter and everybody in all the line-ups started to clap and applaud me. How ignorant can you get? I mean, for a dime.

1993

I was still good friends with Tina and we went with a few people to the Shark Club in downtown Vancouver. We stayed for a couple of hours until we decided to head back to Maple Ridge before we were too bent out of shape. As we were walking across the street, we were almost hit by a car. My first reaction was to kick the side of it with my cowboy boots as it drove by, and once I'd done that we just carried on to the car. The guys driving the car stopped, got out, and started yelling, so I turned around to confront them. What I didn't know was that these guys were the heads of a Chinese gang. There was one guy leaning up against the car with his hand behind his back holding a gun, and another threatening to make a phone call to have me taken care of. I knew the third one must be the boss only because he was wearing an Armani suit. I actually told this guy that I could blindfold him with dental floss because they couldn't see at the best of times. He looked at me and said, "You don't want to fuck with us" in such a calm voice I could only take him seriously. So I said to him, "Why don't we go down here and talk about this?" and he agreed.

As we started to walk down to the corner my friends started to follow, but I told them to just wait there, I would be right back. The same thing happened with his guys. The guy was telling me the car was a rental Lexus and they would bill him for the damage my boot made. There wasn't a mark on the car at all. This was all about the principle. He felt that I'd disrespected him and I wasn't in a position to argue. I asked him, "What about a hundred bucks, would that cover it?" and he agreed. We walked back up to our boys after a handshake and got the hell out of there. I think that was the best one hundred bucks I ever spent. If you ever read this buddy, you're one cool cucumber; that could have gotten real ugly.

I was at that same club another night with a friend, and I was working on a chick who seemed to be a sure thing. My friend wanted to go to this party somewhere in Vancouver he'd heard about. I gave him the keys to my car because I thought I was going home with this girl. At last call I asked if we were heading to her place but I was wrong. She told me that it wasn't going to happen that night, but she gave me her phone number to call.

Now I'm downtown in Vancouver with no ride home. I called over a cab and told him I had no money until I got home, and if he could drive me there I would give him a good tip. He was new in town, having just come from a different country, and didn't know his way around. He had to call his boss to see if it was okay to take me home with no money and his boss said no.

He was a black man and we hit it off right away, so he decided to take me anyway. We talked about a lot of things. He was awed and amazed by the scenery on the way, and said he was glad he had driven me. Now, when we got to my place I had to tell him that I had to break into my house and come out with the money. I can just imagine what that looked like to him, but it was all good and I gave him a big tip. I gave him directions on how to get back and my phone number in case he got lost, and we shook hands and wished each other a good night.

I got a call from Rick and he told me to meet him at the Esso cardlock just off of the Mary Hill Bypass. Once I was there he opened the back of a semi trailer he was driving and started to pass me down these boxes. I had no idea what was in there, but it turned out to be just a bunch of winter jackets that were designated for Ontario. I still have one of the jackets. It being triple down, I only wear it when we get bad cold weather. I guess the point of this is I was there for my friend without asking any questions.

I got a call from Rick one morning and he asked if I had any weapons. All I had at the time was an old 303 British rifle at, so I put it in my truck and headed over to his place. He came to the door with a smile on his face as I walked in with the gun wrapped in a blanket. There was blood all over the floor, and bullet holes through the walls and the tile in the kitchen, as well as a hole in the kitchen sink. I guess some guys came into Rick's place to rob him, but got a rude reception instead. Rick was shooting at them from behind the wall in the kitchen and, as a result, clipped one of them in the process. I handed him the gun and told him I didn't want it back. He was there for me when I needed him, so I had to be there for him when he needed me.

Rick was over one day with his partner-in-crime when I was mowing the lawn. The neighbour had this Cocker Spaniel that loved to bark. When we walked from the backyard to the front we had to go down the side of the house, which meant we would be close to the fence. As we approached the fence this dog started in on us. Rick was jabbing him with the handle of the rake. The neighbour saw what was going on and threw his dog over the fence at us. For a Cocker Spaniel he sure was mean. The dog stood his ground and we took off to the frontyard.

A few weeks later it was Father's Day, and my day to get even. As I worked night shift I had to sleep through lawnmowers and everything else that went on throughout the day. This Father's Day you could hear a pin drop because everyone was busy with their family. My Dad lived out of town so I decided I would get out the lawnmower, and I actually mowed it twice, trying to piss everyone off. After the lawn, I got out the chain saw and started to take limbs off the trees.

I was walking to the front and at the end of the fence there were large cedar hedges. As I approached the hedge the neighbour's dog went for my leg and bit me, breaking the skin on my shin. I tried to kick it and my shoe flew off. I attempted to get at this dog through the hedge but it was fruitless. This just made my blood boil, so with one shoe on I ran down the hedge and into the neighbour's yard.

The neighbour was out in the driveway saying goodbye to his family With so much rage in me, I knocked shoulders with the owner of the dog and kicked the dog so hard in the head it did cart wheels in the air. As it crawled for cover under his owner's truck, I told the guy that if I ever saw that dog in my yard again I would throw it through his fucking front window. I didn't notice that the other neighbour's five-year-old boy had seen everything while on his tricycle. After about 10 minutes I heard the squeaking of his wheels approach me. He said, "You said a bad word." I just said, "Yeah kid, I said a few of them, I'm sorry" and off he went. The dog died a week later.

Mowing the lawn one day I noticed two birch trees that had been cut up and thrown over my fence in the corner of my yard where I would put my grass clippings. My yard was a pie shape so it could only be one of two of my neighbours. I got along with one of them really well, so I asked her if maybe she'd hired someone to clear some trees for her and they'd just thrown everything over the fence. She told me she hadn't, and that she never had birch trees anyway, just cedar.

One day out in the backyard the woman behind me got my attention, and called me over to the fence. She asked if I would be interested in taking down some trees in my backyard, and that she would pay half because all the fir needles were going into her pool. She also told me that the last wind storm had knocked down two birch trees. Now I knew for sure who it was. She had two older sons and, with the pile of wood and two stumps along with two coffee cups in the pile as evidence, I knew then that they'd done it. The stumps were a good size and it had to have taken both of them to get them over my fence. I decided to save my revenge for a rainy day. It does come.

A year later, on my way home from work, I waved to one of the brother's wives because she used to be one of our old neighbours from the street where I'd grown up. The bitch didn't wave back and that pissed me off. She was the daughter of the witch who lived behind our old house, the one that would gave me shit for swinging up high when I faced her house and could look in her yard. I was civil enough to wave instead of being the snob.

Anyway, I was so angry over how she'd just burned me off that I decided the rainy day I had been waiting for had arrived. I had the strength to put those stumps over the fence myself, along with everything else that they'd thrown over that day. Later that day the father of the two brothers came knocking at my door to give me shit for throwing HIS shit into HIS yard. He told me he was going to throw it back, and I told him if he did I would throw everything in his pool because his kids were the ones who had put the stuff in my yard in the first place. I told him to fuck off and not to come back. That was the end of that. Those two brothers were so lucky I didn't hop the fence and beat the hell out of them… sooo lucky.

Glen, who I'd met as a connection for getting my steroids, was in and out of prison most of his life. I went to pick him up from prison on his release, and he already had a plan before he closed the door to the truck. He had met a heavy man in prison who, because of this guy's good behaviour, was sent to work out the rest of his time looking after the trout farm on Alouette Lake. He got in the truck and said, "We're using your boat and your motor." I said "No problem, what are we doing?"

He had told this guy we would bring him booze and cocaine. We loaded the boat up and away we went. Once there we found him waiting on the shore for us. I handed him the coke that I brought for him and he asked, "How good is this?" and I replied, "About seventy-five to eighty percent" He dumped some coke into a syringe and filled it with water from the lake and shot it in his arm right there. A couple of seconds later I could see that it had hit him pretty hard and he said, "Yeah, that's pretty good all right." He then gave us directions to a road that was behind the prison, so later that night we drove more dope to him. When we found the meeting spot there were four prisoners there. I gave them the coke and they all shot up, and Glen and I snorted some coke on the hood of my truck.

I have no idea how they got out of the prison to meet us but I wasn't about to ask. This guy was supposed to pay Glen for the shit that I had brought, once he got out, and then Glen was to give me the money, but that clown never gave Glen anything. He obviously hadn't learned a thing in there. I did all of this for I guy I didn't know. What a piece of shit he turned out to be. That guy died a few years later of a drug overdose.

I remember Glen telling me a story about this cop who gave him a ride. He took his dog to the lake in Merritt where we went from time to time to go fishing. He was taking pictures of his dog there and left his camera behind. He was back on the highway when he realized he didn't have his camera. He was speeding to get there because it started to rain, and got pulled over by a cop who found out Glen had never had a driver's licence. The cop didn't do much about that and gave him a ride to go get his camera. As they were driving down the highway the cop reached down beside him and pulled up a bottle of rye he had in a paper bag. All the cop said was, "I have been driving this same stretch of highway for the past seven years." I guess he was losing it. I asked Glen if he took a swig and he said, "Not a chance, I just kept my mouth shut." Once he got his camera back, and the cop realized he was telling the truth, he drove Glen back to town. Glen called a cab to take him to his car, and then he drove home.

On another night out with the boys, we took a cab home from the bar and I invited the cabbie in for some coke. The next weekend he showed up at my door with this woman asking if I had anything for sale. I knew this chick was a cop so I told her I'd only had the little bit I bought from the bar that night. They left and I never saw him again.

A friend and I headed to a fishing spot I had on the Fraser River one foggy morning. The fog was so thick I couldn't see fifteen feet in front of me. I thought I knew what direction I was going until a tugboat came out of the fog. It was a good thing I was paying attention because there was no time for error. All I saw was the bow of the tugboat about seven feet tall and fifteen feet away from us. I hit the throttle and steered the boat hard to my left, just missing the tug. If that boat had have hit us we would have drowned in that river because no one would have been able to find us. We were turned around and didn't know where we were until we got to shore. We asked a kayaker who was paddling by where we were, so we were able to follow the shoreline, find our spot, and catch our limit. I tell you, if a cat has nine lives, I must have a thousand.

I still had the Grand Prix, as well as the Ford 4x4, and I needed to take the car through Aircare (to check air emissions). I took it through and it failed. I came up with a scam because I had a friend who worked there. I took Doctor Dave's Oldsmobile through and handed my friend the insurance papers from the Grand Prix. Now Dave's car had passed so I knew this wasn't going to be a problem. After I took the car through the test, a pass came up with my insurance information on the papers. It's a beautiful thing when a plan comes together.

It was October and I was off on a moose hunt with a buddy from work. We headed to 100 Mile House, which was known for good moose hunting though too many hunters in recent years had made hunting there pretty tough. We picked this place only because it was a five-hour drive away from home. The only accommodation we had was sleeping in the canopy of Bjorn's truck. With the temperature being well below zero, we bought a Coleman heater and hung it inside the canopy door the first night. We drank a bottle of rye each and passed out in the canopy with the heater on.

Now, because the heater was hung just below the interior light of the canopy, the light lens started to melt. As the lens was melting it dripped onto the heater, which caused the plastic to catch fire, which then dripped onto my sleeping bag igniting my sleeping bag. I only woke up because the flames were burning my feet, and when I did the smoke was so thick in the canopy, that I couldn't see Bjorn right beside me. I could see the orange from the flames at my feet, and started to put out the fire with my hands. After burning my hands I was lucky enough to find a ballcap on my pillow, and I used that to put the fire out. Once the fire was over we opened the canopy door and climbed out. We were so lucky that night, but that was the end of using the heater. The next few nights of our stay I remember ice on the inside of the windows of the canopy. We only stayed a few days and had no luck.

1994

One night, when I got off work, a co-worker flew past me on the Pitt River Bridge. As I approached the crest of the bridge I couldn't see him anymore. As I crossed over the bridge wondering where he'd gone, I could see this hydro pole swaying in the wind. His car had hydroplaned after hitting a puddle, and as a result he'd hit the pole. I pulled over clear of the traffic and ran to his aid. The car was split in two and his legs were resting on the asphalt. The roof was crushed, and was forcing his head sideways so he couldn't breathe. I grabbed the roof, folded it over and held his head up straight until the paramedics showed up.

The car after my buddy got into an accident on his way home from work one morning.

I was trying to tell him who I was, but he was too incoherent to see me clearly. As I was holding his head this other guy yelled out because my truck was rolling forward and heading right into the guy's car. I guess when I threw the truck into park in a panic I'd only managed to put it into neutral. All I could do was watch my truck roll into him and see my insurance rate go back up. I had just got my insurance premium down from a 150 percent surcharge to zero a month prior. After the paramedics arrived I ran to the gas station to call my co-worker's wife to let her know what had happened. He broke his left humerus, left femur, six ribs, and his clavicle. He had a blood clot in his right leg, and almost died when he got double pneumonia. When he was finally out of the hospital, he attended the Grey Cup game and ended up winning the 50-50 draw, which was about $15,000. Sure enough, my insurance went back up from zero to a thirty percent surcharge, but that didn't matter as long as my buddy ended up okay. .

With my insurance rate so high all the time, I had to figure something out to be able to afford to drive. The insurance company only charged the high premium on one of your vehicles so I went and bought a utility trailer. The insurance for the trailer was only $50 for the year, so I could put the large premium on the trailer, and my vehicle could be insured with a forty percent discount. Must have been living in the early 1900s that makes my mind think like this. Scam Artist.

I said it didn't matter, but I was still looking for ways to get even with the insurance company for ripping me off. I decided to try and rip them off. My friend Jake and I decided to stage a car accident and collect the money. The deal was we would pick a stretch of road and Jake would tailgate me while I drove under the speed limit, then I would slam on my brakes and he would do the same, hoping that the guy behind him would ram into him. We found the road we wanted and away we went. As Jake got close on my tail, and when I could see that someone was tailgating him, I slammed on the brakes. I could see the smoke from Jake's tires as I looked out the side mirror, and with a smile on my face I thought for sure the guy behind him had hit him, so I took off. As it turned out, there was no accident and that was the end of that. Lots of people have tried to rip off the insurance companies, as well as Workers Compensation, so it is no wonder they are so hard to deal with now. We can only blame ourselves for that, not being honest and being greedy.

I was at the Jolly Coachman pub in town watching a Vancouver Canucks playoff game. I'd bought some tickets for a chance to win an autographed Pavel Bure jersey. Someone called and wanted some coke so I left the pub to go home and look after this guy. I was only gone about 10 minutes when they called my number for the jersey. Since I wasn't there to claim it, they drew another number. Just another shit end of the stick. Some other prick got the jersey.

A good friend of mine, Kenny, and I decided to go hunting one Saturday. We got as far as the Mission Springs Pub, and then doubled back to the Black Sheep back in Maple Ridge. We were getting quite drunk, and Kenny knew a guy there who thought he was a major biker. Kenny got into an argument with him. I wasn't saying anything until this guy said to us, "You want to party? Let me make a phone call." I looked at him and said, "You make your phone call and I will be right back." He followed me just outside the entrance door while I walked to my truck. I opened the door and pulled out my stainless steel stalker rifle and put in the clip. When I turned around that pimp was gone, which was good for him because I was going to shoot him right at the front doors of the pub. I did see that guy again about six months later in the local strip joint, and when we made eye contact I gave him that evil smile I had and he was gone in minutes. I never saw that guy again. Big shot!

I was friends with NHL player Link Gaetz, who loved to party after he got into a bad car accident that ruined his career. He was an enforcer for the San Jose Sharks before the accident and he got a second chance with the Vancouver Canucks. He went to training camp a couple of times and that was it. We partied for three days and they didn't know where he was. In the newspaper, the caption was "Link Missing" instead of the "Missing Link." I remember us driving his mom's Plymouth Volare down Lougheed Highway at the tail end of that three day bender, and Link saying to me, "It doesn't get any better than this." We felt like shit. We didn't hang around much after this, as he ended up going to the Quebec Iron league to play.

It was Hallowe'en and I had rented a limo to take us to a party at a large hall in Burnaby. I dressed up as Jim Carrey's "Fire Marshall Bill" that year and what a show I put on. I had Roman candles in my inside pocket and won second prize. I also went out the next night to the Haney Hotel and won second place there as well. It took me a couple of weeks to put that costume together but it was worth it. I can imitate him pretty good.

Me as Jim Carrey's "Fire Marshall Bill" during Hallowe'en 1994.

When there is an opening for a new job at my work it is posted on the bulletin board. I bid on one job, and with my seniority I got it. My brother Darin (who worked there too) apparently didn't see the job posting and was going into the office to try to take it from me because he said he never saw the posting. I told him, right in front of everybody in the lunch room, that if he complained about it I would follow him home and kick the shit out of him in his driveway. He shut his mouth up pretty quick, and believe it or not he asked me to be best man at his wedding a few years later. Not too much to write about the wedding, but he eventually had a son before they divorced.

I was still going out with Maria until she came back from a trip to Mexico. I had found out that she'd slept around again. I'm a good investigator, but also an idiot, because I didn't tell her to beat it. I was really starting to get bitter after these relationships, but that was nothing compared to the relationship that I would later have. The stories that I am going to tell you will make your head spin. It's just amazing how much we put ourselves through with relationships that are doomed from the start. We blind ourselves to it and stay anyway, doing more damage to ourselves.

I was now seeing this crazy stripper. I called her "Trucker" because of her foul mouth, but pictures of her were in Penthouse Magazine. I spent the night at her house one night, and at about six in the morning she came out with all this leather in one hand and a whip in the other. I said, "Not a chance, I'm done."

I had my truck loaded up to head for 100 Mile House that morning for a hunting trip. She wouldn't let me leave. I had to run to the front door to get the hell away from this crazy chic, but she chased me down the steps and to my truck with no clothes on. This girl had the biggest fake tits I had ever seen so you can imagine what that looked like. She lived at the corner of a four-way stop, and the cars were starting to pile up from everyone watching the show.

She was trying to grab my keys as I was trying to put them in the ignition. I didn't want to hurt her so I said, "Fuck this, you can have the truck," and I started to walk up the road. There was a jogger running towards me and I said to him, "Do you believe this?" and he replied, "It happens to all of us." Later that night I got a friend to drop me off around the corner from her place, got in my truck and buggered off.

As nuts as she was, I was still involved with her. A short time later, she was going to Hawaii to strip there for a while and wanted me to come and see her. Stupid me, I said, "Sure." She had a ticket for me waiting at the airport.

She had also invited a friend of mine and his girlfriend. They were to arrive in Hawaii before me and I would see them there. Craig called to tell me that "Trucker's" roommate was a heroin addict, and he and his girlfriend were going to find a hotel.

When "Trucker" found out that I knew what was going on, she was going to get a hotel room just for us. She also arranged to have me picked up in a limo from the airport when I arrived.

I got a ride to the Vancouver airport and had a couple of drinks on the way. I walked up to the ticket counter to get my ticket and to check in. I asked if the bag I had was small enough for a carry on. The size was not a problem, so I said, "Good, it has my bomb in it." They never said shit about it, but you don't say things like that in today's world. Once on the plane I found my seat, looked at everyone, and asked if the bombs went up in the luggage compartment and the handguns up front. Some of the people laughed, and some had a worried look on their face. Believe it or not no one said anything to me about the comments I had made, but then again, it was before 9-11.

I had a few more drinks on the plane, and the two girls I was sitting with loaned me their headphones. There was an episode of Bugs Bunny on. I was laughing so hard the tears were running down my face. After the cartoon I pulled off the head phones to apologize to everyone for my laughter, and it was then I realized the whole plane was laughing at me.

We landed in Hawaii, and instead of the limo I was picked up in the back of a pickup truck. Right there I knew that this trip was going to be hell. I got to where "Trucker" was staying and nothing had changed; she hadn't found another hotel room for us. I knew that Craig was there, so I called him to come and get me. He picked me up twenty minutes later in this $120,000 BMW that he had rented. We weren't at his condo half an hour when "Trucker" called me on my cell phone. She was in a phone booth across the street. I asked Craig, "How the hell did she know where we were staying?" He had no idea. I told him this chick was crazy enough to climb up the balconies to get at me. She called a couple more times but I didn't answer and that was the end of her, but I would feel the karma for this one.

The three of us took the Beamer out for a drive and went for a swim. We found a place where warning signs advised that there were large waves. It was therefore a no-swim zone. That didn't stop me. I swam out a bit until this huge wave crashed down on me, forcing my head into the ocean floor and spraining my neck. I was only in Hawaii for four days and my neck was sore the whole time. We went on a pub-crawl two days later, and I was so shit-faced I ended up getting lost. I passed out and hit my head on the concrete. I was laying in this corridor just down from where we were staying, with blood pouring from my head. A guy passing by thought I was dying and came to my aid. He found out that I was just drunk and walked away.

I woke up the next morning in my bed wondering what had happened. Craig was in the room but his girlfriend wasn't. The drawers were all open and all our money and IDs were gone. I woke up Craig to ask what had happened. He said, "Didn't you hear us last night?" Apparently Craig and his girlfriend had ended up a big fight, and they were screaming at each other but I didn't hear a thing. With no money, and without ID, we were screwed. We managed to find $12 in our pants pockets. We didn't even have enough to hire a cab, so we started to walk until we got into a price range that a cab would take us to the airport.

After walking in the hot sun for four hours we found a cab that would take us to the airport. We were telling the cab driver the story and he was laughing his head off. We were going to the airport to get a hold of security and stop Craig's girlfriend leaving the island. I was in the backseat of the cab, and just as we were approaching the airport I went to hand the driver the money. As I tried to do this, half of it flew out the window. The driver couldn't believe our luck, and actually gave us two dollars back so we could take the bus back to our condo for a dollar once we were finished at the airport. Once we'd dealt with airport security, and found out that she hadn't left yet, we hopped on the bus. There was standing room only, and Craig looked at me and said, "Two days ago we were in a $120,000 BMW and now we're riding the peasant wagon.

We asked the bus driver where the nearest money store was and she pulled over, let us out, and told us there was one just a block down the road. Well there wasn't one in site, and now we were in the middle of nowhere. We stopped a cab and made a deal with him, that if he took us to a Money Store and stuck around while Craig got money wired from his dad, we would look after him well. He did, and when we finally got back to the condo, after an eight-hour day in the heat and hung over, there was a note on our condo door. The note read, "Sorry, I'm down at the pool." I told Craig he'd better go down there and get my shit back or I would drown her in that pool. I also told him that if he took her back after this I would put him in a wheelchair. I got my stuff back, and off to happy hour across the street I went.

I kept my distance from her for the next two days. We thought it would be fun to go out on a large pontoon boat. It was nice and sunny out, and off we went. Once we were offshore the clouds rolled in, and so did the wind. The sea got so rough that they were worried that we wouldn't make it back to shore. Everyone was hanging on to something to stop them from going overboard, but we did make it back to shore. There was no refund for us. If we had been in Canada I would have strangled the guy to get my money back. The next day it was time to fly home and I managed to get a seat far away from those two.

When we landed a friend picked me up, and when I got in the car I said, "Get me the fuck out of here." I guess that's what you get for a free ticket. Sorry "Trucker." She phoned me a few weeks later and asked if I wanted to have dinner with the band Van Halen. She was friends with them because she travelled with them at one point. It would have been nice to meet them, but it wasn't worth the hell. However, I still keep in contact with her from time to time.

Craig had a house party after the bar one night. I pointed out two guys that we didn't know. I said to Craig that I thought they were cops, and that he should ask them to leave. Sure enough, one day later that week, driving by the cop shop, I saw the same two guys walking out the front door.

I had one of my parties one night, and I took a picture of two guys I didn't know. Somebody said that he had met one of them before. I showed the picture around to a few people and found out that they were involved in a drug smuggling operation across the line. I did meet up with one of the guys later on, and he wanted me to do business with him, but like I told them, I didn't like partners. It turned out later that the guy had to leave town because he ripped off someone he shouldn't have.

Craig called one night in a panic. He thought someone was going to beat him up. He told me that he slept with a guy's girlfriend, and the guy wasn't very happy about it. I told him that he needed to take his lumps for what he'd done, and that I couldn't help him. He never did take his lumps, he just phoned a cab from the phone booth and left his car in the bar parking lot.

I would normally be there for my friends, but not for something I frowned on. He called me another night while he was outside a night-club and told me that someone was after him, but he didn't know why. I told him I would be right there. I drove my truck into the parking lot sideways and jumped out the driver's door. I asked Craig where the guy was, but he had already left. Lucky for him.

It was the first of the three times the RCMP tried to shut me down for selling cocaine. One night a friend of mine came over in a panic to tell me that a guy that bought off me was a rat for the cops. This guy was busted for breaking into a house and stealing a .357 revolver, so he started working with the cops on the Most Wanted Top Ten hot list, and apparently I was number four. After my buddy warned me, about ten minutes later the phone rang and it was the rat. He told me he had the $70 that he owed me, and that he wanted to play pool.

Wanting to play pool meant that he wanted an eight-ball of cocaine, three and a half gram's. I said no problem, put some laundry detergent in a ziplock bag and headed out the door to meet him in Coquitlam at a local hotel. Once I got there I cased out the joint looking for anybody waiting in cars. It was all clear. I'd realized on the way there that if I gave him this detergent it would still be trafficking, even though it wasn't a narcotic. I pulled up at the front door of the hotel and the rat hopped in. I pulled around to the back. He was wearing a long trench coat so I couldn't see if he was wired. I just told him that I was there for my $70, and that I'd heard he was a rat. He denied the rumour and I dropped him off at the front door.

Once the cops knew the word was out as to the identity of the rat, it was the end of the cops trying to bust me and the other six dealers from that most-wanted list. They would try twice more to get me. When one of the dealers went to court, he told me later they'd read my name out and asked him if he knew me. He denied that he did.

The word on the street was that the RCMP had purchased another ghost car. It was a LeBaron convertible, tan in colour. My house was at the end of a street, and I could see all the traffic from my chair in the living room. I noticed that this car was parked out front of my place on a day when I was leaving to go fishing, and had to think fast about what to do. I walked outside, went right up to the car, and asked if he was lost. He had a moustache, and was wearing a plain white tee shirt. Like why would they send him, when they could have sent someone who could at least blend in with the neighbourhood? He told me that he wasn't lost, and that he was meeting a friend there. I thought to myself, "Yeah right, you're meeting a friend here, what about a coffee shop?" But I just said all right and walked back inside, now knowing for sure he was a cop. He drove away up the street and made a left turn.

I grabbed my coke, put it in an envelope, and hopped in my car. My mail box was at the end of the street and my thought was that if I could get it in my box it would be safe. The mail is federal, and they would have to get a warrant for my place first. I figured with nothing there, there would be no way they could get a warrant for my mail. At least I think that's how it would have happened. As I approached my box I saw that the cop had just pulled around the corner and was watching my every move. I opened the box and put the envelope in, and as I shut the door and locked it, I waved goodbye to him. I went fishing that weekend, and when I got home I went to my mail box and grabbed the envelope, all safe and sound. It wouldn't have mattered if the postman had been there, as all he would have done was add the mail to the box without batting an eye.

I had a few good places to hide my stash in the house, one in particular. The ceiling lights in the bedrooms always have one bulb burnt out so I came up with a good idea. I unscrewed one of them and sat on the couch with a file and filed the end off, but the threads would still be attached. Once this was done I rolled up my baggy, put it inside and screwed it back up there, but not all the way in. So if the cops raided my place they wouldn't think twice about a burned out bulb when the other bulb in the fixture came on. I had to change it up once in a while, just in case one of my customers got a stupid idea and came back for it when I wasn't home.

My buddy and me on the fishing trip I took the weekend I hid the cocaine in a mailbox.

The parties that I had in this house would sometimes get out of control. One night I had a full house, and when I got up from the couch I hit my shin on my coffee table. This was about 4 a.m. and I headed for the garage, grabbed my chainsaw, and brought it in the house. There was panic in the eyes of those partygoers when I came in and fired it up. I went into the living room and cut the corner off the coffee table so now I had lots of room to get in and out. I think that I have a little something loose upstairs.

I was now buying my cocaine from another guy, Allan. He called me over to his place one day and had a couple of lines cut up on his dresser. As well, he cooked some up and made crack. He didn't do drugs after he'd overdosed a few years earlier. He wanted me to test out the product before he purchased a kilogram of it. I didn't smoke crack at that time so I chose to snort a line. I didn't feel anything for about ten minutes, but when I did, it was the best stuff I had ever tried. It looked so shitty though, being as fluffy as it was, but we still talk about that from time to time, and he had everyone asking for it, but he could never get his hands on it again.

It was the May long weekend and my German friend and I were headed for Tulameen (a small town outside Princeton). We were camped on the river with all our friends. After being up for two days doing coke and magic mushrooms, we were sitting in my camper. This guy I didn't know poked his head in the door, then looked back at his friends who were just outside and laughed. I didn't hear what he said, but because he was laughing I knew it was something I wouldn't like. I got my friends to move out of the way from the table so I could leave the camper, and walked outside. There were three of them, so I positioned myself and hit the biggest guy first with a huge right hand, I followed that with a right elbow to the guy on my right, and a left jab and a right to the guy on my left. Within seven seconds, these guys were laying out cold in the sand.

The first guy I hit so hard that I knocked him out of his shoes and you could see that they were still stuck in the sand. They eventually got up and walked away, and I made my way to the front of my truck were we had a fire going. After about fifteen minutes I saw there was a bunch of guys approaching us. I grabbed my chainsaw and tried to start it as a weapon, but for the first time ever it wouldn't start. I then threw it on the hood of my truck and called for the rest of my friends to follow me. These guys wanted their shoes back, and for me to pay for their dental work. We just told them to beat it, and that they were lucky that it was only their teeth that were missing. They took off and didn't come back.

The next day this bum came up to our camp and asked if he could have our beer cans. I said, "No problem buddy, help yourself." His one hand was wrapped in a shirt that was covered in blood. I asked him what had happened, and he said that he asked someone else for their cans, but when he went to grab them they shot him in the hand with a handgun. I offered to take him to the hospital, but he said he would be all right.

The next night, after three days of no sleep and wired on magic mushrooms, I decided to take down this huge fir tree across the river. I had the chainsaw running, and held it over my head while I made my way across the river with all my clothes on. As I cut the mouth I saw that there were hundreds of people cheering me on. I did fall the tree, and the next morning had a beautiful view of the mountains. Another stupid thing I regret.

We needed some dry firewood so a friend of mine drove his truck down to the river bed. As I was handing someone my chainsaw, with one foot on the bumper, he popped the clutch. I flew off the bumper and landed in the riverbed, smashing my head on a rock. We left that morning and I had someone else drive my truck home because I was in no condition to drive. I hadn't eaten anything so we stopped for something to eat. When the waitress went to grab my plate because she thought I was finished, I growled at her. She pulled her hand back quickly and the guys I was with told her that it was a good idea to leave me be. It took a few days to lick my wounds after that weekend.

I got my hands on a mittfull of free tickets to a Vancouver Grizzlies basketball game, so I rented a Budget truck to take us all there. There were about a dozen of us who went, and we were all drinking. I said to Kenny, "What do you say we jump down there and head for the court." He looked at me and said, "You figure?" and I said, "I'm going." I jumped down into the corridor and headed for the court when there were only five minutes left in the game and a time out. I got to the edge of the floor, turned around and did the moon walk to the centre of the court. They had me on the Jumbotron and the whole place was cheering me on until security came out and escorted me off the floor. I could have given these guys a run for their money but this was all for fun. When they got me to one of the exit doors, we just waved to each other and they told me to have a good night.

The next day my Mom phoned and asked if I was at the game, and

I had to ask why. She said that an employee at her work had thought she'd seen me on TV because I was on Sports Page, but I told my Mom it wasn't me.

Everything in life happens for a reason, so I have been wondering why I did this. Maybe I have to come back and finish what I started in order for the Canucks to win the cup. I feel they will finally win it in 2013 against the Philadelphia Flyers. Why I say this is because in 2011 I told the guys at work that they wouldn't win it in 2012, but in 2013 against the Flyers. I said this just before I went to a treatment centre. While I was playing basketball at the centre, a guy was reading The Province paper and an article in the sports section said EA Games predicted the same thing. I even went so far as making my own jersey. I hope I'm right, but it could just be my dream.

The jersey I had made to reinforce my prediction about the Vancouver Canucks winning the Stanley Cup in 2013 against the Philadelphia Flyers.

If that wasn't enough, the next weekend I had my camper on my truck and drove it into work after leaving a party. I arrived at work half cut, and after I had my job assigned to me for that night I headed back to my camper with my partner. We were drinking, and I was snorting coke, until we got a call on the radio to go and fix a rail car. On our way out to the track we passed a switch man up ahead. Dave slowed down, and as we approached this guy he threw his flashlight into the passenger side of the front windshield for no good reason. Dave stopped, got out, and I could hear this guy yelling as I was picking glass out of my face. I opened the door, came around the back of the truck, and started shit-kicking him. I had him on the ground and he was covering up pretty good, covering his face with his arms. I was hitting this guy so hard I was surprised I didn't break his arms. I then got back in the truck and told Dave to drive to the rail bridge, and to tell anybody who asked that he didn't know where I'd gone. I knew the police would soon be there looking for me.

I ran across the bridge with my workclothes and boots on all the way home… about seven kilometres. Once home, it was only a couple of hours later that the union was at my door with my older brother. They told me that the boss and another big shot wanted me back there to explain what had happened. It turns out this guy had a record of wrecking company property, and I know they were glad to see this guy finally get it.

As I worked for a different department than the guy I hurt, we had different unions. My boss, the big wigs and both unions were having a meeting on what to do with me. The other union wanted me fired for beating up one of their members, but that wouldn't happen. My boss picked up an ashtray and threw it across the room, hitting that union rep in the arm. He shouted, "No one is going to fire that kid, it doesn't go any further than this" and walked out. Now my boss was just a small guy compared to the other levels of management in the room, but because the guy I punched out had a record a mile long for wrecking company property they didn't say anything. I wasn't fired. They disciplined me with thirty demerit points instead.

One of the other employees from his department had drawn a picture of a switch man laying out cold with birds flying over his head and the caption was "CAR SHOPS 1-RUNNING TRADES 0. These pictures were sent all over the railway as far as Montreal because it was big news. His department was so grateful they were going to buy me a case of beer because they were happy he finally got it. It turned out that they hated this guy. I never did get that case of beer. This guy was retiring in two weeks, he was fifty-four years of age but in my rage I didn't care if he was in a wheelchair, he had to learn a lesson. I guess you could say I gave him an early retirement gift. I'm so thoughtful.

The poster made by an employee at the railway to commemorate the fight between me and another guy on the railway.

It was a long weekend and off I went to Stave Lake for a campout with all my friends. After the second day of doing magic mushrooms and coke, my buddy and I needed to get more coke. While his girlfriend was sleeping in my camper we quietly unhooked his boat from the van, then we pushed his van far enough away so we wouldn't wake her up. We knew that if we woke her he wouldn't be going anywhere. We drove to a friend's house who sold coke, but he told us he was out. He had just left the camp site earlier that morning and didn't want to put a flap together because he felt as bad as we did.

On the way back to the site on the gravel road, and feeling so shitty, I was looking at the height of the bridges and saying, "That one isn't high enough" – meaning it wasn't high enough to kill us if we were to jump. We got back to the site and his girlfriend never knew we had left.

About a month later I decided to go and see my Dad in Salmon Arm, which was about a four and a half hour drive. Once I got there we headed out to a pub for a few drinks. We got back and I still wanted to find a party. My Dad said he'd had enough, so I decided to venture out myself in this redneck town. His wife said that there was no way I was going out because I would be asking for trouble as I was from out of town. She said that I wouldn't be able to get a cab to come all the way out to their place anyway. I asked her, "If I can get a cab, will you let me go?" and she said sure. I picked up the phone book, called the cab company, and wouldn't you know it, they were sending me a cab. I hung up the phone, looked at her and said, "BYE."

Once in the cab and on our way to town, I asked the driver to take me to where there was some action. He dropped me off at the Motor Hotel, and what a rough-looking place this was. I asked him if this was the only place happening tonight and he replied, "This is it." I walked in and all eyes were on me. With a smile on my face I took a seat. There were only about twenty people there at the time, including a massive guy who had to be about six foot eight and weighing about 350 pounds. This dude comes over, sits down next to me at the bar, and asks me where I'm from. With everyone looking on I told him I was from Vancouver, and just as I said this a fight broke out behind us. I stood up, as he did, to help break up the fight but he pushed me away with a hand on the chest. I let him break up the fight and then he came back and sat down beside me again. He said, "Sorry about that, but I run this place." I said, "Don't put your hands on me again." I then went to grab a wine glass that was hanging in the rack just above me, to bite a piece out of it just to let him know I wasn't fucking around. Once I'd done this he knocked it out of my hand and we both stood up ready to fight, but the waitress got between us and started yelling at me to leave because they had enough problems in there. I stared him down and walked out the door. As I was standing outside I thought to myself, "I am not leaving without a fight," so I tucked my wallet into my sock and walked back in. I then told the waitress that the guy had stolen my wallet and I wanted it back.

Another fight had broken out, and she was telling me that he hadn't stolen my wallet and I should just leave. I walked to the front doors and put my fist through the safety glass window in the door that had all that wire reinforcement in it. I was yelling at the waitress to send that fuck-head outside.

I waited for about fifteen minutes and no gorilla, so with blood pouring down my arm I headed to the 7-11 that was about a hundred yards away. On the way to the store I grabbed the receiver from the pay phone and ripped it off. As a result, I tore my left pinky finger wide open on the sharp cord as it unravelled when I pulled it. I walked into the store, with blood all over, and told the cashier to call an ambulance. As I was waiting for the ambulance outside I saw the cab driver who had driven me there in the first place pull up to the bar to see what happened. I think he heard something on his radio. Now I knew that this prick knew I was going to get into trouble, and that was why he'd taken me there.

Thinking this, I told myself that after I got patched up I would get the hospital to call me a cab, and I would take care of this guy. The ambulance came and took me to the hospital, stitched my right hand up, and told me that I needed plastic surgery to repair the tendon in my torn finger. They said that I had to see my doctor so he could schedule me for surgery when I got home. The nurse on shift said that I would have to find another way home because that cab driver was the only one on shift that night. The cops showed up and asked what happened, so I told them that I was from out of town and couldn't fit in, so things got a little ugly. I also told them to tell that gorilla he was lucky I didn't hurt him. They left and now, with both my hands all bandaged up, I asked the new nurse on shift if she could call me a cab and she said sure, not a problem, because she didn't know how any of this had happened.

I was waiting outside for my cab, and here he comes. Wonderful! I got in and this guy had a smile on his face, and as we drove off I said, "You knew I was going to get into trouble in there tonight, didn't you." He said, “Well, you are from out of town” as we turned onto the highway. I looked around and there weren’t any other cars on the road. I saw the coast was clear and with us driving 60 km/h, I grabbed a hold of him by his shirt and told him that he was coming outside. I had the door open while we were driving and tried to drag him out of the moving vehicle. He managed to grab the steering wheel with his left hand, steer the car to the shoulder and stop the car. As I was pulling him out of the car he had the radio in his hand calling for help. I let him go, and as I stood outside the car I sprained my right ankle on the curb. He peeled out of there and I limped up the hill and hid in the prickle bushes thinking the cops were coming. I stayed up in the bush for about an hour, but with no cops in sight I started to run home on that ankle, which was about eight kilometres.

I got to my Dad’s and there he was to greet me. He just opened the door, I walked upstairs to bed, and he didn’t say anything. The next morning I hobbled down the stairs and took a seat in the living room. With my Dad holding his coffee cup and watching TV, he waited until I spoke first. I told him what had happened, and that I had to leave and get surgery. My Dad offered to drive me home, but I told him to just get me some ice for the ankle and I would be out of there. I hopped in my truck, and had my left arm elevated because of the damaged tendon in my finger. I had ice on my right ankle so I drove home using my left foot. I got to the doctor’s, and went into surgery that night. The surgery was a waste of time because that night I got home, and while I was having a dream I clinched my left hand and the tendon broke again. I didn’t bother getting it fixed again, but the shitty thing about this was that I had to find another golf grip. I tell ya, that phone both won’t look at me like that again. I hope it learned a lesson.

As you have undoubtedly guessed by now I was quite crazy, but huge on respect.

Gus and I went to the bar at the local ice rink and got into a disagreement with one of the owners. It was the same guy who jumped me from behind the night I crashed into the fence and hurt my back. We were escorted out and we headed for Roosters Bar. On the way there I said, "Turn around and take me back to the ice rink." He was telling me I was crazy because there were at least twelve of them there. I hollered at him that he should "Take me back there and drop me off. Even if I have to take on all twelve, I will before I let this happen." He dropped me off and told me I was nuts, but what else is new? I knew the doorman who came to talk to me, and I told him to send the owner down. I waited there for at least an hour but the chickenshit never came out. I only lived a few blocks away from there, so I eventually walked home.

At the bar one night I told everybody I was having a party, and to come over after closing time. I lived on a cul-de-sac that looked like all the others in the area. They went down the wrong street and tried to get into a house that wasn't mine. One of them got stuck in a doggie door, and one other was trying to open a window. One of the neighbours came outside, who just happened to be a cop, and asked what they were all doing. One of them piped up and said that Scott Magri was having a party. The cop told them I lived one street over so they dropped the cooler on the front lawn and got the hell out of there.

About ten years later I was on a boat for this wedding. The girl I was with, we were sitting at this table with another couple. He was telling me that he lived in Pitt Meadows by the high school. I told him I had once lived close to the school myself, and asked what street he lived on. It just happened to be the same house my friends were trying to break into that night, and when I told him that they'd left their cooler there that night he laughed and said that he still had the cooler. What a small world.

1995

My NHL friend was in town for a visit so a bunch of us went out to a pub. We were all having a good time until I started to do a strip show. I took off my shirt, but when I started to undo my pants this guy shoved a bar chair with rollers across the room and hit me in the legs. I asked him, "What the fuck did you do that for?" and he said, "Don't be taking your clothes off in front of my girlfriend." I smashed him in the face and knocked him out. The manager saw everything and asked me to leave. I then picked up the chair and threw it into the glass mirrors behind the bar and went out the back door.

The police station was right beside the pub so I had to think fast. My friend, Craig, had a raised-up Chevy truck with an alarm system in it. I went and jumped into the back of his truck and the alarm sounded. I used reverse psychology and stayed low in the box of the truck, thinking that no one would think I would be dumb enough to stick around. Lying flat in the box I could see people running past the truck, and hear them saying, "He must have gone that way because the alarm is going off on that truck."

I got on my cell, phoned Craig, and told him to get outside and drive away because I was in the back of his truck. He told me the cops were all over the place and no one was allowed to leave. I phoned back and told him to send Link out. Link managed to get out of there and come to my aid. The alarm wasn't sounding anymore when Link approached the truck. He whispered, "Hey Scottie, it's me, Link." and he got in the truck. He didn't even get the door closed before the cops told him to get back in the pub until they found me. I looked up and could see the RCMP crest on the cop's shoulder, that's how close I was to getting pinched, but he never looked in the box of the truck.

It was January and below zero outside, and I must have stayed in that truck for two hours. The place closed and everyone left. Once the parking lot was cleared, Craig pulled up in someone else's car and said, "Come on Magri, the coast is clear." I tell you I never liked the heat so much as after that night in that truck.

That would have been my third assault charge, and off to jail I would have gone, but that would come later anyway.

I went up to my Dad's to go on a hunting trip. He was always very impatient. The first day hunting he was yelling that there was nothing here. I said there was fresh elk shit right in our camp, that they were here, and he should give it some time. He insisted that we leave the next morning and we headed for his place. Once we were there I unloaded all his gear and asked if I could borrow $100 for gas so I could get home. I told him I would write him a cheque for the $100, but not to cash it for a few days until I got home and took some of my stash and deposited it in the bank. I asked him this in front of his wife Mary and she started in on me, saying, "Don't you have an overdraft or a line of credit?" She questioned me for about fifteen minutes and my Dad just stood there watching the whole thing. I couldn't believe what was happening after all the help I had given them over the years on that acreage, and here I was being treated like a piece of shit. I left and that was the last time I talked to my Dad for ten years.

I started smoking crack shortly after that with a couple of friends, Barry and Kenny. When the two of them would show up on Friday I would say to them, "Resume your positions." We only did this for about five weeks before it started to get out of hand. My life was bad enough, and I came to the conclusion that if I kept this up it would only get worse, so I quit. I stuck with just snorting coke about three days a week because it went hand in hand with drinking.

All three of us went to a pub one night at the Cat and Fiddle. These three guys started to have an argument with my buddy Barry, and the bouncers threw those guys out. One of them was waving me to come outside, and Barry wanted to go, but I said, "If they are there when we leave we will deal with it, in the meantime let's have a good time."

It was last call and we noticed that these three guys were still out there, but were now wearing all black. It had been three hours since the incident, and I guess they went home, changed and came back. I don't know who they thought they were but they were going to get taught a lesson. I asked the owner of the bar if he minded if we went out there and beat these guys up before coming back in for last call. He said no problem because he was coming out to watch. I took on the big guy and, because I wasn't mad, I decided to give this guy a lesson. I was jabbing this guy so much he was begging for a right. Just when you couldn't recognize what he looked like, he raised his hands and said he'd had enough. I just said to him, "Good, that's real good." My friends had beaten up the other two. We went in for last call.

Another night when I was there, I was in a bad mood. I handed one of the bouncers my drink and headed for the bathroom. All the urinals were all taken up, as well as the toilets. I reached up and pulled the chandelier out of the ceiling and threw it against the wall and told everybody to get the fuck out. These guys couldn't get their flies up quick enough, and now I had the whole bathroom to myself. I finished and walked out to the doorman, and when he handed my drink back and asked what was wrong, I just took a bite out of the glass and threw it on the ground, smashing it while spitting out the broken glass. He didn't say anything. Would you?

My buddy Allan was telling me about this girl he was bringing to the bar that night. I knew her from high school, although I never did talk to her. She was the hottest girl in school and I was looking forward to seeing her after all these years. She was hotter than ever and I started to put on a show for her. I jumped on the floor and started biting her shoes and growling like a dog. When I stood up laughing with everyone else I could see from the look in her eyes that she loved me right away, Yeah, I'm crazy.

A couple of days later the phone rang and it was her. She wanted to know if I wanted to go to the movies with her. I told her I wasn't too sure, and to let me think about it. She couldn't believe I had to think about it, but I had to check with Allan first. I called him up and asked if it was all right if I took her out and he said, sure, go ahead, she's not my girlfriend. We went out to the movies a few days later, started making out, and ended up at my place. We had sex twice that night, and man did she have the nicest nipples I had ever seen, just like battery posts. She actually swallowed that night, and only that night, and you know what happened next… she moved in with her four-year-old son that month because she knew what card to play. She never told me she had a ten-year-old daughter until several months later.

Her son, Brock, was such a perfect kid I fell in love with him right away. I would have twenty kids if they could all be like him and his sister. He would catch on to my humour from all the crazy friends who would come over. One day, when we were getting ready to go out somewhere, he put on a show. He was about seven then and all dressed, standing in the bathroom doorway with one hand on his hip and the other on the door frame. We didn't notice at first, but he had this smile on his face, and he said, "Are we ready to go?" He had his fly open and his penis hanging out. Laura and I were laughing our heads off, and so was he.

I was never an affectionate guy by any means, and would always push Laura away. She was a hard one to get close to anyway because she was such an angry person. I was sitting on my bed one morning putting on my socks and she was giving me shit for something. I was just ignoring her, saying, "yeah, yeah, yeah," and then she smacked me on the shoulder. My blood boiled immediately and I kicked her in the stomach, knocking her to the ground. While she lay there gasping for air I told her to never, ever lay her hands on me again and walked away. It was pretty rough living together because I was partying three days a week, and all of a sudden I had this girl and her son living with me. I guess she was looking for a father figure and a husband, but I was neither.

I headed to Roosters Country Bar after a day on the golf course. I still had my golf shoes on, and I was dancing on the dance floor. My golf shoes had spikes back then and every step I made the shoes would get stuck on the floor. I still managed to finish the dance but it was pretty funny. I can just imagine the damage I did to that floor.

1996

Laura was working at the White spot and I was at home. The phone rang and it was Allan telling me to get to his girlfriend's house in Hammond right away. He was in a panic and I asked him what for, because Brock was in the tub and I had no insurance on my truck. He said never mind, just get there fast. I grabbed Brock out of the tub and quickly dried him off, and we hopped in my truck. When I got there I told Brock to go into the house with the other kids. Allan had just picked up his coke and a couple of days later someone robbed him. He found out who had taken it, and had one of the culprits sitting in the passenger seat of a car in the carport. We had to get this guy to talk so we could get his partner.

I told Allan's girlfriend to call Laura at work so she could come and get Brock. When she showed up I told her to take my truck home. I then backed up her car and opened the trunk to put this guy in so we could take him somewhere else. Allan said for me to wait because another friend of his was on his way. In the meantime I started in on this guy. He wasn't telling me anything until I started kicking him in the face. He gave up his partner and I came up with a plan to get him.

I told the guy in the car to phone his partner and tell him that he was at the beer and wine store and they wouldn't sell him booze because he didn't have a driver's licence. We got a description from him so Allan and his buddy would get the right guy. I stayed with the guy in the car while those two went for his partner. When they got hold of the partner they beat him and threw him in a ditch. We let the guy that I was watching go, and told him the amount he owed plus interest, and not to leave town. My hands were washed of this episode. I did what I was supposed to do and I don't think that guy ever paid Allan.

Laura had bought a car that had a cooling problem I was trying to fix. It was front-wheel drive, and I was replacing the water pump. I spent six hours trying to fix it and it still ran hot. My back was so sore from being bent over all those hours that I had trouble walking back in the house. I told her I didn't know what was wrong with her car. I couldn't believe it when she looked me in the face and said, "You can't fix fuck all." Well I had two options, I could hit her in the face, or take it out on the Filter Queen vacuum. I decided to pick up the vacuum and throw it down the hallway. It bounced off the couch and through the glass in the coffee table. She looked at me and said, "You want to throw things?" She then picked up the vacuum and threw it out the front door and onto the driveway, slammed the door, and said, "There you go." Her son Brock saw the whole thing, then went outside, brought the vacuum in, and put it back together.

After going out and not coming home for days, Laura would be there in the front doorway waiting for me. She only took my shit for about a year before she started sleeping around on me, and I don't blame her, I mean, the only feelings I had for her was when my sperm travelled through my penis. This one time when we were at Roosters, I ran into one of my ex-girlfriends, Tina. I didn't know that Laura was standing behind me so when Tina grabbed my cock I grabbed her box and Laura saw everything. Laura ran out the door crying, and I just shrugged it off like I didn't give a shit… and I didn't. I couldn't even hold hands or kiss any of my girlfriends in public, because my reputation was so well known I didn't want anybody thinking I was getting weak. Crazy, eh?

What a real piece of shit I was with girls. I remember her telling me a few years later that she would get excited when she heard my truck coming down the road, but at that time in my life I wouldn't have given a shit how excited she was.

A buddy and I were out driving around in my truck one afternoon drinking beer. I had my binoculars in the truck and thought that it would be a good idea to drive with them. It was hard enough driving drunk, and then trying to see through the binoculars. We didn't get in a car accident that day, but I guess luck was with me again. I don't recommend this, but that's your decision.

1997

Laura decided to get a boob job. After the surgery, I notice that her nipples were cut back. I asked her why the hell she'd done that because they were beautiful. She told me that it was me who wanted them shorter. I'd never said a thing about that, and asked why she hadn't told me she was going to do this before the operation. I wondered at the time, who was she seeing who would make her do this surgery? It was simple… she was so insecure that someone she was seeing behind my back at that time, or someone she'd seen previously, probably told her that she should do something with them. Why would I want her to change the best part of her body… the part I loved the most… or should I say, liked the most?

I found out she was seeing the leader of this big organization because he called the house one day. I talked to this guy, not knowing who he really was, and then with no please or thank you he told me to tell Laura that he had phoned. Now I knew who he was. When I hung the phone up I stood there staring at it, wondering whether I should go down to his house and blow his fucking head off. I thought these organizations were supposed to be built on respect. Well, how disrespectful could one man be to another than by doing what he did. I realized that if I shot him, I would have to kill myself, and she wasn't worth it. It wasn't because I was jealous, it was because he was disrespectful when he called the house.

I heard from a buddy that he wanted to apologize, but I'm still waiting. I did stay with her, and I think the only reason I did was because I knew I treated her like shit and I deserved everything she did to me. I thought to myself that was just the way I was, and it didn't matter who I was with, I would have treated every girl the same.

It was Hallowe'en night and I was up by myself snorting coke while Laura was in bed with Brock. I started to get paranoid, and saw a police car outside my house. I took my coke and flushed it down the toilet along with Laura's, who had started selling. The cops never did come in, and I don't know if I was too high and seeing things or not. I had to tell Laura in the morning what had happened and man was she pissed, but what else was new?

I had to go and get more so we could both get back in business. Laura had had a problem with coke prior to our relationship, when she'd lived on Vancouver Island, and had gone to Narcotics Anonymous to get cleaned up. There was one time when she and I smoked crack together, but as far as I know she never did touch it again.

After that incident on Hallowe'en I only sold coke for about another month or so, until the neighbour up the street told me the cops had parked around the corner for a couple weeks watching me. I stopped selling right there and then, and never sold again. They wanted me too bad to keep gambling.

Laura's daughter was living with her Dad, who had a few problems of his own, and I said to Laura, "That's no place for a child so let's get her out of there and bring her here." I was no prize myself, doing coke three days a week and drinking, but at least Laura was sober, and we had food in the house. Her daughter lived with us from then on, and she was just one of those kids who never asked for anything.

I was always there to help anyone who would ask. My older brother was always selfish but I would help him anyway. I gave him a hand one weekend putting in some fence posts in his yard. While we were doing this I thought to myself, "Where are all his friends, why aren't they here?" I think that was because he was never there for them. Do you see what happens when you don't help others.

That week my truck didn't work and I asked him for a ride, and he got pissed off because he had to go out of his way to pick me up. After that happened I never helped him with anything again. We never did get along anyway, so it didn't make any difference to me.

Laura's boy Brock wanted to take up BMX riding, so I went out and bought him a new bike. When he came home from school I told him to go to his bedroom and clean it up. Little did he know that I'd put his new bike in his bedroom. He was so happy, and off we went to the track. His first race of the night he came in last and started to cry. I took him aside and told him that babies cry, so you get back out there and beat those kids. He won the next two races and finished first, taking home his first trophy. He was in it for a year, and was doing really well, but lost interest the next year.

Laura and I headed out one night to Roosters. I wasn't a dancer and she got asked to dance by some guy. She came and asked if it would be alright, and I said sure, no problem. After the dance, she came and sat next to me. This guy actually came up to me, to thank me for letting him dance with my girlfriend, and shook my hand. He came back a few minutes later to talk to Laura and that would have been fine but he turned his back on me with his ass in my face. I took that as strike number two. One more and he was going to sleep. This guy then walked over to his buddy and started talking to him. They were both looking in our direction and laughing, so I knew it wasn't good. Strike three.

I put down my glass and headed over there. He was about four steps away and I drilled him in the side of the head. I could feel the bones crushing in his face as my fist sunk into his skull. He hit the floor so fast you would have thought someone had shot the legs out from under him. I knew some of the bouncers and they took me aside to tell me to leave. I said sure, no problem, but I thought I'd hit the guy too hard and I wanted to go apologize to him. So they walked me over there and, with him sitting on a bar stool and people helping him, I apologized. It was hard to do considering his eye was hanging out of his socket and the side of his head was so swollen he looked like the elephant man. A lot of good the apology did because I would end up in jail a little later for it.

Anyway, no one told me that his brother had been escorted out, but he was waiting for me outside. As I walked out and waved goodbye to the doorman I got kicked in the stomach and fell to the ground. While on the ground, I looked up at this guy going berserk, who was yelling for me to get up. I looked at him with that smile on my face and stood up. I threw two quick jabs to his face, close enough without hitting him to let him know he'd fucked with the wrong guy. By the look on his face, he knew he was in trouble. I threw a left and a right, knocking him out as his teeth went flying through the air. The doorman said that I should get into a cab and get out of there before the cops came.

Three months later the cops called at the house looking for me. This guy needed two surgeries to put his face back together. I broke his upper and lower jaw bones, and his lower eye socket, all in that one punch, and his brother needed some dental work. I wasn't home when they called, but Laura was, and when the cops asked her about that night she said, "Those guys deserved it" instead of keeping her mouth shut and just telling them I wasn't even there. Everybody who worked in that bar knew me, and they weren't going to give out any statements, except one waitress who hated me and the group of friends I had. That girl gave a statement and I was a sitting duck. I was charged with my third assault.

About six months later I was drinking again at Roosters and Pat, the brother of my old roommate, was sitting on one of the bar stools. I approached Pat and asked were his brother was. He said, "I don't know where my brother is" and then offered to pay the debt from when Al used to live with me. I said to Pat that I wanted Al to pay the debt because he was the one who owed me the money. Again, it was the principle of the whole thing. I finished the conversation and went on my merry way around the bar. After a few minutes I saw Pat walk into the washroom, and I went to tell him that I was going to tack on some extra interest. Once I got in the can, I told Pat that instead of the $750, he should tell his brother he now owed me $1,000. Pat shook his head side to side and said, "He doesn't owe you a $1,000." Right away I smashed him in the face, and he flew back into the tile wall and slid down to the floor out cold.

There was a guy taking a piss at the urinal, and I looked at him and said, "You wait here, and when he wakes up you tell him its $1,200" and I walked out. I never did see the money, and with Al working for the railway himself he took a transfer to Golden, B.C. about an eight-hour drive into the interior. Of course, with an assault charge pending I thought that if this guy sang I was in real shit, but I wasn't worried. I would have used a favour on him anyway.

My lawyer made a deal with crown, because with this assault charge being my third, they were looking to throw me in jail for a year if found guilty. The deal was, I was to plead guilty, receive three weeks on the ankle bracelet, take an anger management course, and face one year of probation.

On my sentencing date they shackled me and the other prisoners, and took us off to jail to wait for a bracelet. On the way in the sheriff's van, there was a young kid about twenty years old, and I could see he was terrified. As we approached the prison gates he asked in this scared voice, "What prison is this?" I looked at him with my smile and told him it was maximum security.

With our hands shackled in front of us, and chains at our feet, I was going to put my hand on his lap just to fuck with him, but I didn't have the heart… he was already scared enough. There were three of us getting the bracelet that day, but they only had two available. Since I was the biggest they gave the two bracelets to the other guys and kept me in there.

They called me into a room and one of the bulls told me there would be a good chance I would be challenged. I just smiled at him as he told me to try and keep my nose clean because it didn't look like I would be there long. The bulls do their homework on a prisoner so they know who they're dealing with. When I walked into the cell block all eyes were on me because the bulls had warned them all of a real beauty coming in. Soon as I sat down this guy ran up to me, offering me his book to read, but I rejected it. It turned out the prisoners were calling this guy "her." They were having their way with him, and he was looking for protection. There were only two black guys in there, and one of them, I was told, could get you things. The other fellow was my cellmate.

The socks they gave me were torn so bad my toes were showing, so the guy who can get things went and got me another pair. My cellmate lit up a joint and asked if I wanted some, but I didn't as I did not smoke pot. He looked at me as though I didn't want a drag because he'd had his lips on it. That wasn't the case at all, and he knew that later, because when he offered me a drag from his cigarette, I said, "Yeah, sure" and he changed his tune. I asked where the ashtray was, and he said they took them out of there because someone used one for a fight.

That night I didn't have a pillow so this guy gave me his, and he slept without one. The next day I was reading a newspaper in my cell and I heard a few guys talking about me, asking if anyone knew how long I was going to be in there.

I guess the bulls had told these guys what a psycho I really was because everyone stayed clear of me. I got called out of my cell by the bulls, and I thought to myself, having had no sleep, what the hell do they want? I went up to their desk and they told me that they didn't give a fuck what that judge had said, they could keep me in there as long as they wanted. One of them then told me to salute another one of them. I was so tired I didn't argue, I just turned and saluted him and said. "There you go," and they all started to laugh and sent me back to my cell.

It was only an hour later that they called me, and the bull I'd saluted got me out of there, took me home, and set up the monitor for the bracelet in my house. On the way to my house he said that the two of us could make a good pair bouncing a bar. I said to him, "I think that I have seen enough." I was given certain hours when I could leave the house so I could go to work.

The prison didn't scare me but the food did. I haven't hit anybody since. LESSON LEARNED.

After a couple of weeks going stir crazy, I called up the sheriff and told him my Mom wasn't doing so well and I had to go see her. He asked me how much time I needed, and I told him four hours. He said, "How about three?" and I took it. I grabbed my clubs and headed for the nine-hole golf course. I had to pull my socks up like an idiot to help hide the fact that I was on the monitoring program, and I finished the round and made it home with just minutes to spare. Once off the bracelet I was off to anger management.

The teacher was cool as a cucumber, as you might guess. There was one guy in there whose wife had sent him because of the anger he had for his neighbour. After the third session I interrupted him, and asked him if he had any criminal charges or anything on his record. He told me he had never been in trouble, ever, so I told him to go home that night and rip that guy out of his house, and then give him the beating he deserved because the first two assaults were free. Everybody was laughing, and the instructor said to him, "No, no, don't listen to Scott." This other time the instructor was trying to set an example by saying, "Now what would happen if you're at home, your favourite TV show is on, and the power goes out?" I said, "What? Are you kidding? There goes my grow op, that's the worst thing that could happen." I didn't even have one at that time, but I had everyone laughing and the instructor changed the scenario.

I tried to start up this scrap metal business by salvaging rail car parts from the wreckers and selling them to companies that rebuild them. I went to go see this bigshot accountant about my idea, and he told me to be careful. He told me that organized crime had their hands in those places, and that he quit his job downtown over it. He told me he'd been working for the government and put two guys away for two years for fraud. One day when he was coming down the escalator from his office he was greeted by those same two guys, and they told him that they just wanted to let him know they were in town. Then they shook his hand. He quit that day and went to work for himself. He was right about organized crime having their hands in these places. One day I was at a scrapyard, telling these two guys what I was looking for. A few days later when I returned, they both had shiners.

I went to another company that was scrapping a lot of rail cars, and sat down with them to talk business. I told them to bid more aggressively for the rail cars from a railroad company in Canada that was scrapping a lot of old cars. A few months went by, and with me paying rent on a small warehouse, I never received a phone call from the scrap company. I called them up to find out what was happening. They told me they did what I had told them to do, and they had flown in the representatives from the companies that I was dealing with. All they did was pick my brain to find out about everyone I was dealing with. I said to him, "So you fucked me" and he said, "That's business." I had that guy's business card in my hand and found his address in the phone book. I paced in my living room for a couple of days wondering whether I should go pay this guy a visit or not. I realized that my hands were tied, and that if I put my hands on this greedy prick I would end up in the river, so I just let it go and quit the business.

1998

I got a letter in the mail one day and it turned out that the guy I hit in Roosters was taking me to the cleaners. They wanted $27,000 out of me and my lawyer told me to hurry up and pay because if it had been him, he would be asking for over $100,000 for the damage I did to that guy. I told him I would handle it, and things would finally come to an end the next year.

Laura, her parents and I were planning a trip to Hawaii, so she bought me a diving course to take because she had hers and wanted us to dive together when we got there. One night, at diving school, we did some training in a swimming pool. While we were at the bottom of the pool I could tell that the guy to my right was dazed and confused and starting to drown. I grabbed him, brought him to the surface, and swam him to the edge of the pool.

I found out this guy drove a Brinks truck, and as you would guess my wheels started to turn. I felt this guy out for a couple more classes, but there was no way this guy was going to do what I had planned, even though I'd saved his life.

The diving course came down to the test, and I told myself that this was one test I was going to master. I was good with math, therefore I was good at reading the PADI chart fairly well, and I said to myself that this was going to be a breeze. At least that's what I was thinking.

In class one day the instructor was talking about the third dive of the day and how long you could stay down for. I looked at the chart, did the calculation, and told the instructor that according to the chart you would be dead on that third dive. The rest of the class and the instructor all agreed with me. The next day the instructor phoned PADI and told them they had to change their chart. I don't know if they did or not, but you think they would have. I studied that book three times, and when I wrote the test I got the worst mark in the class. I read one question wrong, and that meant I calculated the chart backwards so I got all the chart questions wrong. I was the first one finished, and thought I'd aced it. When the instructor handed me my results and told me I got the worst mark in the class I grabbed a hold of the desk and was going to throw it through the front window. He told me that even though I got the worst mark I was the best diver in the class, so he passed me anyway.

We only dove once in Hawaii, and I grabbed the flashlight from the guide and went into a shark cave. While I was in the cave I spotted two six-foot sharks. I can't remember if they were black- or white-tipped sharks, but I thought that was pretty cool.

It was October and off I went on another hunting trip. While I was away Laura gave Craig a ride home to his place after the bar closed. This was the same friend who had called me a couple of times to come to his rescue. His brother, who lived with him, came over after I got back and told me that he could hear them upstairs in Craig's bedroom. Craig came over a week later with his brother and tried to tell me that nothing had happened. His brother said that he was mistaken, but I knew it was bullshit. I just tried to blow it off, like I did every time Laura cheated on me. My heart had been kicked around more times than Beckham had kicked a soccer ball, so this time was no different.

1999

Laura was on the hunt for a newer vehicle, so her brother set her up with a car salesman he knew. As you might guess she started sleeping with him, so I packed up my bed, TV and clothes and moved out. It just so happened that my Mom's house was vacant because she was working in Penticton at the time and had the house up for sale. I threw my bed in a spare room and stayed there while her house was for sale. When I went back to my house a few days later to grab my camper that was in the driveway, I noticed a Camaro parked out front. I grabbed my keys, opened the front door, and there was Laura standing there. She had this car salesman in bed, and I asked her how long this had been going on but she didn't answer me.

I guess I made it a little difficult for the realtors because of my shift work. I was sleeping after graveyard shift one day and a realtor brought a couple through the house without giving me notice. They woke me up and I was standing there in my underwear, so I tore a strip of this guy. His excuse was he just wasn't going to show the bedroom I was staying in. After telling the realtor and his clients to get the fuck out, I called his boss. I told him that if this happened again I would show up at his house at four in the morning and do more than wake him up. I then asked him whether I'd made myself perfectly clear, and he replied, "Crystal." I had no problems with them after that. The neighbour was next.

The neighbours that surrounded my Mom's house all had dogs that barked all day, keeping me awake. This guy next door was on unemployment insurance and didn't get up till noon every day. I would have respected him, but he was just a lazy bum. I had just returned home from a hunting trip, and hadn't cleaned my chainsaw yet. I used the chainsaw to cut the moose into pieces because it made things a lot easier. I was out cutting some of the limbs off the trees that divided the two properties because I would have to duck under the branches when I mowed the lawn. He came out and asked what I was doing and I told him. I then told him that I was sick of everybody pissing me off with their dogs barking all day, and that I didn't like people. I showed him the chainsaw that was covered in blood and the guys eyes almost fell out of his head. He turned around and went back inside, and I continued my task with that smile on my face.

Rob from work and I went to Logan Lake for a recreational hockey tournament. It was supposed to be for fun, but the teams were all made up of junior players on their way to the NHL. We played anyway, and our poor goalie, holy cow was he bruised. The last game, we had to give him a twenty-sixer of tequila because he couldn't get out of bed in the morning; he drank that whole bottle down before we were on the ice at 11 a.m.. At the end of the game he got a standing ovation because he'd had over a hundred shots fired at him. In that game, we lost twelve to one. I tell you, I wish someone had that game on tape because he played better than any goalie I have ever seen in the NHL. It was amazing.

It was time for our work golf tournament, and I was laying down on the first tee box waiting to tee off. I was talking to the family assistance guy from our office, and telling him that I didn't feel like being there because of everything on my mind. He just told me to stay and try to put it all behind me for the day, and to try to enjoy myself. I agreed and off I went. The first shot I made went right into the water. I ended up with a bogey on that hole, but turned everything around after that. I got an eagle on the third hole, and was sitting at even par going into the sixteenth. I made a drive, and then a three wood shot off the fairway onto the fringe. I only had a six-foot putt for another eagle, but I was startled by a dog that started to bark up on the hill behind the clubhouse. I started to sweat and bogeyed the hole. I went on to double-bogey the next two holes and finished with a 77, winning the tournament. I took home all the trophies that day, and drove home with a smile on my face.

2000

The Mustang I used to pay my debt.

I finally made a deal with the lawyer of the guy I'd hit in the bar. I told him I would give him my 1992 GT mustang and $7,000 that I had in RRSPs as long as I could hang onto my truck. I drove the car to my lawyer's office and put the keys through the mail slot, left the cheque on the seat and called a cab. I was home in bed, looking at the Sesame Street wallpaper that was on the walls and saying to myself, "It doesn't get any better than this."

My old girlfriend Tina was getting married at Meadow Gardens Golf Course and I was invited. This is a classy clubhouse, and a lot of people get married there. I went for a walk to the lounge upstairs and they had this grand piano that played by itself. I grabbed a drink from the bar and took a seat at the piano. The piano was facing the lounge, and with no one there I turned it on and pretended to play. After the first song people started to drift in to watch me play. I kept a straight face, and was able to keep playing, and by the time I finished the fourth song the place was packed, with everyone clapping after each song. On the fifth song I started to see what I could get away with before they all caught on. I started to cross my hands and play, then I turned around and played with my hands behind me. As soon as I started to play with my feet the cat was out of the bag. Everyone was looking at me as though to say, "How did he pull that off and we never caught on?" I just walked away laughing my head off, and so did everyone else.

Even though Laura and I were separated, occasionally she would still come over to my Mom's. This one night she dropped by and we headed for the bedroom. My Mom's cat was in my room and meowing like never before, so I grabbed him and put him out in the hallway. While we were lying in bed I felt something across the back of my hair, and then it happened again. I got up, turned the light on, and saw this huge rat about ten inches long from head to tail. I got out my pellet gun, cornered it in the room, and shot it. Pretty creepy but I still got a hard on. She later ended up getting pregnant from one of those times coming over and insisted she was going to have it. I would do the right thing and move back into the house with Laura and the kids to support her decision. We ended up buying into her mom's house, where Laura grew up, because we didn't need a down payment. Laura's mother and I got along for a while, but then that started to diminish. Mothers-in-law!

This year was a little quieter, other than the relationship I had with Laura's mother.

I had sold my .338 stainless stalker rifle to a guy who sold potatoes out of a truck. This had happened while I was living in the party house about five years earlier. The deal was that he would buy it for $1,000 and a bag of potatoes. Because he he didn't have any more potatoes with him on the day of the exchange, he said he'd drop them off the next week when he was back in the neighbourhood. The potatoes never came.

Five years later I was in the new house we had bought from Laura's Mom when the doorbell rang. Who do you think it was? This could only happen to me. Surprise! It was the potato man. Imagine, after five years here he was. But, the question was, where were my potatoes?

I asked if he remembered me and he said that he didn't. I told him that I was the one who had sold him the gun, and that the deal was he would give me $1,000 and a bag of potatoes. He now knew who I was, because he said the potatoes weren't part of the deal, so I started to put my shoes on to go grab a bag out of his truck. He tried to tell me that I couldn't. I told him he could give me one bag, or I could make a phone call and before he got to the end of the street I would own his truck and all the potatoes. It was his decision.

He went and got me a bag, and when he got back he started whimpering and whining that they cost him $10, and I should give him that at least. I decided he wasn't worth the hassle, so I gave him the $10 and grabbed the potatoes. When he handed me the bag I told him that I had been so pissed off that he didn't honour the original deal that I was going to hunt him down. He said I wouldn't have found him anyway, as he lived in Princeton. I told him that it would have been easy finding him because one of my best friends lived there. I just told him to beat it and closed the door.

I was a shop steward at work because I needed extra protection for what I was trying to accomplish. Our job was to inspect rail cars and repair them. After we would go out into the field to inspect the cars, the managers would go down the track and pull off the defect cards that we would place on the cars. These cards indicated what was wrong with them, and by removing them they were letting unsafe cars go through every town. It was a disaster waiting to happen. I started reporting the problem to the government and shit started to fly, at least it looked that way.

The company didn't know what to do with me, so they decided to have a meeting with our union and discuss the situation. While this meeting was going on up in the yard tower, I was sent out to couple up a train and air test it. I locked up my track, put the air on the east end of the train, and started my way towards the west end. As I got about ten cars in, the train started to move eastward. This was happening because there weren't any handbrakes applied, and as the brakes started to release the train started to roll.

Now I started to go into a panic because the train was heading for the main line and stripping all the switches as it was making its way east. I knew there wasn't going to be a good outcome so I put my own safety at risk and started to jump on the train one car at a time, tying the hand brakes on until it came to a halt. That train did a lot of damage to the trainyard that day, shutting it down until the next morning while all the switches were replaced, but it could have been a lot worse.

Now here is the funny thing, the company is having a meeting about me at the same time as I'm trying to stop a runaway train, which they all could see out of the office windows of the tower. I can just imagine what they were all saying about me when this was all going on: "Who hired this maniac?" was probably at the top of the list. All the employees working for Transport Canada had all worked for a railroad before, and they all know the deal: "Scratch my back and I will scratch yours."

I gave the government about a thousand violations and they didn't even give the company a $5 fine. The problem, as far as I could see, was that it would be cheaper for the railroad to admit guilt if caught, and to pay off the families who lost loved ones, than it would be to change their ways. I went to the national representative of the union and said that it was time the union got lawyers on this because nothing was changing. He didn't agree with me, so I phoned the head of the union and told him to fire this asshole because he had nothing but bottom feeders working for us. I told this national rep what I had done, and he would try to get even with me a few years later, but in the end I would win just like I always do.

All the information that I gathered went to an annual transportation safety meeting. This meeting was held in Ottawa with the transportation companies, their unions and the government. Because of the information I had gathered, it was easy enough for the government to see that there needed to be more monitoring of the rail companies. I knew a guy who had friends with the union assholes, and he told me the government put more than $1,000,000, but less than $10,000,000, into a special fund to help monitor the railroad; he didn't know the exact amount. Nobody told me shit. They took all the credit, but who really cares, the railroad runs a little better now.

I started a hockey team and went out and got sponsors so we didn't have to pay for uniforms. We were doing okay but needed a little help, so I went scouting. I remembered playing drop-in hockey at this rink one day and saw a guy playing like Wayne Gretzky. He was amazing. I found him and asked him if he wanted to join our team. He agreed, and now we had a new team member. The first game this guy played for us I was at the hospital with Laura while she was giving birth to my beautiful daughter. We didn't win that game, but I took home a bigger prize, my brand new daughter, Chevelle.

I was kicked out for fighting for three games, so I went upstairs to watch our team play as the bar had windows all around so you could watch. Our team showed up to play with only seven players, but thank god Danny, our sniper, showed. He played the whole game without a break and we won that game. While I was upstairs watching, these guys were talking about my star player, Danny. They were talking about how much money he owed their team when he used to play for them. They were talking about waiting for him in the parking lot after the game. I walked over to those guys and told them they'd better not lay a hand on him or they were going to deal with me. I told them every team has their star players and Danny was mine. I then told them they could do whatever they wanted to him after the season. I knew what they were talking about because he never had the money to play for us, but I told everybody he was paying.

I was the manager so I hid everything in the books. We had this guy on our team who skated on his ankles. He came up to me before the playoffs started and asked me if I wanted him to sit because he wasn't that good. I told him that I didn't care how good he could play, he'd paid his dues so get the fuck out there. He put a smile on his face and skated on out. I even had a couple guys on the team come up to me to try to get this guy to sit out because they wanted to win the championship. I just told them that wasn't going to happen, and that maybe I should bench them. We came in second that year. I didn't want to manage the team anymore, so Scott offered to do it next year.

2001

Laura was now working at a bar in New Westminster, and I noticed that she would wear dresses to work. This was unusual, so I did a little investigation. It turned out that she was seeing a guy who owned a limo, and would wear dresses because it was easier for her to remove her panties and fuck him in the back of his limo while the driver took her to work. I was still dumb enough to stay with her. but a short time later I left her for the second time. That prick died of cancer a year later.

I decided I had had enough of Laura's bullshit and moved out again, but I would later return for more abuse. I rented an apartment with a friend of mine, who used to live down the street from me when we were growing up. It turned out that he had a drug problem and was on probation. Someone owed him money, so he grabbed his shotgun to go collect his debt. However, while he was high, and before he could leave the apartment, he tripped in the doorway and the shotgun went off.

Part of his probation was to piss in a cup any time the court called. At one point he didn't come home for three days. I was going to call the cops and put in a missing person report, but I couldn't because of his probation. On the fourth day I opened his bedroom door and there he was, all beaten up. He gave me a line of bullshit about what had happened, but what can you do. I came back from work the next morning and he was gone, leaving me a note telling me he went into treatment.

When Laura's mother moved out of the house and into a condo, I moved back in. When I was moving I noticed that a rifle from the closet was missing. My old roommate, the one who went into treatment, took it, probably traded it for crack, and now it was on the streets with my prints all over it. Lucky for me it never surfaced.

With the mother-in-law gone, that freed up the basement bedroom. I had Kenny come over and we made this room into a grow-op. I put nine lights in there, and on the first crop I made $27,000. When it was time to crop out Kenny was sick, so I had his friend come and help me replant. He had a grow-op of his own and was having troubles with his partner. You see what happens when you have partners? That's why I was always a solo businessman, and a one-man wrecking crew. You don't need an army when you have balls and brains. His partner would send his heavies over to his place and push him around. I told him that all he had to do was ask me to take care of him and it would be no problem. It took a few more times with these heavies pushing him around before he'd had enough. I had to help this guy because he helped me.

I drove over to his partner's house knowing that the guy's daughter was in Children's Hospital. I don't recall why, but I knew they had to remove her legs the next morning. What a terrible tragedy for a young girl.

When I finally talked to him, I told him that if he sent his guys over to bully his partner again, he would have me to deal with. I also told him he had to pay his rent on time. The first of the month came and buddy didn't have the rent, so I called him. I said, "Well, it's the first of the month, where's the rent." He just said, "You can have the grow-op." Now I had two grow-ops. I was such a nice guy that people used to pay to hang out with me. Oh, wait a minute, that was protection money. Sorry!

One of the hockey jerseys in question. It was the principle of the matter that counted.

Hockey season was here and I was waiting for the call from Scott. I ran into a co-worker who had been at the rink the night before and he told me he had seen our team playing. I told him we didn't have a team this year and he said, "They had your jerseys on." I got in my truck and drove over to Scott's house, and lucky for him he wasn't home. I left a note on his front door that read, "If I don't get my jerseys back today I am going to break every bone in your face." He called within half an hour later and I went and picked up my jerseys. I had calmed down enough that I didn't slap him around because he did give me back the jerseys that day. I'm a man of my word.

I left on a hunting trip with Allan just after a root canal. This trip would be the beginning of the ruination of my life. My mouth was killing me and he gave me two Percocets for the pain. After all the car accidents and fights, all my pain went away and I felt like I was 20 years old again. You will find out the hell that those pills had on my life as we go on, because I started taking them every day after that.

When we got back from our hunting trip I thought that it would be a cool thing to buy one of these 2.2 kg chocolate bars that I saw in the mall to give away to a kid on Hallowe'en. I thought it would be cool to give one of these away every Hallowe'en, and to take their picture with it, and to make up a picture wall of all the bars I would give out every year.

On Hallowe'en night I waited for the right kid to come up the stairs. I had this little kid come to the door dressed up as a cow, and he had to be about four years old. He had one of those little plastic pumpkins in his hands. When I opened the door he said, "Trick or Treat" and I asked him if he had been a good boy that year, and he nodded his head. "Yes." I said, "Well then, do I have the chocolate bar for you." As I gave him the bar I thought that he would drop his pumpkin with excitement and grab the damned bar, but that didn't happen. Instead his mom walked up the stairs, grabbed it, and said thanks without even a smile on her face. I didn't get the joy I expected or the appreciation, so I never did it again. I shouldn't have let it bother me because it makes me a hypocrite. After all, I've always said, "Just because one person lets you down, it doesn't mean you stop doing nice things for people."

Laura and I had just had a battle, and we happened to be going in opposite directions on the stairs at home. Neither of us moved aside and we bumped shoulders. Stupid me. I was the one going down, and she turned around and kicked me down the stairs. Where is a Filter Queen vacuum when you need one? After I got up I looked at her with a look that said she was lucky I didn't kill her for this. It's just amazing what shit some of us put up with before we finally call it quits.

I was making lots of money at that time, and I decided to find a place to rent while I renovated the house. We rented the house across the street. Was that meant to be or what? I put a baby monitor in the basement so I could hear if someone was breaking in and taking my weed. I had a plan to protect my weed if this happened. I had a gym bag by the front door with rope, tape, hand cuffs and a few other things I would need to tie someone up, as well as my defender loaded under my bed to grab on my way out the door. I don't know if it was lucky for me, or any potential thief, but nothing ever happened.

I had another grow-op in Mission, and with the three grow-op's I managed to put $200,000 into the house. What a beautiful house it was, and it was the talk of the town. Laura's son told me his friends at school thought I was in the mob. I guess he thought that because of all the expensive cars that would come over, as well as the money I gave him. I always had a couple of inches of cash with an elastic band wrapped around it in my pocket. One of my friends would show up in his Mercedes, and he was high up the ladder in the criminal world around the Lower Mainland, but it didn't do him any good because he was fatally shot right in his own driveway in 2010.

I worked sixteen-hour days building the house and tending to the grow-op's, I didn't take a day off for a year. I did take a year off from my real job due to all the stress, and because I wasn't sleeping very well. With your head under railcars you have to have your wits about you, and when you're not getting sleep you have a real chance of an accident occurring. I did go on some anti-depressants for most of that year. I had disability insurance from my job with the railroad so that I could be paid while I was off work. I would fight the insurance company a year later because they said I wasn't disabled enough so they wouldn't pay. Yeah, that's right, working too hard on my illegal business to work my real job. What's up with that?

Me and the builder doing renovations on our home (above), and the finished games room (below).

While renovating the house, I always used safety glasses when cutting nails. I was trying to fit in a door, and realized I'd missed one nail. I could see the safety glasses across the room but decided not to grab them, I thought it was only one nail so big deal. When I went to cut it, the nail flew off and stuck in my right eye. My friend Kenny was standing right there and saw the whole thing. I was nervous about pulling it out, thinking my eye might deflate, but I pulled it out anyway. I went to the hospital to get it looked at and there was only a scratch on the eye. The piece of nail, about three inches long, ricocheted off my eye and stuck right in the corner. I guess you could say I'm a lucky person, Yeah right. Kenny said he didn't care what the doctor said, he'd watched me pull it out of the white of my eye. It will never hit you anywhere else; it will always go for your eye.

2002

A real estate company in town was putting on a golf tournament in Kelowna, so Allan and I decided to go. We went up the day before because I wanted to get even with Laura. We popped some Viagra, hit the local rub and tug, and took a couple of sweethearts up to the hot tub. Having sex with a hooker was hardly getting even with all the hell that Laura had put me through, but it was fun anyway. I tell you, that Viagra made my cock so hard a grizzly bear couldn't chew it.

I always loved muscle cars so I went online to a website for General Motors to give them a suggestion. This website said that any suggestion you give them, they would get back to you the next business day. I gave them an idea to bring back the 66 Chevelle. I told them how I thought it should be built, and to bring it back in 2006 so they could call it the 66-06 Chevelle SS. I waited for a reply but never got it. I sent another request and never got a reply for that one either. Then I wrote them a letter, and nine months later I got a response. All it said was something like, "We like hearing from our customers and their input." It was only a few sentences long, and then the next year there was something in the paper about the Camaro they were bringing back.

Now, to me, it was as if they'd sat down and talked about it, and decided to bring back the Camaro instead. I know that I probably wasn't the only one to tell them this, but why did it take all this hassle to get a reply. I don't know if that is what happened, but I didn't want anything for the suggestion. The only thing I asked was for them to build one Black Cherry in colour… only one. I would still like to see them bring back the 66, before we get rid of oil, which will happen some day. Better yet, make them with some crazy, high output electric motor. The new muscle cars.

I was having a bad day and Laura called about a dental bill for her older daughter's teeth. I had been off work and did not have any insurance. I told her to call Annie's dad and ask him to pay the bill since he had never paid child support. She phoned me right back and said that he had laughed and hung up the phone. He was on welfare, and being a professional student, he was smart, but not smart enough.

He'd told me months before where he went camping free at Stave Lake on the weekends, and I never forgot that. I went to his house to confront him, and the neighbour came out, so I asked whether Mark had already left to go camping, though I didn't even know if that's where he was.

The neighbour told me he'd left about an hour earlier. I headed for the spot where he'd told me he went, and bingo, there he was. I got out of my truck and said, "Well, you can scream all you want out here and no one is going to hear you." He looked a little worried, but he thought that he could get in my head because he was my stepdaughter's dad.

My intention wasn't to lay a hand on him, just to make him a little upset. The things I was saying about him and his family, I had him in tears, so much so that he grabbed a machete out of the back of his truck. I was hoping that he would come after me with it so I could have a reason to snap his neck. I continued to put pressure on him, and as he was crying I started to take his belongings from his truck. He didn't come after me with that machete so I put his shit back into the truck.

He calmed down, and since I'd accomplished what I wanted he agreed to pay me the next week. If you can believe it, we actually had a drink together. As soon as I left he called his daughter and told her what I had done. He never did pay me, but what can you do? I couldn't punch out my stepdaughter's dad.

Allan and I bought this used air conditioner for a future grow op. Allan and I had that grow-op together in Mission, and I only did business with him because we were best friends, and it worked out for a while. We had this thing rebuilt, and when we decided we weren't going to use it we sold it to this guy we both knew. The guy called me up after he had it installed and said that it was too small, and that it wouldn't cool his lights. I went and picked it up, gave him half the money back, and said

I would get the other half from Allan for him.

I went on a trip, and while I was gone this guy called my house and left a threatening message on my phone. When I got home I called him up and told him it hadn't been a very good idea to leave that message, because the next time I saw him I was going to beat him so bad his mother wouldn't recognize him.

I was picking something up at the local Safeway. I was walking towards the fruit and happened to look down one of the aisles, and there he was. He saw me coming and he looked like he shit his pants. There were cameras all through the store so all I could do was threaten him. I grabbed onto his shopping cart and shook the shit out of it. At the same time I told him that I would be waiting outside for him. It was a Saturday afternoon so the parking lot was packed. I decided to get him another day because I didn't need any witnesses. I'll bet dollars to donuts he spent the night in that store because there was no way he was coming out while I was there. Never saw that guy again.

While I was making all this money, I was fighting with my doctor, as well as the insurance company from work, and the company that insured my mortgage. My doctor and I got into an argument, and he told me to go back to work after I had already taken eight months off. I went to grab my file out of his hand and he told me I couldn't have it, to leave and not come back. I called him a fucking asshole, and told him he was the one who had screwed up the paperwork that fucked me from getting paid.

I then hired two lawyers, and with my finishing touches I eventually got paid. The first lawyer I hired told me that this was a case I couldn't win, so I took care of things myself. I sat at a table in his office for one hour and photocopied everything I needed. I proved that the doctor was incompetent, and that it was his fault I was off for so long. I showed the insurance company the doctor's clinicals, that the lawyer had got for me. It showed he never did a follow up on my sleep apnea problem.

Three days after I had that fight with the doctor, I went to go see a chiropractor. I also showed them a letter that I got the chiropractor to write, telling them I had the worst case of stress he had ever seen, which he did say. I was in to see the chiropractor three times a week for three months. I also had a newspaper clipping saying how serious depression was, and that doctors should start to take it more seriously. The next day I received a call from the insurance company telling me they were issuing me a cheque for the full amount owing from all the months when I wasn't getting paid.

Now I went to the company that rejected a claim to cover my mortgage payments and my 1999 Dodge 4x4 truck. I told the insurance company that if they didn't pay me I would see them in court. I was going to subpoena all the specialists involved in the newspaper clipping. I told them I would be asking for $250,000 instead of the $47,000 that they owed me. The next day they called and said that my cheque was in the mail. Fuck am I Perry Mason or what? You just never take no for an answer. I never have, unless it's from my Mom.

I wanted the union to pay my lawyer's bills because I felt that they hadn't represented me as they should have. I was right, and this big shot union boss told his little guppies not to help me at all. This, he thought, was his way of getting even with me for having gone over his head a few years back. The grievance chair that we had was good friends with this prick, and he came into the lunchroom at work while I was playing cribbage with Bob. He was against the table to my left, leaning forward and putting his face in my space, and telling me that I wasn't going to get any money from the union to cover my lawyer's bills. I took his shit for about five minutes, then jumped out of my seat so fast that before he knew it I had him pinned down on the table with my hands around his throat. With my right hand raised ready to smash his face in, I heard Bob yell, "No Scott, no." It took everything I had not to do this guy in, because if I had I'm pretty sure I would have lost my job. I let him up and walked out to where I was working for the day to cool off. He came back out to try to get me to hit him because he had phoned his boss (the national representative) and that's what he was told to do, hoping to get me fired. I knew that, so all we did was yell at each other. I knew I would win later anyway. I always win.

The second lawyer I hired was a union and corporate lawyer from Vancouver. He walked me through how to get the union to pay me. He told me to stack the union hall with members on my side, and then put a motion on the floor. The day of the union meeting one of the bosses came up to me and handed me some papers. The company wanted to do an investigation on my absenteeism. As I read what it was for, I spun around and put my elbow through the safety glass in the lunchroom door.

It was time for the meeting, and when it came time for anyone with new business I stood up and put a motion on the floor that I should get reimbursed for my lawyer's bills. They denied me, and so I raised the motion again. Now, the rules say they can only reject a motion once, and if brought up again, it has to be voted on. It was put to a vote and passed, so the secretary wrote the cheque out for the total of $4,133.26. He picked up his bag and left the building.

The next morning I told my boss what had happened, and that I needed to get to the bank first thing when they opened. I knew the shit was going to hit the fan, and the national representatives would want their cheque back, so my boss gave me a company truck to get to the bank. I looked on the cheque to see where the union's bank was located, because if I went to my bank they would have had time to put a hold on the cheque. The union secretary made a mistake on the cheque that I didn't notice right away. When the cheque was written, he'd left out the word "hundred" in the amount, but the bank never noticed it either, and it got cashed.

It just so happened that I was going on a trip to Maui two weeks after I got the cheque, so it looked like I took the money and went on a holiday. I took advantage of this though, and took that big shot's address with me. I went and bought a postcard in Maui and put on the card, "You should come here. It's great, and thanks a lot. I couldn't have done this without your help. Ps: This trip cost me $4,133.26." I heard that when he got this he did cartwheels, and I loved every minute of it.

The poster a co-worker made to commemorate my victory against the union. They were only up about an hour before the union tore them down. Sore losers.

The Union was trying to write me up on harassment charges because of a poster that was being put up around the workplace. I had posed for a photo at work when one of the guy's had his camera with him, and he went home and made this wanted poster. We all got a good laugh, but obviously the union wasn't very happy. The harassment charges never stuck.

I had something different planned for that national rep before I decided to send the card. I got a hold of this guy who was a collector – in other words, a "bone breaker" – and got him to follow me to this asshole's house. Once this guy knew where he lived, he knew where to go when I gave him the phone call. While we were standing down the way from his house this guy was jumping up and down with excitement, wanting to go in right then and there. I said to him, "What if his kids are in there?" and he said, "All the better." I told him that he couldn't do it right then because the cops would drive straight to my house. I had to give this more time. I told him that when I gave him the call I wanted this asshole in the hospital so I could go visit him. Then I had better thoughts, and did the card instead. I hear he still talks about that post-card. The mental way is the best way… it can last forever.

Now, I had another investigation a week later for the window I broke. I did a lot of crazy things at work over the years, and I'm lucky I still have my job. One of the bosses there had a police scanner he would listen to on the weekends, and on Monday he would ask me how the weekend was, because he would always hear my name on that thing.

A co-worker and I got a flat tire out in the yard one night and headed back to the shop to fix it. We were almost there, riding on the rim, but about 200 yards away from the shop this guy didn't want to drive any further on that rim. I told him the tire was already wrecked but he refused to drive any further. I got out of the passenger door, ran around to the driver's side, and tried to pull him out through the open window of the truck. He opened the door and I threw him out, but when I went to beat him I could see that the light on the radio was on. He had the talk button down the whole time, and now I thought everyone had heard me. Thinking this, I knew now I couldn't beat this guy because I would have been a sitting duck. It turns out nobody heard anything except some muffled sounds. I actually finished the shift with this guy after we fixed the tire.

I cleaned the whole lunch room one weekend, and when I came in on Monday the place was a pigsty. I grabbed all the garbage cans, emptied them all over the floor, and said to everyone, "You want to be a bunch of pigs, than live like them." I took my lunch outside to eat and now I had the shift supervisor trying to tell me to clean it up. I told him that wasn't going to happen, and that if he wanted it cleaned up he should get someone else to do it because I'd already done it once. Somebody else cleaned it up.

Just a few more things out of the hundreds that I did at work. I punched a towel dispenser off the wall, and threw a thermos through one of the lunchroom windows. One day, when I'd had enough and was going to quit, I threw my radio at a safety light, smashing it to pieces.

We were all having a snowball fight in the shop at work one winter and I was losing. I got so pissed off I picked up a truck spring that must have weighed twenty pounds or so and threw it at a guy. He could see that I had picked it up, and everyone ran for cover because they all knew that once it hit the ground the spring was going to bounce all over the place.

Being on the night shift for fifteen years you learn where to sleep like a homeless man. I went to catch a nap in a caboose one night, and once inside I rolled up my jacket for a pillow and threw it in the corner of the bunk. It was dark in there and I couldn't see much, so when my jacket came to rest I heard this drunk guy mumbling. I guess I woke up this bum who was sleeping on that bunk when my jacket hit him in the face. I just said, "Sorry man" and grabbed the bunk right next to him without a care in the world.

One time I went inside and put on the oil heater from the snow-plough that was in for repair. I didn't know how high I had it, just that it was on, and I went to sleep. I woke up from a dream that I was on fire, and when I did the heater was glowing red. The temperature in there must have been at least 150 degrees. The first breath I took after I woke up, the inside of my nose burned. I kicked the door open and dove out onto the asphalt. I was sweating so bad, that my clothes were soaked right through. I never did that again. I would sleep on the lunchroom bench instead; safer that way.

I would normally come into work on the weekends drunk. There was this fat guy at work who thought he was all muscle. I got into a little argument with him in the lunch room one day, and decided I would teach him a small lesson. He was bragging about how he thought he was all muscle. I told him, "Yeah, before you can get your hands up in front of your face, I would have hit you 10 times." He thought it wasn't going to happen and just laughed at me. I threw two quick jabs so close to his face he probably felt the breeze through the hairs on his nose. I then hit him with a light right and knocked his glasses off his face and onto the floor. I know it is wrong to hit someone with glasses on but I didn't actually mean to hit him, only to let him know who's boss. I think he got the message that night.

Later, I was pared up with the same guy while waiting to get our job for the night. I looked at the boss and said, "That figures, the rare time I get the truck job, I have to work with that fat fuck." I then kicked the eyewash station off the wall and threw it through the boss's office window. The boss we had on the weekend was a good shit and we covered it up.

The same guy was stealing pop cans from this wooden box we had made to collect money for the family of an employee who had died from leukaemia. We would donate the money to the leukaemia foundation at the end of the year. I walked into the lunch room one night and caught him with a welding rod fishing these cans out through the hole. I told him that if I ever caught him doing it again, it would be the last time he ever used his hands. I told everyone on shift to let me know should they see him taking cans. I never saw it happen again, and nothing was ever reported to me.

The boss we had during the week was a real pain in my ass, like I wasn't in his. One night I had four rail cars fixed before first coffee, and was lying on the bench in the shop. He came in at exactly 2:10 a.m. when our coffee time was over, and kicked the table right by my head. He told me to get to work and we exchanged a few words. I went back to my area and thought about this for a few minutes. I thought to myself that he needed to be taught a lesson.

I got into the forklift, raised the forks and headed for his office. He could see me coming, got out of his chair and put his back to the wall because he thought I was coming right through the window. I slammed on the brakes and stopped about two inches away from the window. I then drove the forklift around and put the forks against his office door so he couldn't get out and went for lunch. On the way past his window I gave him my middle finger and told him to fuck off. He had to call someone on the radio to move the forklift so he could get out.

That guy sat in his office for the next two days with the lights off, just staring at me and wondering what to do with me. He never did shit, only because he knew what would happen to him, so his hands were tied. I worked those two days with a smile on my face. It felt great.

The only reason I still have a job is because I was one of the better workers. That's right guys. Worker! I got this nickname "Forty-six-and-a-Finger" because a crew of guys and I fixed forty-six rail cars in one shift. The second part of the nickname came a few months later when I ended up taking the end of a co-worker's finger off. It was an accident with the equipment. It could have been avoided but I am always in a hurry to get things done. Sorry George. I did grab George's glove, cut it open with a utility knife, took the piece of finger out and put it in a bag of ice hoping they could sew it back on. It was too messed up for that, but at least I tried.

Every time I got in trouble for something I would always tell the truth. I would take my lumps and my boss respected me for that. He liked my personality. I know that it seems unbelievable that I can do all this shit at work and still have my job, but it was all for a reason. I don't work like I used to, that's for sure. I'm too tired, and too damned sore.

The car foreman, who was the boss of our whole department, was a good man and he looked after me. If it wasn't for him I would have been fired a long time ago. Over the years, he's done more for me than my own father ever has.

This guy that I was working with wanted a goose for Christmas dinner. There were geese all over the railyards, so running over one was a piece of cake. I was driving the work truck and ran one over for him. The rear dualies ran it over, so needless to say, we had to find another one. The next day he was working with someone else and I ran into him in the yard. He told me that he still wanted a goose. I picked up a rock and threw it at a goose standing between the tracks. I hit him with the first shot and he dropped like a sack of hammers. I ran over and grabbed it by the neck and spun it around trying to break its neck, but with no success. I took it over to the back of my truck and beat it over the head with a piece of steel. I then brought it over to Doug and said, "There you go kid, there's your goose." The guy with him had this astonished look on his face, like he had just witnessed a murder. I guess he had.

While working in the shop there were always pigeons sitting on the roll up door to the shop, so one night I started to hit the power button up and down like they were riding a log in the water. Eventually two of them fell to the ground. I had a girl working with me so I didn't want her to see the next step. There just happened to be an axe leaning up against the wall and I took it outside. I kicked the pigeons out the door and out of site. She could see the axe swinging through the shop window, but I had to put these birds out of their misery.

I look at everything I've done in my life, and if I could take that back I would. I have total remorse for my actions, and even now, if I see a spider on the ground I avoid stepping on it. Even putting salt on slugs and watching them curl up was wrong, I can see that now. All the other creatures of this planet have a reason, and they have their own journey to make so don't ruin it, embrace it. You have to realize that some of the barbaric incidents I have done in my life have to do with my past lives, at least that's what I think.

This one guy at work was always borrowing cigarettes from me, so one day I put a ladyfinger (small firecracker) in the end of one and gave it to him. As I lit the smoke with that smile on my face, boom it went off and looked like a flower from the blast. He never asked me for another one. He learned a lesson there. Buy your own.

A guy at work we called Boo-Boo was always doing everything for his mate, Doug. I came in from inspecting a train one time and noticed that Boo-Boo was standing outside the bathroom door. I knew something was wrong and asked him what had happened. He told me that this asshole Englishman we had on our shift had lost an argument with him. He said that when this guy lost the match he couldn't take it, so he jumped onto the lunchroom table like a child and kicked Boo-Boo's coffee cup off the table. I said, "Is that right, well I'll fix him."

When I got into the lunchroom I opened up my lunch box and grabbed the two Japanese oranges I had. With the yard foreman and a few workers in there, I started to lay into this guy, saying anything I could about him and his family to get him going nuts. Once I had him pissed off I threw the oranges at him several minutes apart as I worked on him. He was pinned in the corner by the dartboard with nowhere to escape . He was yelling at the foreman to do something, but earlier that night he'd been screwing the foreman over, so the foreman was loving every minute of it. Once I finished with him he ran to the boss to complain. That didn't get him anywhere, either, because I was good friends with the boss, too. We had a lot of different foremen through the years, probably fifty between all shifts, but it would have been more confusing for you if I'd named them all here, so I just left them out.

This incident didn't end there because the next week, while I was working out in the trainyard, he jumped onto the table and kicked my mug off, breaking it. He worked the early shift, so when I came in from working on a train Boo-Boo told me what had happened. The guy had already gone home but I got even with him.

I was having one of my crazy parties at the house when I got this brainstorm. I told everyone I had something to do, and that I would be right back. I drove to work to grab this guy's lunch kit, knowing he would go berserk. When I got there nobody was around, which was a bonus. I opened his lunch box to see if he had anything of value in there so I could leave it behind, and it was a good thing I did because he had heart pills. I left those on the table and threw his box over the fence and onto the highway. That guy was so pissed off because he couldn't figure out who had done this to him. He started to stay out in the trainyard instead of coming in, until it got cold. That lasted about seven months. It was sure nice not to have that asshole around for a while. Boo-Boo died in September of 2011 in a bicycle accident.

It was Christmas back in 1992 and I was driving my 66 Parisienne. We got so drunk at work Christmas Eve that the boss took my keys from me. They would always turn a blind eye to this on Christmas Eve because they never had Christmas parties before. We were supposed to keep it a little discreet, but I brought that cooler right into the lunchroom. Once I gave him the keys I headed for my car. I opened the hood and grabbed the key I kept for emergencies, fired up the car and drove away. I only remember about five seconds of the drive home, looking out one eye. Once at home, and after I'd had a nap, I opened the blinds to the living room and discovered I had parked my car inches away from the front window. All I saw was chrome. Another close call.

Back in 1990 the boss on shift came and grabbed me to drive him downtown. He'd had an impaired charge so he didn't have a licence. We had to go look at this railcar that needed repair, and man was I nervous, driving with the boss in the truck. We didn't talk much at first because we didn't know each other. As we were driving along the Barnet Highway a slow song came on the radio, so with the boss looking out his window I reached over and put my hand on his lap. He right away turned to look at me, pulled his leg away and said, "Fuck off, you fucking queer." We both started laughing and the ice was broken. We were good friends after that happened. I had a lot of respect for him because it didn't matter what happened on our shift, it stayed on the shift.

One time I phoned in sick, and I told them on the recording that I couldn't make it that night because I had CRAMPS. When the foreman on shift played the tape, she thought I said CRABS, and now I was the laughing stock of the place. Only me!

We had this bigshot come for a visit at the shop one day, and he came up to me and asked what I would do if I was in charge of safety for a day. I told him that I would start locking these locomotives up like Fort Knox because of the threat of terrorism. He looked down at the ground and said, "Good point." I later asked my Dad how someone climbs the ladder in those big companies, and he told me you have to kiss a lot of ass and buy a lot of booze. Buying the booze wouldn't be so bad, but kissing ass was not going to happen. I don't kiss anyone's ass, I don't give a shit who you are.

The file they have on me at work. Seems I've been a busy boy over the years.

2003

We were back in the new house and I was at the building supply store to pick up some plumbing parts. They had a display of chain link fence set up right in the middle of one of the aisles. While I was looking at the parts my daughter, Chevelle , opened the gate, and as it wasn't bolted to the floor it became unbalanced. It fell on her, hitting her on the head and pinning her to a shelf. I picked up the whole thing and threw it into the glass display case in front of the counter. I swear, you could have heard a pin drop in that place after I was finished. I grabbed my daughter and headed out the door. She suffered a large bump on her head, but otherwise she was okay.

Brock and I took our motorcycles out to the lake one day. I didn't have a helmet on, all I had was my ball cap on backwards and my sunglasses while I was riding. You have to look cool, right? I was riding ahead of Brock, and when I looked back to see where he was I steered the bike onto the soft shoulder. The front wheel turned sideways and over the handlebars I went. I was going about 50 km/h, and as I was flying through the air I knew I had to tuck and roll. After about four somersaults, I flew back up into the air and landed on my feet. A car coming up the road saw everything, and when they approached, they couldn't believe what they'd witnessed. I still had my hat and my sunglasses on, and I didn't even have a scratch on me. Who the hell am I?

Wayne and I were out on our annual moose hunting trip. We were out driving around the first day at this new spot, just looking for places to hunt the next morning. On the way back to my camper we saw a cow and calf moose walk across the road and into the bush. We ran up to where we saw them go and I put my sights on the cow and pulled the trigger, at least I thought it was the cow. There was so much excitement that both Wayne and I were shooting at these animals. We ended up shooting both the cow and the calf, only because when the calf was standing on this elevated hill it looked like the cow because it was so much bigger than the other one. I should have known which one was the calf because their snoot is a lot shorter than a cow's would be, but we were too excited I guess.

When we walked up and saw the cow on the ground, and the calf leaning up against a tree covered in blood, we realized what had happened. I told Wayne to finish off the calf but he couldn't do it, so I leaned up against a tree, and the calf's eye took up my whole scope. I pulled the trigger. I was thinking to myself, why is Wayne hunting if he can't finish the job. His heart is a little too soft, I guess, but he's still a good kid.

We gutted these two animals, loaded them into my trailer and headed back to camp. We had a problem now, because we only had one tag for a moose in that area, and it was closed for calves. We decided to get the hell out of there and head for home. We tagged the calf for the region next to us, which was open for calves, and made it to the main road in the clear. We got the hell out of there safe and sound, and planned to skin the moose once we got back to Maple Ridge.

We got home, went over to a friend's house, skinned them and headed over to a butcher we knew. After a week I got a call from the butcher and he told me to get down to the farm. The moose had what they call fluke worm, and was rotting from the inside out. Apparently they get this disease from eating other animal's shit or from pesticides that get sprayed on the weeds to keep them from choking the freshly planted trees. We had to get the meat out of there.

We loaded up my truck but we couldn't take the meat to the dump, so we decided to dump it along a back road in the ditch. We would pull over to my left and start throwing out pieces until a car started up the road. Then we would have to close the tailgate and start driving again until the cars passed us. We had to repeat this several times to get rid of all the pieces. I mean, we must have had at least 1,400 pounds of meat in the truck. The whole thing was wrong, but there was nowhere to go to get rid of this problem. It made it to the papers the next week because a jogger had seen the evidence and reported it.

I remember my Dad's friend telling us a story about the mistake he made one day out hunting. He shot an elk that he thought was legal, but it turned out to not have enough points. He gutted the animal, cut it up, and loaded it in his truck. He drove to town and brought it to the conservation office. He told them what had happened, but they still gave him a $200 fine. He'll never do that again. I have learned what is wrong and right, and even if that were to happen to me again I would definitely do the right thing and take my lumps for it. There are rules.

It was Christmas time and we were all sitting in the living room of my house talking. Chevelle was in her bedroom and she didn't like how noisy we were. She came out of her room, down a couple of stairs just so she could see us, and then told us to shut the fuck up before going back to her room. I should have corrected her, but all we could do was laugh.

We were at a restaurant, and while Laura was paying the bill, Chevelle and I went to the car. We were in the car for a while until I looked over at the door to the restaurant and said, "What is taking her so fucking long?" Chevelle then leaned over from the back seat and repeated exactly what I said. I didn't laugh then, I apologized for my behaviour and told her that it was wrong. Even though Laura and I swore all the time (it being our second language) I never did hear it again from her.

2004

The following year I found this cabin out in the middle of nowhere to rent for our yearly hunting trip. There were four of us going up on this hunt, Allan, Wayne, Shooter and myself. Now Shooter got the name because he did a drive-by on this house, but his real name was Tyler. Shooter wasn't allowed to be in the possession of any firearms while his trial was pending, but we gave him one to use anyway.

Wayne and I drove up in my truck, and we weren't an hour out of town before we started to snort coke. The drive took us fifteen hours to get to this cabin. I tell you I had the worst headache of my life by the time we got there because of the eyestrain while concentrating on driving when I was ripped out of my scull. Well, we finally got there, and after putting the road kit away I tried to lie down for a few hours. A lot of good that did, didn't sleep a wink.

There was a section of the forest service road where we were hunting the next day that had a lot of sign crossings on one part of the road. I would call this part of the road the "four o'clock rush." This meant we would catch a glimpse of an animal every time we came around the corner.

I parked the truck up the hill so I could view the crossing. Sure enough, when four o'clock came around a cow and a calf came out from one side of the road to cross to the other. I took a shot at the calf because that's all we had a tag for. I hit it, and it started to limp into the bush. We drove down and I headed into the bush after the calf.

Now a calf might seem small in a domestic cow, but with a moose they would stand five feet tall from the hind and weigh about 400 pounds. I walked right up to the calf and he was crying for his mother, looking from left to right trying to make up his mind were to go. I brought up my gun and couldn't focus because he was right in front of me. The only way I was going to get this animal was to put down my gun, jump on his back and put my knife in his throat.

Just as I put my gun down on the ground, he bolted to his right. This all happened in about five seconds, and if I had another two, I would have been on his back.

I waited ten minutes before I went in to look for him, but you should wait twenty minutes because they will seize up after time, and won't be able to move from the loss of blood. I came up to a puddle of blood about four feet square where he'd laid down, but soon as he heard me he started on foot again.

I came across three more blood puddles like that, and followed the blood trail until it ended. No sign of him, but if the injured calf met up with his mother she could nurse him back to life. This is definitely a sport that separates the men from the boys. Shooter died in a boating accident in March of 2010.

2005

Laura and I were at one of her friend's house for dinner one night. The guy that lived there knew about me, and hinted that someone owed him money. We went in the other room and he told me he wanted him killed for the insurance money. When he'd loaned this guy some money, he'd made sure the guy signed an insurance policy. He didn't pay back the money and it was curtains for him. I got a hold of some people to take care of this for him and had it all lined up. The only problem was, they couldn't guarantee it would look like an accident. It had to be an accidental death in order for this guy to receive any money. With that at risk he called it off and saved the $50,000 it was going to cost.

Allan had one of his workers, Jay, looking after our Mission grow-op, and another guy from his contracting company, Lee, was working overseas building a golf course. A rumour got out that Jay was sleeping with Lee's girlfriend, so Lee got on a plane after hearing about this from Allan and flew home to deal with it. Allan picked him up at the airport in his Hummer and drove him to the Mission house. Allan pulled into the driveway and Lee ran into the house looking for Jay. He was throwing shit around and yelling, so the neighbour came out and asked if he should call the cops. Allan told him that everything was under control, and Lee got back in Allan's Hummer and peeled off. Jay called me in a panic because he didn't know what to do. I told him to stay there because I was on my way.

When I got there I asked if he knew were Lee lived. We got to Lee's house and I told Jay to wait in the truck. He warned me that there would probably be a few guys in there. I told him the more guys the bigger the mess. I kicked open the front door, ripped a picture off the wall and threw it down the hall. I then picked up one of his kitchen chairs and threw it into his gas fireplace, smashing it. Lee and these other guys knew how crazy I was and just stood there. I walked up to Lee and told him that if he ever went to that house again I would kill him. After I left, the phone rang and it was Allan, and the war began. A couple days went by and we had a meeting. I asked him, "What were you thinking taking this guy to our place of business and jeopardizing it?" He agreed and everything was cool, and that place ran for a few more years.

I needed a larger air conditioner for another grow show I was building in Hammond. I was building this for a friend from work, but he would fuck me in the end. I bought this air conditioner from a guy Allan knew from South Africa. I had already met this guy before and knew he was a piece of shit. I asked Allan if this conditioner was any good and he told me that it came out of a place of his, and that there was nothing wrong with it; they just needed a larger one because the summer was too hot, and this one wouldn't keep the lights cool. I bought it, hooked it up, and wouldn't you know, it didn't work.

I called this piece of shit from a work phone in the morning so he wouldn't recognize the number. He gave me the run around and I told him that now we had a problem. I grabbed Bob from work and headed over to his place after work with the air conditioner. I backed up to his gate and threw it off my tailgate while he watched from his front steps. The steps were about seventy-five yards from the gate and he wasn't coming any closer to us. I wrote on the side of the unit how much he owed me and put some tax on it. Allan covered the amount because I told him that if I didn't see the money before I ran into him, I was going to cripple him. This was one of Allan's workers and that's why he covered it, because he knew if I ran into this guy it wasn't going to be good.

With too much on my plate I decided to use this friend of mine that processed weed. I would cut down all the plants, bag them, and hand it all over to him. He had a group of people who would trim the plants, put the buds on the screens to dry, and when dry, bag it, sell it, and come and give me the invoice with my money. It sure saved me a lot of hassle.

2006

I was approached by this guy who did a couple years in prison for making ecstasy, to go partners in a grow-op in Burnaby. Since I didn't have to put any of my money into this, I agreed. There was another guy who was in with us from a gang in Burnaby. This was working out well. On our third crop the neighbour came over and told the landlord he knew what we were up to, that he thought there was a grow-op in her basement. She came down and told us what had happened, so we decided to get the weed out of there and process it somewhere else.

I told a couple of the workers to go up the street and get two pieces of plywood and two boxes of contractor garbage bags from Rona hardware store. We cut down all 1,900 plants and put them in these bags. The box of my truck was full. I used the plywood to hold down the bags and cinched everything down with some rope. I had to put the rest of the bags in the back seat. I looked like the Grinch that stole Christmas for fucks sake. I was the one driving, so we all agreed on some rules in case anything went wrong. I told the Mexican gangster (he died in 2010 of a gang shooting)] that he was to follow me, and if I was pulled over he was to run the cop over.

Off we went, and we didn't get four blocks away before my phone rang. It was buddy and he told me that he had a flat tire. I told him to pull into the gas station up ahead. I couldn't sit there because I was stinking up the city. I told him that I had to get the fuck out of there, and to wish me luck. Once I was on the freeway my truck started to sputter. The catalytic converter packed it in and the truck died right there on the side of the highway. As you might imagine I started to panic, so I got on the phone and called a towing company. I told them that the truck was overloaded and we needed a flat deck tow truck because of the weight. I didn't want the truck on an angle in case the bags should fall out on the way to the place we had lined up to process the weed.

While I was waiting for the tow truck, the other guys had fixed the tire and pulled up behind me. I told them to get out the flat tire and make it look like we were changing it, so if a cop drove by he would think we were only changing a tire. The tow truck showed up, and when the driver opened the door to put it in neutral I looked over to buddy and gave him the sign to club this guy if he said anything about the smell. He didn't, and when we got to the house he unloaded my truck and I gave him a big tip. It's hard to believe this tow truck was carrying me with $300,000 street value worth of weed in the back. I made all the right decisions on that mess, but that was the end of that grow op, and what a shame that was because we had thirty-two lights in there and it took me a month and a half to build it. It should have been in a magazine, it was built that well. It had full watering irrigation, CO_2 burners with digital meters, heaters, dehumidifiers, air conditioning, everything that I needed to control the room as if it was outside. That room pulled two pounds a light only because I had the Mexican looking after it as I lived too far away to take care of it. He did an excellent job for a green man. It was making us an average of $150,000 every two and a half months because we sold it by the pound. Not bad.

I went away on my annual hunting trip and, while I was gone, Laura was hanging out at this guy's house. When I got home I found out about it, and by the third day she wasn't home yet. All the kids were at home and I found out where this guy lived, so I headed out. When I got to the guy's house I walked inside and there she was, sitting on the couch, just exhausted. It turns out she'd been doing ecstasy for three days. This house was known for having ecstasy orgies, so I guess that's what she was doing as I doubt she was just sitting there watching TV for three days. I looked at her and asked if she wanted to come home, and she sat there for a bit with a smile on her face, and then nodded yes.

One night I watched her pack a bag and leave, to go downtown to spend the night with the guy that was feeding her ecstasy. Things were really on the rocks after this one. We both agreed it was time to pack in this horror show, but stupid me, I ended up staying for just a little longer.

Laura was always trying to make some money, which was good, but it cost me more than what she made. She started selling specialty candles and ordered about $5,000 worth. I told her that this wasn't the way to do this business, that you needed to get orders from people and then order it. I told her that we weren't a store, but she did it anyway and only sold a few, so I had thousands of dollars worth of candles on the shelf in the garage.

She did the same with a make-up line, but that cost me $7,000. I had a drawer in the bedroom that I would fill with cash because she would be the one that paid the bills. She was good at paying the bills but helped herself, and bought thousands of dollars worth of purses and other items without me knowing. After paying about $10,000 a month on the mortgages and rents for my other locations, along with the overhead, I still managed to clear about $20,000 every two weeks.

Laura was out with this couple clipping weed for this guy, and when they were finished this guy asked Jeff (the husband) to take the weed in these Rubber Maids and drop it off at another location for an extra $200. Laura said that she didn't want anything to do with it, but Jeff laughed and told her to just get in the car.

On the way to the location they got pulled over in a speed trap. The cops asked what was in the Rubber Maids, and they were busted. The cops asked whose it was, but everybody kept their mouth shut so they all got charged. This was the right thing to do, but because Laura said that she didn't want anything to do with it, Jeff should have paid the lawyer's bill.

I had the best lawyer in the Lower Mainland and Laura walked before the papers were even processed in court, but it cost me $8,000. I told this Jeff that he now owed me the money, but they didn't have a nickel to their name.

My hands were tied on this because this couple just happened to be my step-son's best friend's parents. Now how would that look if I beat the shit out of the guy. I never did get a nickel from that asshole. Laura was somewhat on his side only because at one time she was sleeping with his brother.

I was starting to use Oxycontin after the Percocet didn't do anything for me anymore, and I was about to know what hell feels like. Taking Oxycontin would change my personality so much, that I could be pretty embarrassing. My daughter said something that hit me right in the heart one day, she told me that other dad's didn't act like me, but did that stop me? Not a chance.

I got a knock on the door and here stood two kids wanting to shovel my driveway. Every time it snows here it rains the next day, making it hard to shovel. This was the rainy day after the snow storm and these kids were soaked. I had a huge driveway, and they said they would do it for $20, so I said, "Fly at it." Now I knew the job was too big for them, but I wanted them to learn something. About one hour later I could see that they had had enough, so I got on my boots and headed out the door. I said to them, "Bigger job than you thought, eh?" They nodded in agreement and I reached into my pocket and handed them each $20. They even asked if I wanted them to finish the job, but I told them I thought they'd worked hard enough that day, and to head home and get warmed up. The rain shovelled the rest for me.

2007

Laura went to pick up her son and his girlfriend at the movie theatre one night. When she tried to pull out there were two drunk teenage girls at the end of the driveway. Laura had to honk the horn to get them to move, and when she returned they were in the way again. Laura honked the horn again so she could get in the driveway, and when she got out she said something to them.

When she was inside, Brock's girlfriend said that one of them had called her a slut. That was it, Laura walked outside and beat up the two of them. The two girls walked up the road and called 911. The cops showed up and charged Laura with assault. Again I had to call my lawyer and that cost $7,000 to get the chatrges dropped, and Laura had to give the girls an apology letter. The charges were easy to drop because the girls admitted that they threw a pop bottle at one of our vehicles. The night this all happened, and the girls admitting they had thrown a pop bottle at one of the vehicles, I walked outside to see if there was any damages. I did this because I already new I had a dent in the tailgate of my truck, and I was going to blame this on the girls so I had a little fire power. I walked around my truck looking for damage, playing stupid, and once I got to the back of my truck, I pointed out the damage that I said wasn't there before. The girls' parents didn't have the money for the damages, so they took the letter instead. One good thing about this was that I didn't have to pay for the lawyer's bill, Laura had to pay it with her share of the house from the separation the following year.

The family and I were down in Disneyland for a vacation. One of our daytrips was to go to Sea World and Legoland. We had to take the bus, and we weren't five minutes into the ride when the driver made a comment about hockey. He said something like, "How's your hockey teams doing down in Canada?" and then said, "Oh yeah, the Mighty Ducks won the cup last year," and laughed. I piped up from the back of the bus, saying, "Why don't you pull this bus over and I will show you how us Canadians play hockey." I never heard a peep out of him the whole two-hour drive after that.

The Americans are wondering why they have a weight problem, so I will tell you. I was down at Birch Bay, Washington for the weekend and needed a few things at the store. I was looking for barbecue sauce and could only find this container that was almost a half gallon in size. I asked someone working there if they had anything smaller, but she replied with this puzzled look on her face that that was the smallest they had. I couldn't believe how big everything was, and, of course, it means you usually eat more if it's there.

We were at this restaurant and they brought us this huge platter of appetizers. I said to the girl, "We didn't order this," and she said that it was what everybody gets free before their meal. I said, "If I eat this, I won't be able to eat my dinner," but she walked away leaving it on the table. I started to look around at how much food was being wasted, and it got me to thinking how people are starving all over the world, and how it didn't make sense.

I was curious to see whether the restaurant had a bin in the back where they put all the wasted food, to see how much food they'd wasted at the end of one day. It would probably blow your mind. Canada is no prize either. Obesity went up thirty percent in the last ten years.

Medieval church leader Thomas Aquinas took a more expansive view of gluttony. Aquinas went so far as to prepare a list of six ways to commit gluttony, including:

Praepropere---eating too soon.

Laute---eating too expensively.

Nimis---eating too much

Ardenter---eating too eagerly {burningly}

Studiose---eating too daintily {keenly}.

Forente---eating wildly {boringly}.

A friend from work entered me into a Gong Show contest that a Vancouver radio station was putting on, which had a grand prize of $20,000.

He entered me in the contest because of this chainsaw sound I've been making since I was eight years old. I went and auditioned to go on the air and I had everyone laughing. They called me up, and now I was on the radio. There were three other contestants that day, but because I got the best vote I now was in the final. The radio station told me that it would be on TV, at the River Rock Casino or at the Commodore ball-room downtown. I got ready for the final, and I even had a few sponsors. This one company gave me a chainsaw to borrow, that his mechanic gutted for me because I had plans for it. I wanted this saw to spit out sawdust while I was making the saw sound on stage. I also had a log that was made of Styrofoam, right out of a movie set, that I carved their radio station logo on, so when I finished my show I could roll it towards the crowd.

I spent a month getting this saw mastered, and spent $700 in materials. With them playing me at least three times a day on the radio I thought I was a shoe-in, but I really wasn't. Because they kept playing me all the time the other contestants were calling in to complain, so if I were to win this thing they would all think it was a fix. When all the contestants were done, and the station had their finalists, they suddenly changed the rules. They told everyone to go online to pick their favourite contestant, and I wasn't chosen. I even had Fire Marshall Bill thrown into the act.

The disk jockey who put on this whole thing has a golf tournament every year, and my plan was to enter just so I could go and throw his golf clubs in the lake, but then I would be at his level. I watched the contest on TV, and with what I had planned I would have won the thing by a landslide. The guy who won was the very first guy they had on the air, which looked like a fix to me. Special thanks to John at A-1 ALL POINTS Sales and Service, in New Westminster for sponsoring me for the show. He had his mechanic take the motor out of a Husqvarna 3120 so I could use it in the show. You're a good man Johnny. I would also like to thank the guy's at Northview Enterprises in Maple Ridge for their help as well.

I got to be good friends with a guy who did the concrete work at my house. He was such a laidback guy that he sometimes didn't get around to collecting on some of his jobs until long after the job was done. When he finally went to collect they would tell him that he should have asked for his money when the job was done because they'd now spent his money on other things.

One day I was starting to get a little worried because he wasn't answering his phone. When I got to his house and opened the front door to yell his name I could tell from the tone in his voice that he wasn't doing very well. I walked upstairs and sat at the kitchen table. I noticed that there was an envelope that read "Last will and testament." It was June 27 and the date on the envelope was June 26. I didn't let him know that I'd seen the envelope, just handed him $100 and told him to go down to the pub and have a couple of beers, which was something he liked to do, and to think about what he wanted.

As I was leaving I could see something out of the corner of my eye. I looked down the hallway and he had opened the attic door and tied a rope to the rafters. He was getting ready to hang himself before I walked in. I didn't say a thing, and told him that I would call him later. I did phone him that night and he was still alive, but when I couldn't get a hold of him a couple of days later I drove over to his house again. The doors were locked, his truck was in the driveway, and there being no answer when I knocked I thought the worst.

I knew a guy from work who lived up the road, so I went there, put his ladder in my truck and headed back to break into his house. I put the ladder up to the roof and climbed through his window, but luckily found no one inside. He called me later that night because the neighbour had told him I was breaking into his house.

Before I could explain, he knew why I was there. I told him that I was just worried about him and he just replied, "I know you are, little buddy." One week later I dropped by his house, and one of the neighbours told me that they hadn't seen him all week. I found out later that he'd just left everything behind, leaving his house to the bank, and went back home to Ontario were his parents lived. I haven't heard from him since, and man do I miss that guy. He was a good friend.

I went to go see this psychic, and what she said to me made my head spin. I asked her whether there was anybody looking after me because I could feel it all the time, and she described what he looked like. She told me that he wanted me to see this picture of himself that my Mom had in a small brown album, fourth page in.

The photo of my grandfather that the psychic, Debbie, wanted me to see. It was in my Mom's photo album.

I called my Mom two weeks later and asked if she had such an album. She said she did. She went and got it, and I asked if there was a picture of Grandpa in there. She started looking and found it, so I asked her what page it was on and she counted… fourth page in. She mailed it to me, and now I have it framed in my living room. He's sitting on the stairs of his front porch eating a Popsicle and looking straight at me. He's my guardian angel, and he was also a foreman at the same place I work. In addition, he was a professional boxer.

The psychic knew about my short-lived boxing career. She told me that I'd been hurt early in my career, and that that was good because later on I would have gotten hurt to the point it would change my life, but I was a good fighter and would have been real good. My Grandfather died when I was only four years old.

The psychic also said that I would quit the railroad within five years, relocate and work on cars. She said I would have all my toys, and I would fix up cars to sell them, and that was how I was going to make my money. She kind of stuttered, with a grin on her face, when she told me this, so now I had to figure out how I was really going to make my money. I would go back and see her in 2011.

As far as Laura and I was concerned, the icing on the cake came when Laura and I were fighting one afternoon. I mean we fought every day, but this time she told me that she has slept with so many guys that she'd lost track. I flew off the couch, and before I knew it I had her by the throat on the ground. I can see how someone could kill another person and not remember it. I didn't remember leaving the couch because I was in a real state of mind. I didn't hit her, but I decided I'd had enough and moved out in January 8, 2008, for good, and onto the next lessons.

2008

I moved out and grabbed an apartment at a place they called the "Heartbreak Hotel" in town. It was full of single parents with kids, hookers and drug dealers. I had a 23-year-old brunette come over one night, really nice, and I really didn't care about anything but myself at the time. It was 10 p.m. and I took her into the bedroom. When I was done I got dressed and went to sit on the couch. With the converter in my hand I looked up at the clock and it was 10:10 p.m. I chuckled to myself, what a stallion?

Laura came over one night for something and I asked her if she'd ever left work early while we were together to go home with guys. She told me she did it all the time, and then came home to me to make it look like she'd finished her shift. What a sweetheart.

Doctor Dave and his cousin and I were going to Kelowna to look at some property. My ex-girlfriend Maria lived there. I called her to come and spend the night with me at the hotel. I took ecstasy and some Viagra with me. I was told you don't get a hard on when on it, which is why I brought the Viagra. I got all liquored up and took this ecstasy so I could pound my ex all night with help from the Viagra. When I got up to go to the bathroom I passed out on the floor. I didn't know what had happened. All I could hear was her asking me what I was doing on the floor. I never did end up doing anything with her that night, and when I got home I asked my buddy what had happened. He told me that it's bad to mix those two drugs together, and I should have asked him first. Too late. Lesson learned.

I always had a love for the 1966 Chevelle Super Sport, so I was having one custom built. It took two years for this guy to build, and the original car came from California. By the time it was finished it had cost me $50,000. I had left Laura and the house in January, and the guy who built the car called me in February to tell me that the car was finished. I couldn't afford this now because I was paying Laura $6,500 a month plus my own bills. I went to the bank and got a line of credit against the house because the bank manager didn't know we'd split up. I got the loan for $30,000, borrowed $10,000 from a close friend, and paid the rest in cash. I told my friend that if anything shitty happened to my grow-ops and I couldn't pay him back, I would sell the car immediately and pay him.

I was driving the car one day and was planning to keep it in the underground parking at my apartment for the night. I didn't feel good about this so I drove it back to Doctor Dave's place where I had it stored, and drove my 1999 Dodge 4x4 back. I got up in the morning to go to work and my truck was gone. I reported it stolen, booked the day off work and went to get a rental car. The RCMP called me a few hours later and said that they had found it. They'd caught the guy who stole it down a deserted street. I couldn't see the truck until they were finished with it, and after it had been towed to ICBC.

I was a little worried because my partner, Allan, had come back from Mexico with $2,000 worth of steroids in his suit case, and he'd put it in a saline solution bottle to hide it. I had bought it from him, and it was sitting on the back seat when the truck was stolen. I got called to the cop shop to identify some of the items they had in their possession from the guy who ripped off my truck. Once there I grabbed my sub-box and the CDs that they had. I told the cops they didn't have to tell me who took my truck, all they had to do was write his name on a piece of paper. One of the officers pushed away from his desk with a smile on his face. I did tell the cops that I knew it had to be someone in the building because the doors to the underground weren't damaged. He looked at me and said that I shouldn't leave anything in the truck because this guy was real close. That was telling me I was bang on.

When I got back to the apartment I talked to the landlord. I said I thought the guy who'd stolen my truck lived in the apartment just above the entrance to the building. She said, "No, the guy we have problems with is in suite 101." I said, "Thanks" and she replied, "Oh no, what have I done?"

I waited until her husband got home so I could get a little information on the guy. Before I did this, I went to go see a friend of mine who knew someone who would go into his apartment and make a real mess of him. I then got a call the next day to come and look at my truck at ICBC, and to answer some questions. While I was there looking in my truck to see what was missing, I asked the adjuster, "Why do the bio-medical people go through the vehicles before you?" He told me they do this to every vehicle, just in case there are drugs inside bottles and other stuff. I knew then he was trying to tell me that the cops had found the steroids, but luckily nothing was ever said about it. They had to send the truck to a body shop because the lock was punched out of the driver's door.

When I went to go see the landlord, Larry, I told him the guy in 101 would soon be out of his hair. He told me to stay away from him because the cops were going to raid his apartment that night or the next day. I told him if the cops didn't come get him by the next day, I was sending a guy over there. He agreed with me, and said that he would even give me the key. I think the reason the cops were going to move in on this guy was because I had told ICBC that I knew who'd stolen my truck, and that he was going to get the beating of his life, and they didn't want me to ruin a six-month sting operation they had on the guy.

I got a description of the guy from the landlord, and when I entered the apartment building you would not believe who held the door open for me. Yes, you got it. The guy I was looking for, from suite 101. He looked right into his mailbox and said, "Oh, I have some mail, I guess I'll go get my key." He thought that using reverse psychology, I wouldn't think he had anything to do with my truck, but little did this idiot know that I'd invented reverse psychology. I could have beat this guy right there, but I just walked away and let things happen. Apparently this guy and his girlfriend ran an escort service through their apartment on Fridays and Saturdays. For this to happen his old lady would buzz the guy up to the apartment and the horny prick would hand over some money. Once the money was handed over, her boyfriend would come out of the closet with a butcher's knife and chase the guy out and keep the money. He would also break into the mailboxes in the buildings, take all the credit information and order credit cards.

The cops did raid his apartment the next night, and Larry told me that he shit and pissed his pants. They found stolen credit cards under the carpets by the hundreds. They arrested both of them, but let his old lady out a couple of days later.

I was doing laundry, and when I went back to get my clothes they were gone. I knew it had to be her because when the cops kicked their door open, they broke it off the hinges, and when I'd put my laundry in the dryer I noticed the door was back in place in the door frame. Then, when I went to get my clothes and discovered they were gone, I noticed the door wasn't closed all the way. You could only close the door completely if you were inside, so I knew that someone had closed it as best they could when they left with my clothes.

I called the RCMP and told them what had happened, and that if I didn't get my clothes back by ten o'clock that night I was going into her apartment to do it right. They told me that wouldn't be a good idea, and I told them they should have left her locked up. I told the cop that I'd had it with everyone, and that I'd finally lost it. The cop told me that if my clothes weren't back by ten she would see what she could do. Because I didn't have any proof, I knew there was nothing that could really be done, so after I took a couple of hours to calm down I realized that this wasn't going to be a good idea and kissed my clothes goodbye.

If that wasn't enough, one night I walked across the street to the 7-11 to grab some milk. As I walked up to the entrance there were four or five teenagers standing outside the store. I grabbed some milk and headed to the cashier. As I reached into my pocket and pulled out the wad of cash with the elastic band around it, I noticed this sketchy kid and his friend eyeing it up. Now I would usually take out what I needed before going to the counter, but for some reason this time I didn't. These two kids walked out the door before I'd finished paying, and when I headed out the door I noticed that all the kids, including the two from inside, were gone. They'd taken off too quickly, so I knew something was up.

I looked across the street to my apartment building, and I could see some heads moving in the dark parking lot of the building. These little fuckers were going to try to rob me because the four guys outside knew where I'd walked from, and were waiting for me to come back. Who did these little brats think they were fucking with anyway? Knowing that there were at least six of them I did something smarter. I called a cab and got him to drive me across the street. I got him to pull up to the underground gates and handed him the key to open it. I looked over to where these kids were, and could see that there were more than six of them, so I had made the right call. The cab drove into the under-ground, I paid him and went to my apartment. Way to go parents. You raised some great kids. It is you who needs the beating.

Being separated was very stressful and I started to do the 80mg Oxy-contin pills… real heavy. I was at the point where it was costing me $400 a day. I was so bad that I couldn't look at myself in the mirror because I would start crying, knowing how bad this drug had a hold of me. I would take my daughter with me to get my drugs whenever I couldn't drop her off somewhere until I got back. I would always say to myself how sorry I was to my daughter, that she had a drug addict for a father, and how I put the addiction before her. I tell you that if I could shut down the pharmaceutical company down that makes this evil drug I would in a heartbeat. Those fucking cocksuckers are killing people every day just to fill their pockets. Why is it that the medications you need to survive cost the most? Because they know you will pay anything, and it's not any harder to make than Aspirin. There's your government.

I went to go see my dealer with my daughter in the truck, and he handed me a sample of an 80mg Oxy that someone was making, and he swore they were the same. After taking this I got into an accident with my daughter in the truck. I rear-ended this lady, and when we were exchanging information I remember her looking at me with this sickened look on her face. I guess I looked like I was wired out of my mind. I remember having a hard time focusing and talking, so I guess that had something to do with it. I was headed to the store to buy my daughter a toy, but realized that I was too ripped to drive. I then headed home. I don't know what was in that pill, but obviously I shouldn't have taken it.

You know you're bad when you start putting your kids in danger, but when you're so fucked up it doesn't matter, you will do anything for your fix. How disgusting. I'd had five grow-ops at one time, and now I was down to two, and money started to get really tight. I handed off my weed to a friend of mine and his partner. I waited by the phone to go pick up the money as they told me it would only take about an hour to do the transaction. I got the call and was told that the guy they were dealing with took the weed and didn't return.

I wasn't in a good situation in my life to have this happen to me. I was told that it was going to be covered just as soon as my buddy and his partner figured out what exactly had happened. I waited a couple of days and then I made a call to Allan. Allan knew my buddy's partner, so I told him, with tears in my eyes, that I was at my wits end and I was walking out my door with my shot gun and a box of shells, and I was going to kill the guy. He told me to just hang on and he would see what he could do. He called me up, told me to go meet the other guy the next day, and that he had half my money right now. I did get the rest of it a week later, thank God, but no more dealings with them.

A guy from work who I went into business with on that grow show changed his mind on the deal we'd made two years earlier. I took all the money from the last crop and told him to go fuck himself. He ran his place for about another year, and then somebody robbed him and that forced him to pack it in. That Karma is a real bitch isn't it?

Barney and I went out one night to the Black Sheep Pub. Barney was the guy who took off on me in the house boat. Once we were inside, Barney saw a guy who owed him $37,000. He pushed him around and told him he wanted his money, and then I had a short talk with him. After we sat down again I said to Barney, "I think I better go have another talk with that guy because I don't think he took me seriously." I went and sat down with this guy, right in his face, and told him in a calm voice that he should pay because he didn't want me coming for him. The next Monday he sent his brother over to Barney's and paid the full amount.

I decided it was time to go and get some help. Before you can enter a treatment centre you have to spend time in detox. I went to detox in Kamloops before I was scheduled to go into the Kamloops's treatment centre. I was there only an hour before I left because I thought I knew more than the doctor, and that scared the hell out of me. Just before I decided to leave, they'd given me 900mgs of Gabapentin. They gave me my keys and away I went. As the medication started to work I started to get drowsy. I woke up twice doing 170 km/h on the shoulder of the highway. I made it home in one piece, surprisingly enough. What the place should have done was to keep my keys until the next morning, and told me to go get a hotel overnight.

When I got back to town I tried to stay clean. I was seven days sober when I went to go see my lawyer about my pension. Laura and I were trying to settle the finances between us, and I wanted to make sure she did not get to touch my pension. He told me that I had to give Laura $54,000 for her half of what my pension was worth. I told him he must have made a mistake, and he told me I should go home and read the pension papers, not just throw them in the backseat. Hearing this, I went and bought some pills to drown my sorrows.

After about a week I looked at the pension papers and called my work to find out that the lawyer was $20,000 too high. I went back to see my lawyer, and I said that maybe HE should read the pension papers better. He told me that he eventually would have found the mistake. He's the professional, so I said, "No, you wouldn't have, because you already gave me the total." I had used this lawyer on three occasions, but I never used him for the big stuff. The last time I used him was to draw up the separation agreement between Laura and I.

My older brother Darin was walking down the aisle again after his divorce… slow learner. I was on the wagon, trying to kick the pills again. I had my Chevelle all polished up for the wedding. Sleeping was a problem as I was going through withdrawal. I was having a tough time trying to sit still in the church. It was also really depressing, sitting there while my brother was getting married and everything was going good for him, and I was in the middle of a separation, with a huge drug problem. Just before the sermon was to start my brother realized he didn't have the wedding rings. The rings were at the hall where the dinner was being held that night, locked up in a Ford Explorer. Since I had the fastest car there I volunteered to go get the rings. I didn't know where this hall was, so I took one of the bridesmaids with me who knew where the place was. I peeled out of the church parking lot sideways down Dewdney Trunk Road like a scene out of *Smokey and the Bandit*. We got the rings and made it back in under ten minutes.

After the service, Doctor Dave and I headed back to his house for a couple of drinks. On the way there I told Dave that I needed some coke to wake me up if I was going to make it to the dinner. We grabbed the blow off a dealer I knew, and off to his place we went. After a couple of rails, I started to get paranoid and had to tell Dave that there was no way I was going to attend the dinner. I went home and snorted the rest of the blow, then my phone started to ring. I never answered it, I just pulled the cord out of the wall and chilled. Drinking or doing blow didn't make me do Oxy, and I would always do the pills by themselves. I didn't ride the wagon for too long after that wedding, and it was back to hell for me. I've been to hell and back so many times it felt like I should buy property there. Or is hell here?

I was missing so much work again that my boss pulled me into the office and asked what was going on, so I told him. I got along with my boss so well I looked at him like the father I never had. If it wasn't for him I probably would have been fired a long time ago, and left pushing a shopping cart. After seeing that psychic again in 2011, I actually think that my Grandfather put him in that position at work just to look after me, and to keep me employed. I told him that I was going to go get help and start all over. I remember lying in the bath tub shaking and crying from the withdrawal, and I was going to throw the toaster in the tub but the cord wasn't long enough. I managed to hold it together with help from this addiction doctor I was working with, Dr. Donald Hedges. He is apparently number two in B.C. for helping people with their addictions, but I would have to say he's number one in my books.

When I went to see him to put me in a treatment centre, he also told me that I couldn't smoke in there, and I would have to quit that too. I was also addicted to Dristan nasal spray, and you weren't allowed that in there either. I quit all three habits before I went to treatment. That was how determined I was to kick my addictions. I managed to stay clean for six weeks before I went into the treatment centre in Vancouver.

One of the withdrawal symptoms is insomnia, and that can last up to one year. I would get about one hour of sleep a night, and after the sixth week I started to sleep for about six hours, but it only felt like I got ten minutes of rest. This was the hardest part of the whole thing. Once at the treatment centre I noticed there was a smoking pit, but the doctor had told me you weren't allowed to smoke at the centre so I would quit smoking as well. I guess I owed him thanks twice.

A few of us guys went up to the media room one night to play some poker. We found some chips in a board game and some cards, so the Texas hold-em game began. One of the men got into debt with someone, and I didn't know he hadn't paid until the allowed one-hour walk the next day. As we were walking, the person who was owed the money mentioned that this guy hadn't paid him yet. I said, "Really?" and so we walked into this dollar store and grabbed some pliers, a hammer, some tape and a screw driver. We smuggled these things in the girl's purses and the hoodies on their jackets. That night, back up to the media room to play poker, we pulled out the tools and put them on the table. On the walk the next day that guy went to a bank machine, paid his debt off, packed up his stuff, and left.

One night in rehab I was watching TV with this black guy. We were watching the U.S. presidential election and he said to me that Obama was going to change the country, and I said, "Yeah, well we can't even get half of the forty people in here to do their chores, so how is he going to get everyone in the country to do theirs." He looked at me as if I was from outer space and said, "Wow, that was deep and you're right." I hope he is doing okay. I should have got his number.

I remember this little black girl about five years old who would swim at my Dad's apartment complex when he would pick me up for the weekends when I was little. I would always look forward to seeing her on the weekend because she was the most beautiful little girl I had ever seen. I mean look at Halle Berry. WOW, she's amazingly beautiful, but I have to admit, I think I'm in love with Serinda Swan. Feisty and delicious. I guess my point here is "STOP BEING RACIST" – love everyone equally.

I think there were a few times over the years that I was using that I almost overdosed on those Oxys. I hit the floor a few times out of breath, and after reading some books in the treatment centre I realized why. The books stated that Oxycontin slows down the respiratory system, and if you were to overdose, even the best paramedic couldn't save your life.

I had bought a house just before I went into the treatment centre, just after Laura and I signed our separation papers and sold our house. I wanted this all done before I went in so that when I came out I would have a fresh start. After all the work and money I spent on that house, I only got $2,500 out of it. When the lawyer handed me the cheque I drove over to one of my co-worker's house to show him. I asked him if he wanted to see something funny, and when I showed him the cheque I laughed. With only $2,500 to my name after the separation I needed a partner for the house that I found.

This house was an older home on one acre and there was lots of peace and quiet. I completed treatment and was looking forward to a fresh start, at least that's what I thought at the time. My partner and I put twenty-four grow lights in the garage. We fenced the property, had the shop and the house fully alarmed but not monitored. If the alarm went off it would call my cellphone first, and then if I didn't answer, it would phone my partner and he was to come over to my place armed and start shooting everyone. We have what they call "rippers" – thieves who will break into your house and rob your weed. If you're home they will tie you up and beat you for something to do while they steal your weed.

Everything was going good, and we were making an average of $100,000 to $120,000 every three months. Being all messed up for the last few years I didn't venture out very often. One night I was invited to a friend's house for a party. I didn't drink and I was clean, but I didn't stay clean for long. This guy covered in tattoos walks up to me and shakes my hand and says, "I finally get to meet the notorious Scott Magri." Even though that was the old me it still made me feel good, because to me that was the only thing I had accomplished in life.

I would run into people from time to time who would call me the legend, all because of the way I could handle myself. The truth is I never wanted to hurt anybody, I just wanted to be normal and fit in.

Before I left Laura I was still working on the house, and I had put down a down payment with a contractor for the bar to be built for the games room. Now that I wasn't living there anymore I asked for my money back several times while I was living in my new place, and I was being very patient because Craig worked for this company. I heard that his boss had bought an old truck to restore without giving me my money.

I told Craig to tell his boss that if I didn't get my money by that Friday I was going to pay him a visit. Friday came and no phone call, so I packed a bag with some clean clothes, and went and bought a new pair of shoes to complete my "Beat Kit", all to change into after I'd beat the hell out of his boss and ditched my bloody clothes. Just as I left the sports store with my new shoes, my phone rang. It was Craig telling me to come by for my money. If he had waited ten more minutes his boss would have been in the hospital. What a piece of shit. He was buying a truck before paying me? What did he think was going to happen when Craig told him all about me and what I was like?

I was working downtown fixing a few rail cars, and went to the Old Spaghetti Factory for lunch. My mate sat in the truck to eat his lunch and I went off to have lunch by myself. I was sitting outside on the patio looking at all the traffic and bums on the streets.

All of a sudden everything went quiet and I could barely hear the dishes in the kitchen. Instantly there was no traffic and no homeless people. This beautiful woman had walked past me and all I could smell was her intoxicating perfume, but this magical moment only lasted for about fifteen seconds and then everything got loud. A bus drove by, making a big dust ball, and there were two crackheads buzzing up to this apartment to my right, and a bum trying to grab the bun off my plate. I thought to myself, "What the hell just happened?"

I have no idea what that was all about, other than that with all the hell that I had been through lately, my head just went on holidays for that short period of time. It was almost like heaven, but how would I know what heaven looks like? I came close to finding out a little later when things turned for the worst and I tried suicide for the third time.

2009

I was five months clean when I was over at Laura's house dropping something off for Chevelle. She offered me a Percocet. She didn't believe I had quit for that long, but that's the evil in her. She knew that if I took it it would put me right back to where I was. I thought to myself as I drove away that maybe if I just got a few of them I would finally get a good night's sleep, considering I hadn't slept for the past five months. Once I got home I called her back and said I would take ten of them. I took those ten and before you knew it, I was back to taking the 80 mg Oxys. They have a saying in recovery, "One is too many, and 1,000 aren't enough."

I had noticed the RCMP chopper flying over my place for the past couple of weeks and that started to get me worried. I got a phone call from a friend a month later and he wanted to meet me at the Husky Gas Station up the street right away. Once there he told me that my name had come up, and the cops are going to bust me within the next forty-eight hours. We got about eight guys together and started tearing down the grow show at my house over the next couple of nights. We moved everything into a storage locker and got rid of all the dirt at a friend's farm. There wasn't a crumb in the place and now it was three days later and no cops.

I finally put it all together as to what had happened, and figured the old lady down the street had ratted me out to the cops. I remember my partner telling me that the little old lady down the street had come over to our place and was telling him that her best friend was a cop.

This old lady also asked me a couple weeks before the bust what days I had my daughter, and I'd told her Thursday and Friday. I got the tip on Tuesday, so that meant forty-eight hours later would run into Thursday, which meant I would have my kid, so they waited until Saturday when she wouldn't be there.

I didn't pick up my daughter that week because of what was happening, just in case they came back before Saturday. I was driving down Lougheed Highway on the Friday and an undercover cop car raced up on my ass with two of them in it because they saw I wasn't wearing my seat belt. Once they drove up close enough to run my plate number they backed completely off, and now I knew for sure they were coming. The next morning, at 10:30 a.m., I was sitting on the couch and heard a warning siren coming from the frontyard. I went to the kitchen window to look and the cops had my place surrounded. I had left the sidegate open so they wouldn't wreck my nice gates at the end of my driveway when they showed up. I walked out, and every one of them was yelling at me to get on the ground and crawl towards them with their guns on me. There had to be twelve of them there, they had the green team, and I think a few members from the gang squad. The green team is the squad that shuts down grow-ops. They hauled me away even though there wasn't a crumb in the place.

They couldn't arrest me, so they had to bring me back to my house about forty-five minutes later. Since they hauled me away in my bare feet, when I got out of the cop car at my place I said to the cops at my gate, "What, you didn't sweep off my driveway for me?" It didn't look like they liked that.

They had a warrant for theft of hydro, but I had already put the original meter back on before they came so there was nothing to find. I thought that they took me away because they wanted to bug my house so I was very careful after that day.

When they dropped me off at my house, the undercover cops took me aside and had a talk with me. They found a poem I had written in the treatment centre, as well as the information I had on my Mom's relative, George Brinton McClellan, who was the thirteenth commissioner of the RCMP. My Mom's first cousin, three times removed, was the commissioner who had saved the horses for the musical ride, and we actually have the musical ride emblem on our locomotives at work.

Here's another weird thing, I was talking to my old neighbour the other day and she apparently talks to spirits. She asked me if I knew a guy by the name of George who had died. I told her my dead relative was the only guy I knew with that name. She said that he had something to do with me, and now I know why I only ever spent one day in prison for all the shit that I have done all these years, he's carrying my ass too.

George McClellan, 13th commissioner of the RCMP.

Anyway, the cops told me that they thought they were coming into a different person's house until they saw that stuff and met me. They said they had to come all force because of my background, and that there were guns registered to that address. I had all the guns out of the house, and my Chevelle and my new twenty-seven-foot travel trailer were gone before they showed up. I remember telling myself one day, looking outside, that I would have given everything I owned away to wake up the next day not knowing what Oxycontin even was.

That night my partner and a friend of his were out drinking to drown his loss. My partner phoned me up the next afternoon and asked if I'd heard him the night before. I said what do you mean, and he told me what he and his friend did to the old lady rat down the street. When I first moved into the house my partner was working on the fence, and that old lady told him that her house was the one with the mailbox that had the cute bunnies on it. With my partner knowing this, he'd gone to her house that night with his chainsaw and cut her mail box down. It now sits in his games room, and the old lady was probably a little scared knowing that we knew she was the one who ratted us out. At least I hope it was her.

I slept with my defender loaded beside me in my bed, and all my other guns under the bed all the time, so imagine what could have happened to me if I hadn't been tipped off. I took my truck into downtown Vancouver and paid $300 dollars to have it swept for any electronic devices they might have planted and they found nothing. I didn't talk about anything for six months in that house. I always went outside on the front lawn to talk about any business. With the grow show shut down for a bit I was short of cash, but I kept my promise to my partner about the money I owed him. I sold the Chevelle for $38,000 and paid him off. That one really hurt. I mean, I had waited since I was twelve years old for that car, and never mind the twelve grand I lost on the sale.

I did take Chevelle camping one weekend before I had to sell the trailer. I took some Oxy on the way back to the campground and passed out at the wheel again, running over a steel pole at the gates to the campground. It tore the front corner of my truck apart and everyone was watching, wondering how I didn't see it. My daughter was always telling me to watch out, and she'd grab the dashboard when I drove. Things like this are an example of how an addiction takes over your life, and that not even the safety of your own child will stop you. It tears me apart when I think of those days.

I sold my trailer to support my habit because I didn't have any money coming in other than my paycheque from work, and that wasn't very much because I was rarely there.

I was at Tim Horton's getting a coffee and noticed the wife of a friend of mine was in there crying with this women friend of hers I had only met once before. The friend had a son who was bipolar, and he seldom took his medication. They were crying because the son had flipped out on his Mom while putting gas in her car at the Chevron down the road. When he walked away to cool off, the mom and my buddy's wife drove up to the Tim Horton's. I called my buddy and told him that his wife was in there and really upset. He said he knew that crazy dude had just flipped out on them, and that he was on his way from work to get her. I told him that I would stay until he got there in case the guy came back. It was only a matter of a few minutes before the guy recognized his mom's van in the parking lot. It was parked right outside the side door, and I could see him sitting in the van all in a rage. I told the manager to call the cops because this guy was ready to snap, and to lock the doors to the building. They did exactly that, but in the meantime he got out of the van with a security club in his hand that was used to lock the steering wheel, and started walking toward the front doors pointing his finger at me. This guy was so out of it that he walked right through the front glass doors like they weren't even there. He was coming right for me and my first thought was, "Today is the day I die."

His chest was all puffed out, and he weighed about 250 pounds so he was bigger than I was. As he was getting closer I took a stance in front of the women to protect them, and decided that if I had to, I would try to crush his jaw. I didn't want to try this because I knew he was bipolar, and that when they don't take their medication it's like they are on LSD. I thought that even if I smashed his jaw into pieces he probably wouldn't even feel it, and then I would be in trouble.

His eyes were looking in different directions and he was no longer focused on me. He walked right by me and went up to the counter cursing and swearing, but didn't threaten anybody. He only stayed in there about thirty seconds, and then went right back out the broken door. The police took him down at gunpoint a block away. He was charged with mischief and now I was a witness. I didn't want any part of it, but he eventually got off anyway without me testifying, even though they had it all on video.

Like I said earlier, just because something went sour from helping someone out, that doesn't mean you stop helping because you might need some good Karma one day. I'm still waiting for mine.

2010

My partner and I decided that we'd given our house enough time to cool off, so we set the shop up again but with only five lights in it until we decided what we were going to do with the place. After the cops had come there once and found nothing, that gave us a green light to go ahead because they would have a hell of a time getting another warrant. I also had the head of the green team's number because he had given it to me in case I wanted to talk. I decided to play a little reverse psychology by telling him about this guy that I knew. This guy never got touched when his partners got pinched, so I knew he was a rat and would sell out his own mother to save his ass.

I called the cop and told him about his grow-op, and that I thought it was strange that they never did anything to him even though they knew about him. I asked for an explanation for this, but he couldn't tell me why. He said he didn't know anything about it because he wasn't working for the green team at the time. I didn't feel like a rat because I knew that the cops already knew about him, and now that the cops knew I knew everything about this rat they wouldn't even come close to me, because they wouldn't want a rash on their hands.

We covered the whole inside of the shop with lead so when the RCMP chopper flew over they couldn't detect any heat from the shop. They could even drive up with their heat gun and not get a reading. You always had to be one step ahead of them. After we got one crop off, we put in another thirteen lights to make it eighteen.

Now, living like a caged animal, I thought it was a good idea to secure the house the best I could since my daughter was still staying with me a couple days a week. I made some bars to fit across the doors out of steal that would stop anyone from kicking them in while we slept at night. I also would sleep with a loaded shotgun in the corner with the safety on. What a way to live.

The way we had it set up this time, I couldn't control the temperature evenly, or the humidity, so we did the shits and weren't making a lot of profit. With my addiction right out of control, and having no large amounts of money, my head started to play games with me. I went out one night for a couple of hours and ran into a coke dealer I knew. I bought a gram and headed for home. I cooked it up over the stove using ammonia and turned it into crack. Then I took a pop can and made a pipe and smoked the gram away. I was already in a bad state of depression, and now that I had no more crack panic started to set in. I thought that I had no way out so I decided to leave this planet.

My daughter putting gas in my 1966 Chevelle. It's one of two photos I was holding when I tried to commit suicide.

I did my homework on the internet about how much medication I needed to overdose. I wrote a goodbye letter, with tears dripping on the paper, and left a disc of music that I liked so they had something to play at my funeral.

I got dressed in my nice clothes and comfortable shoes, and took three bottles of pills. I took the whole bottle of my prescription sleep medication, as well as a full bottle of Gabapentin, and a bottle of Clonidine. I then lay on my back on my king size bed holding onto pictures on my chest, and asking God to take me. I had a picture of my Chevelle with my daughter standing beside it, and the picture of my Grandpa the psychic had talked about. It took about an hour before I started to feel myself slip away, and I looked at the clock and it was one a.m. I passed out just after looking at the clock and my soul went somewhere else for about three hours. I don't know if I was dead or not, but I did see the other side.

They say from what I described that I had an out-of-body experience. I was at a place where there were people as far as the eye could see. They were all having such a good time, all of them screaming with joy, and some guys from the sixties were passing a football around. There was a car parked on the street with the trunk open and playing music. I just stood there observing all of this, and no one saw me, even though I was shoulder to shoulder with the guy throwing the football. This was no illusion, nor was this a dream, because everything was real and I had no emotions whatsoever. I think it was all up to me if I wanted to take that step forward or not, but I didn't, obviously.

I think that what changed my mind was this blonde girl riding on a merry-go-round. She was about seven years old, and was wearing a light blue dress and a dark blue bow tied to her back. I figure from the dress, she was from the fifties. While I was watching her I think she must have reminded me of my daughter, and all of a sudden my eyes opened and it was four a.m. I was so pissed off that I was still alive that I immediately began thinking of another way to kill myself. I didn't feel sick from all the medication, nor did I throw up. I couldn't walk very well for a couple of days, and my speech was all messed up. As crazy as it sounds, this wouldn't be my last attempt. What I got from this experience was that there was something I had to do here, and that I had to come back and figure it out. I don't know if it was heaven because what does heaven look like? All I can tell you is that there sure wasn't any evil at that place, that's for sure.

After the near-death experience, I started wondering, even if jumped in front of a moving train, whether I would only suffer a broken arm or something. The last fifteen years these doctors have been telling me that I need to treat my high cholesterol. I had a level of bad cholesterol like a seventy-five year old man, but my good cholesterol was off the charts and that was saving my life. They also told me that for sure I have had heart attacks without me knowing, or even a small stroke. I know now that I'm here for the long haul, but a stroke is something I don't need, so I'm going to try some medication for it only because I feel there is a lot more I need to do in this world. Otherwise what would be the point of me living any longer.

My buddy Allan was moving and he called me to see if I would be interested in buying his bedroom suite and some railroad pictures. I said that I would, but I couldn't pay for anything at the time, but he had no problem with that. I went and picked up the suite and hung the pictures on the wall. The pictures were collector prints, and were worth some cash. Allan and I never talked about how much he wanted for these things, but he told me when I had some money we would talk about it. The withdrawals were starting and I didn't have any money. I called a guy off the internet who bought prints. I told him what I had, and he said that I would be better off selling them piece by piece, because I would get more than he was prepared to offer for the whole lot. He was being honest.

It's amazing how desperate you can get just to get your next fix. In hopes that this guy would feel sorry for me I told him that I didn't have that much time because I was dying of cancer and I needed the money to take my kid to Disneyland before I died. After telling him this story the offer didn't go up, but I drove them over to his place and sold them to him for $1,200; they were worth $9,000. I know what I did was wrong, and I will regret this the rest of my life. At first I thought to myself he was a heartless piece of shit, but he did tell me I would be better selling them separately.

I pawned all my DeWalt tools and my camera for money. I then sold all my other rifles, only because one night while sitting on the edge of my bed I had my .300 Winchester Magnum in my mouth. I was seeing if I would be able to pull the trigger with it in my mouth or not. I had written another letter to my brother, and had planned to blow my head off down in the shop that night. I actually went down there and set up a chair. I managed to find some money so the whole thing changed one more time.

I called my Dad, now that we were on speaking terms again, and asked if I could come up there for a few days because I needed to get out of town to clean up. I had already been there once before to try and clean up, about six months prior, and I could tell from the tone in his voice that he didn't want me there even though he said it was okay.

I decided to go back up to my Mom's house instead, knowing that her door was always open. I went up to her house that weekend and cleaned up, but that wouldn't last for long. I came home and went on this new drug, Suboxone, for a while, until I got back on the Oxys. With no sleep because of the withdrawals, and trying to stay clean, I wasn't thinking one night when I put my cat outside. I always brought him in at night because of the coyotes around. He would run around at four in the morning because he had to go outside and I needed all the sleep I could get. The second night he never came back, and I remember yelling and crying to the higher power , "You took everything in my life from me, and now you take my best friend." I also said, "When I get up there, I am going to renovate that fucking place for doing this to me." I knew everything happens for a reason but I couldn't figure out why they pushed me this far.

As time went on, and everything started to make sense to me, I realized that my Dad had made his bed, and now he would have to lay in it. I'd already tried to tell him how I felt about the day he let his wife walk all over me, but he still didn't get it. I feel that if you bring children into this world you take on the responsibility to help them until the day you die or you shouldn't have any. I'm not even going to waste my breath trying to make him understand anymore because I've tried too often already. He did leave a message on my phone in March of 2012, but I didn't return the call only because he would be the same guy, and it's going to take more than a phone call to fix the damage.

I went back to the pills a couple of weeks after my cat went missing, and when I was taking my daughter and a friend of hers to the PNE one day the house was robbed! I had the alarm system on so that when someone opened the shop door the alarm would sound up in the house. So on the way to the PNE my phone rang, it was my house number and that meant my alarm was going off. I called my neighbour and asked if she had seen anyone at my place. When she walked to her driveway she could see two guys hopping the fence before getting into a Chrysler 300 and taking off.

I made the decision to take the grow show down only because of the notes I'd made on the calendar in the shop. I was sure that they knew when we were going to crop out, as we would write it on the calendar. I was right about this, because they came back when I wasn't home again. I did the math, and if we'd kept the show going the weed would have been drying two days on the screens when they came. There was a black cloud over that house right from square one. It was a living hell.

I was at the neighbour's one day, talking outside, and he had a son who was bipolar. His son was about ten years old and wore glasses, and got picked on at school. Sound familiar? As I was talking to his dad his son walked up from school and had something in his hand. I said to him, "What do you have there, kid?" and he said, "My pictures." I told him how good they looked, and then he turned to his dad. He walked away with his head down and I said to the dad, "Didn't you look at his pictures?" He said, "Yeah, I did" but he didn't pick them up and look at them or tell his son how good they were, he just glanced at them.

As I looked at the hurt on his son's face, it reminded me of myself, and right away I said to myself, "There goes another kid that's going to be ruined." Like I said earlier, it doesn't take much for a kid to feel he's not wanted. All you parents out there need to do a one-on-one with all your kids so they feel special, that's the secret.

I asked the kid if he wanted me to show him how to fight and he looked at the ground and replied, "No." Then, about ten seconds later, he piped up with a small smile on his face and said, "Yeah, I do." I told him I would call up a friend who had some gear and we could set up my garage. I called up Doctor Dave but he had given all his gear away already. I didn't have the money to buy everything I needed to train him, so I guess he will have to learn on his own. It was probably a good thing, because the things that I would have taught him would have gotten him into a whole lot of trouble. Look what happened to me.

I got home from work one day, and after I had a shower I heard my cat meow. Now, this was the cat that never came back. It was so clear that I went outside looking for him. I also looked in all the closets but nothing. They say that animals will give a sign to tell you that they are all right, once they are gone. It was a bit of a relief, but I would rather have had my best friend back, because he was with me through all that hell, but I know I will see him again.

Even though I was all messed up, I always paid my child support. Sometimes it was late. But over my dead body would I ever not pay, even though that ex of mine was telling everybody that I didn't pay her, and that I was a piece of shit. I actually feel sorry for her because I know that Karma is slowly setting in on her now. Everybody who has fucked me over in my life has paid the price for it in one way or another. I shouldn't even use the word Karma because there is no such thing, because life is all supposed to happen that way.

I never ripped anybody off to feed my addiction, but I did borrow money I couldn't pay back. I was also taking money out of Laura's bank account only because I was hitting the 'OTHER' button at the bank machine and thought I was taking it out of my own savings account. It was really coming out of our old joint account. I had told her over and over to cancel it after our separation. I gave the bank my signature to cancel it after the separation, but her signature was also required. As per usual, weeks went by and she didn't sign off.

I had $500 on me and phoned a friend who was good with computers to find out which one I should buy. There was a sale going on at Best Buy and I bought the one I was told to get. As I was sitting at home looking at it in the box, I couldn't figure out why the hell I had bought this thing because I hated computers. No patience. I told myself that I needed to get the cable guy over to hook the thing up. I thought that it would be good to look at all the cars on the Internet, and to look up some old friends on Facebook, but that wasn't the real reason.

Little did I know that the man upstairs had a bigger plan for me. While sitting on the couch high, I thought that now would be the time to start writing a book because I had all this time on my hands. I had no more grow-ops to look after, and I was seldom at work, so it was perfect timing, but all this timing was for a reason.

I started to get these weird chills all the time, running up my spine, and the hair all over my body would stand up. It started to happen as soon as I started writing, and it was then I knew what I was supposed to do with my life.

I had kept so much shit inside me all these years and it was finally time for it to all come out. I would write, then push the computer away, but for some reason I would pull it back and write with tears in my eyes. I knew now what I was here to do, and that it was important to finish this task because there wouldn't be time to do it all over again because this world is ready to explode.

I was trying to find some information about how to write your own book, as I had no idea how to start. I found out about this course that an author was putting on at the local college. On the day of the course there was one person who stood out like a sore thumb. I sat down with my computer bag and started to look for a pen. This guy threw a pen across the table for me and I'm thinking to myself, "How did this guy know I was looking for a pen?" I still have that pen. I said, "thanks" and I continued to look in the bag for some paper, and he said to me, "Do you need some paper?" I know it was easy to figure out what I might have been looking for, but he would also later put a short story he'd written in my binder. After the course I went to give that guy back his pen but he was gone. I didn't even see him leave, nor did I see him put this story in my binder.

I didn't know about the story until a few days later when I was looking at some of my notes and that's when I discovered it. It took me a bit to figure out why he put it in my binder, or why he was even there. He was sent there for me, I thought, only because what he wrote was real deep and it all made sense. It has everything to do with my challenges in writing this book and I've added it just below.

Why does opportunity knock so often?
OP KNOCKS
Faced with a mirror and a vision,
people are armed and ready to fight,
fight for success, fight for money, fight for life.
There is a sound that is heard when the vision meets the mirror
and the connection is most permanent, what is it ?
KNOCK
Not three times, and not from the back end of a ruined car,
It is the sound of victory,
as one thought is placed in the front of your mind
And the often old, useless,
pointless ones are pushed over the imagined cliff,
Through the glass door, out of the locked cell or into the abyss.
KNOCK!
Thanks

Back when I was selling cocaine, I had my hands on some hot booze. One of the bottles was Alberta Springs Sipping Whiskey, and it had the year I was born on it so I kept it all those years for a special occasion. One night I had a friend over at the house, which I seldom did anymore. I had this bottle in one of the washroom cabinets, and I had just picked up a bottle of Percocet.

I could see from the couch that when Marcus was in the kitchen he was being very quiet before he went to the washroom. I got up and looked in the kitchen cabinet where my pills were, and noticed that the bottle was moved. I looked in it and sure enough there was about ten of them missing. I put the bottle in thc drawer and sat back down. Marcus came out and went for that cabinet again. I could see his arm reaching for the door and now he saw that they were gone. Now he knew that I knew he'd taken some, and he couldn't get his shoes on quick enough, telling me he had to go. By the time I got up to see him out the door he was already in his van. I went and checked the bathroom, and sure enough he had cracked that bottle I had been saving for twenty-two years. Like I said, when you really look at your friends, there are only about five of them you can trust and rely on, the rest are just users.

2011

When Laura and I had split up, and she bought her new house, I told her she was in over her head. She was crying to me that she had no money, and that someone else was going to help her put a grow-op in her basement. I decided to help her only because I knew my daughter would take the brunt of it all with Laura not having any money. I had some people build her grow show for her, and I taught her everything I knew. She was doing well, and now I was finding out that she was leaving my daughter home alone til two o'clock in the morning by herself. So here's my daughter home alone at ten years old, and a grow show in the basement just waiting to be robbed. I was no angel, but I never left my daughter home alone.

I tried to work with Laura on this but she just told me to fuck off and don't call her house anymore. I tried again the next day and got the same response. So I had no choice but to call the cops. I had to call the cops because Laura had custody of Chevelle, so if I called child services I would have had to battle in court, and that would have taken years. I needed her out of that house now.

I had to tell the cops that Laura had a grow op in the house, and that she was leaving my daughter in the house by herself. I told the cop I had on the phone that I was calling from Richmond, and I was heading to her house which was about an hour and a half away. It was about 1 p.m., and I told the cop that when I got there about 2:30 p.m. I was going to kick in the door and grab my daughter. I wasn't going to let another night go by. I didn't want to take a chance on my daughter being left alone and have some guy break in at night and rob the grow show. They told me that I couldn't go to the house and do this, but I told them that no matter what, I was getting my daughter tonight. It just didn't feel right to call the cops even when I needed them because I was a criminal myself. The cops apparently already had a rap sheet on her house from other complaints and were just waiting for an excuse to go there. I was never a good father, doing the things I did, but I guess if I had been better I wouldn't have these lessons to share with you.

They (child services and the cops) showed up at Laura's house, and when Laura answered the door she told them to get the hell off her property because they didn't have a warrant. It was lucky that Chevelle was at her friend's house and didn't have to witness this. The social worker knocked on the door again and told Laura she had two options. One, she could let them in so they could see that the house was safe for Chevelle , or two, she could hand over the child. Laura told them I could have Chevelle, so the social worker then called me and said I could go and pick up my daughter at her friend's house as she would be staying with me. Chevelle was pretty upset with me because I took her from her mother, but it was the right thing to do. She did tell me that she would never forgive me for doing this, but I knew in time she would when she understood.

Laura changed her tune the next day because she does love her daughter. I told the childcare worker that Laura said stupid thing's all the time because she has a short fuse, and that she would change her mind really fast. I think Laura just snapped because she was at the end of her rope. Working afternoons at her regular job and cleaning houses through the day, she was done raising kids. She had the grow show removed, and five days later she let the cops in for a walk around. Everything was cleaned out and I handed over Chevelle, only because she did have legal custody and the childcare worker told me that now I would have to go to court to get that changed.

Without money coming in, and facing depression over detox from the Oxycontin, I tried to kill myself for the last time. I was now claiming bankruptcy and the bailiffs had come and taken my truck. I had no credit, and my house was gone too, It was time to get the hell out of here, I thought.

My other Grandpa was in long-term care and wouldn't be driving his car anymore. At 91 years of age that was probably for the best, and he decided to give me his car. I had it parked in the garage. I cut up the garden hose into three pieces and taped them together so they would fit nice and snug in the tail pipe. I had it all set up to go ahead with this that night when I realized I didn't have that much gas in the tank. I didn't want to fuck this up again. I pulled the hose out of the window and tail pipe and went to get $10 in gas with some change I had. By this time I'd had some time to think about what I was going to do and put it on the back burner. It wasn't my time to go just yet.

My little brother had given me a sealed envelope some time earlier with all the information on his assets, and what to do if something were to happen to him. Even with all the hell that I had gone through in my life, I never opened it up. I tried to end my life three times instead of opening the envelope to find out where his money was. The only thing I stole during my addiction period was a few pills out of my dealer's ziplock bag when he wasn't looking. The only thing.

I got a call from the mortgage holder's lawyer about my house, and he told me the bank wanted me out by the end of the month. I started to panic because now, with no place to live, I thought I would be pushing a shopping cart.

While I was trying to figure everything out my dealer was telling me that if I tried Valium I would never go back to Oxycontin. I took his advice and tried some. I went home and swallowed them, and started to make my Grandmother's chocolate sauce. While I waited for the sauce to heat up I laid down on the couch. I woke up with the house so full of smoke you could have cut it with a knife. I ran into the kitchen and threw the pot outside off the back balcony. That was the end of the Valium. In the house where I was raised, three times I came home drunk and used the deep fryer only to wake up with the house full of smoke, so you think I'd have learned my lesson about leaving something on in the kitchen and having a nap. I've learned it now… it took four times but I've finally got it.

I got my shit together with the help of Suboxone, and managed to stay somewhat sane so I could find an apartment in Pitt Meadows. For the first time in a long time I wasn't involved in crime, and I felt I could rest with no worries. I always thought that my life wasn't my fault because I was born with a learning disorder and weak eye, but they say you pick your life and your parents before you're born, and I now believe this. So all of this was my fault, until I learned later that someone else had made this life for me. Knowing that everything happens for a reason, my life all started to make sense.

The first day I saw my counsellor I was telling her that when I was at my worst, while living at the house on that acre, I wanted to pack up some clothes and head to Field, where I had spent a few of my younger years, and stay there. She then asked me what my first memory was as a child, and that if I could draw a picture of it, what would it look like. I started to tell her about the time when my Mom was pushing me in the buggy and she was wearing her blue fur coat, and that it must have been October because it was cool outside and there were no leaves on the trees.

As I was telling her this I started to cry. She asked me why I was crying and I didn't know, but she did. She told me that it was because I'd felt safe, for that was a time when my Mom fed me, rocked me to sleep, burped me when needed, and that meant it was the last time I felt secure, and after that, my life started to take a fall. It all made sense to me then after all these years, of my attraction for moving there. I'd felt safe there. Amazing.

What a special person this counsellor is, and I'd only gone to see her because the childcare worker who was at my house dealing with the removal of my child had told me I needed to talk to a woman counsellor rather than the guy that I was seeing from time to time. I had told this to the male counsellor, and he said there must be a reason for this so he set me up with a new counsellor, Ramona.

Now that I was in the apartment and working on my recovery, I called up Barney, who I owed money to, because I thought he was a friend. Now this was the same person that I had collected that $37,000 for, as well as the same guy who had taken off in that houseboat while we were fishing. I called him up and asked if he could meet me in the morning for breakfast. I only wanted to be a man and explain what had happened to me, and that I hoped he could understand. He said for me to call him in the morning and hung up the phone, but didn't realize his phone wasn't hung up properly. I heard him bash me to the guy he was with, calling me a cockroach, pill popper drug addict, and that I owed him money. This is a perfect example of the people in the world who haven't learned a thing.

If I was the man I was five years ago I would have hopped in my car, crashed through his pearly gates, kicked open his front door and smashed his face in without batting an eye. I'm not that person any more, thank God. I did so much for him. I got him the money that was owed to him, sent my meter guy over to his house to slow down his meter, had an electric company drop everything they were doing and head over to his place to put up a pole in his yard so he could get the power back on. I did this so he wouldn't lose his crop and I hooked him up with an Italian that I had met who had an excavating outfit.

I never asked for anything from him, and he blew me off for $1,200 I owed him. How pathetic. I hope he gets it, because I believe you keep coming back here until you learn your lessons, and then you keep moving on to a new life until you have learned everything that you are supposed to do. Only then is it off to heaven, but not before. If he ever apologizes to me, it would be a sign that maybe he's getting it, but he has a lot of work to do for himself.

I borrowed money from a few people that I could never pay back. That was so hard for me to swallow because I was always someone you could rely on. I will pay those debts off if it is the last thing I do.

My Mom had now sold her house in Penticton and moved back to Pitt Meadows in a mobile home park. I would go to my Mom's trailer park for a swim in the morning, and then sit in the sauna to help with the withdrawals. They could last for months, or even a year or two. They even come back from time to time just to see if you've changed your mind or not. This was the biggest fight of my life. I would sit in the sauna with the lights off, and I couldn't figure out why I did this. I always had the pool to myself, as well as the sauna, as people seldom used it. I finally realized that this reminded me of the quiet place I would sit, think and cry, in that hole I'd dug in the backyard way back when, and I started to cry. It was then I knew this was the reason I turned the lights off.

At noon on May 19, 2011, I decided to take a walk down the trail that went alongside the Katzie slough. I used to drive over the slough just about every day, and now saw that it was just a ditch. I parked the car at the entrance to the path that was made as part of the project for the bridge. I locked up the car and headed down that path in search of the spot where I'd once fished. I would pass by several dirt paths that headed towards the slough that people made to get access to it. I managed to pick the right path at one point, and ended up at the spot where I had once fished, but didn't realize this until a short time later. I came to the edge of the slough and tried to figure out what direction I had to go in search for my spot. In my sandals, climbing over prickles, I tried to find my way through the bush in search for that very spot.

Before I headed down the path from the first location I noticed this golden eagle flying overhead and talking to me. He landed on different trees, and when he landed on a branch from which he couldn't see me, he flew to another one so I was in his sights. I thought this was odd, but eventually realized what he was trying to tell me a few minutes later. I came to a dead end down this one trail and headed back, telling myself that there wasn't a chance in hell I was going to find my old fishing hole because everything had changed. I made my way back to where I'd originally started. This eagle continued to talk to me while flying from tree to tree. I was now standing on a fallen cottonwood tree. I looked over to the other side and noticed this large shady area, and it turned out to be a stump from a tree that had blown over in a storm. I then looked to my right and saw a tee in the slough, just like where I used to fish, I knew then this was the spot.

I'd fished under that tree that had now fallen because it would shade that part of the slough, keeping it cool. I looked up at the eagle again, and while I was watching him tears started to run down my face. I knew then what he was trying to tell me. He was telling me that I had to do something about this slough or he wouldn't have a home. I found this slough and it gave me that safe place I needed to get through the horrible childhood I was still living in. I knew that it was my turn to pay back the favour and I will.

This bird was crying to me for help just like I did when I was a little boy, and it was there for me. As I made my promise to do whatever it took to get that slough back to how it was thirty-five years ago, I headed back to the trail and came across this photographer. I asked him if he was taking pictures of the eagle and he told me that it was a camcorder, and that he was going to film the two birds that were there. He told me that there were two of them over there and they had a nest way up the tree. At first I found it odd that the only nest along the slough in that area was just above the spot where I had once fished, but they were there to send me a message. I hope one day we can do something to bring back the slough I once fished, so it can give another child a safe place to go.

The problem there is that the farmers are using fertilizers and it has made the slough vegetation grow very fast, and I don't think the fish really like fertilizer. Would you? The natives told me that they also re-routed the slough so they could put in this subdivision, and now instead of the slough running into the Fraser river, the river runs into the slough, which means the slough water doesn't go anywhere, it just sits there stagnant. Now we've got this Stephen Harper who wants to screw things up even worse, and he belongs to the church?

I met this girl through a friend of mine and decided to give it a try. After five weeks I started to put things together. She was actually helping her ex-boyfriend with his heroin problem, and was trying to get him into treatment. I told her to come and get the things she had at my place. It was then she said that this thing we had going on was just bad timing. I never did sleep with her, probably a good thing. If she had just been honest with me I would have helped that guy myself, even though I had my own fight on my hands.

THE PSYCHIC

On March 31, 2010 I had an appointment with Debbie the psychic. I wanted to know if I was on the right track or not. As it turned out, I was. I first told her when I walked in, "You better tell me something good because I'm ready to jump in front of a train." She told me that she couldn't read me if I had a closed mind, and I said, "Don't worry, I'm ready for this."

She told me that I had finally figured out why I was here, and that I was put here to experience all the hell this world has brought me in order to write a book so that the whole world could learn from my mistakes. She said I had done a fantastic job. She said I have a message to send to the world. Hearing this made everything that had happened to me all make sense.

I asked her why I have an attraction to the Coliseum in Rome. I feel that I must have fought there because how did I know how to fight. She did say that I did fight in that era, although she couldn't tell me if I had fought in the Coliseum or not. She then showed me the card she'd been holding before I asked her this, of a Roman man wearing the clothes that they did in that era. She said I could have died a horrible death, and I told her that I felt this as well.

I also asked her why my back is so sensitive, because I have this cringe inside me when someone pats me on the back. She told me it was because in Egyptian days I would move rocks around with ropes crossing over my back that left permanent scars. In addition, I was also whipped. This could be the reason why I can work all day in the heat without wanting anything to drink. I would have something to drink if it were there, but I would never stop what I was doing to go get a drink.

She told me that back in 1890-1910, in the criminal underground, I was one of the men that everyone went to for assistance. It was my job to get things done, and that's who I am today. She's right, because everyone would phone me when they had a problem or needed something. She said that I am at the end of my healing, and I have to finish or none of this will happen, and then she looked into my eyes with this serious look and said, "YOU HAVE TO FINISH THIS." She told me that I have two more lives to come back and learn, and I think I know what I have to learn.

1: I have a sewer mouth on me and there aren't enough bars of soap in the world to wash my mouth out, like my Mom used to. I can do the right thing and not swear, but deep down I like it too much because to me, they are only words, it's what they mean that is bad. I guess I will learn my lesson one day.

2: I like muscle cars, even though I know they are bad for the environment. They're something I don't need, but want.

3. I am very judgemental before I know anything about a person. I judge them on their work ethics, body language and attitude. These are things that will have to wait because I have bigger problems to fix, the world.

She told me that I should dream large because I have no idea what this book is going to do for me. I won't have any luck with the first two publishers, but the third one will make me successful, and I won't have to worry about a thing because they will look after me and protect me from the evil business world. She sees that not only will the book be successful, but actually visualized the story happening, maybe a movie.

She also said that I did leave my body to see the other side, as I said, and she called it something but I can't remember what. My younger brother needs to read my book before it hits the shelf because it will shake him up pretty good, and he needs time to process what I have written. I met the publisher in seven and a half months, and he is walking me through everything as a friend so I can publish it myself. I met this guy when I was making that Canucks jersey, so there has to be some truth to the game, otherwise I would have never met him.

She told me that a life is like a house, and that I had stored so much in the attic I couldn't even close the door to keep everything inside all those years. Writing this book is finally giving me the freedom and the rest that I need. She also said that there is a planet moving outside the Milky Way that has 1,000 times more energy than any other planet in the solar system. This is why we are having all these earthquakes and tsunamis. She said there would be two more mishaps that are devastating, before December 21, 2012, and that she felt sorry for those people. On the day in question everybody was going to feel a type of energy that they never felt before. That will be the start of the earth turning around for the better.

Isn't it odd that hopefully this book will be on the shelf in 2012? I asked if it was a coincidence that this book was going to be out in 2012, and before I finished saying this she was shaking her head, no, so I guess I'm right on schedule. She said I will meet my soulmate in two years, and she won't leave my side, nor does she see a divorce or anything close. Maybe I will walk down that aisle after all. If this happens I would like to have that wedding singer from the movie, *The Hangover,* and I would love to have the wedding in the Coliseum, but I think I'm asking too much. A guy at work said to me just after he broke up with his girlfriend, "How can I ever love someone else when I love myself so much?" I was just howling. That's what I thought about myself, but not anymore. However, it's still funny.

Why is it always the guys who have to make the first move? Is it because we have a penis? I mean, if you like a guy, girls, just ask him out. What's the big deal? You might never see that guy again, and there's nothing worse than saying, "Damn, I wish I would have said something."

Debbie also said that she doesn't get to read people like me that often. I asked her what that meant. She told me that there are five words used in the universe and I don't use any of them. I call a spade a spade and I say what I am going to do and do what I say. As well, I put people in their place, even if the truth hurts. People might think that I'm an ass-hole, but that's because they don't get it. President Lincoln always said: "What makes a great leader is one that speaks from the heart, even if the other person doesn't like it."

I have to tell you that I don't care for people who go out of their way to do little or nothing to get their pay cheque. This just makes my blood boil, and I have been pulled into the office more than once for picking on those ones because they all go crying to management so they can hide behind all the politics there. That's okay, because if you are scared to get a blister on your hands, or even some dirt on your work cloths, you're not a man at all.

If you take the time to think about why things happen to you with an open mind, you can always figure it out because there is no such thing as luck or coincidence.

I also asked the psychic if I would ever see my Grandfather again, she chuckled, and said, "Oh yeah, he will be waiting for you." I can hardly wait. Everybody has a higher power, you just need to find it so you will have somebody to talk to. She also said that HE never leaves my side, and has saved my ass I don't know how many times. I think I have a good idea when those times where. My

My grandfather the boxer, who fought in the 'paperweight' division, and was champion in 1925. Yes, there was such a thing. He's in the B.C. Sports Hall of Fame now.

Grandfather sold newspapers back in the twenties and had to fight for his corner in order to sell papers. He had the busiest corner in Vancouver, at the corner of East Hastings and Main Street. My aunt told me that a Chinese gang tried to take the corner away from him twice, and he got stabbed in the back in one of the brawls, but he stood his ground and never gave that corner up.

He also worked for the same railroad as I do, and the first day on the job I was approached by all the old guy's with stories of him. His parents were from Sicily so he was a little hot headed. They told me that when he would get mad at somebody, you could hear him yelling from one end of the shop to the other. Afterwards, he'd walk away to cool off for twenty minutes, then he would come back and apologize. But once he'd apologized to the man he would start getting pissed off and begin yelling at him again. Everybody there loved him for who he was. They had great respect for him, and I guess it had something to do with the fact he was a tough son of a bitch. His name was Ignacio, which means "fiery one." The name Ignacio came from Ignatius, a Christian saint who was arrested and sent to die in the coliseum with two lions.

My Aunt and I actually got my Grandpa into the B.C. Sports Hall of Fame. He was a paperweight champion in 1925 in Vancouver. They had never heard of such a class. You can go to BC Place, and you will see his little display. I'm honoured he was my grandfather.

LESSONS LEARNED

When you think of people losing their child in a horrible crime, there are no words to experience the feeling those parents have unless it happens to you. This is a learning lesson for those parents, for reasons unknown, but believe me people there is a happy afterlife. That girl I saw during my brief look into the afterlife was having the time of her life, and so are your lost ones, so stop ruining the rest of your life blaming yourself, because it wasn't your fault. It's all part of the plan, and when it's your time, they will be greeting you with open arms.

At my funeral the only song I want them to play is, *Another One Bites The Dust,* and I will be looking down, laughing my head off. I think that place I visited was a place where we go until it is time for us to live our next life, and when our lives are all lived, and we've learned everything, it's off to heaven we go.

I know people from other religions and they steal, lie and are greedy because they think if they go to church on Sundays everything will be good, because they're going to heaven anyway. I believe it doesn't work like that because think about it, do you think heaven needs any greedy ones fucking that place up? A person at my place of work, who carried a Bible and read it every day, was actually the biggest thief we had. To add insult to injury, he was the padre in his church every Sunday.

Many people pray to God, which is fine, but I think what is really happening, is he is praying for us. We have to change. Remember what I say: "Nothing changes if nothing changes."

There is only one religion, and that is LEARNING. There aren't a bunch of virgins waiting up there if you kill people. I know, because that feeling I had when I saw the afterlife, it was greater than any sexual experience I have ever had, so you're not going to want sex anyway.

If everybody thinks there are different gods, and they all want you to do different things, don't you think they would all be fighting with one other up there for what they believe in? There's only one religion and you're living it. Mother Teresa doesn't need to come back here anymore because she didn't care what she ate, where she lived, or what she wore. All she did was help people. If you're someone who has a bad disease like cancer or any other death-causing illness, you should not be sad, for this is your lesson, and it's the same for someone with a disability. You should be proud of yourself, full of pride, good pride, because you have accomplished what you were supposed to experience, for this is your lesson.

If you have lost a loved one you will be reunited with them soon enough. This is just a place to learn things, your body is just something to carry your soul around in. You need to carry on in your life for that is your lesson… lesson presented until learned. If your life seems torn apart you need to find a way to move on, and then you can help other people who have experienced what you went through. For now, you are a teacher, as am I.

There was a girl who wanted to raise $300 for the water shortage in Africa before her ninth birthday. Before she reached that birthday, however, she died in a car accident. By August 29, 2011 they had over a million dollars in donations for her cause. I believe that girl was put here to start this fund, and once she had it started they took her back so people could see the importance of her cause. It is horrible that it takes someone's life in order to open our eyes. I asked the psychic if I was right about this and she said I was.

Buddhist Saying:

You die when you are complete, the cause of your death is not the reason you have died.

Rose Kennedy wrote a famous quote:

"It has been said; 'Time heals all wounds.' I don't agree. The wounds remain. In time the mind, protecting its sanity, covers them with scar tissue and the pain lessens. But it is never gone."

After all this, it still wasn't enough for me to get help, at least not yet. When I worked the weekends I would get a lunch from Quiznos. One time, while I was ordering my sandwich, I noticed this plant in the corner was almost dead. The plant was as dry as could be, so I told the lady and she said, "I know." So I said, "If you know, why don't you water it." I paid for my lunch and told her to grab a glass, and she watered the plant. The next week when I went in for lunch there was a large red flower growing out of the top. I said to the lady, "Do you see?" and she replied, "Yes, I do," and I told her, "That's how it works."

I knew that I'd started to change because of what happened at Tim Horton's one morning. While I was waiting in line at the drive through, a guy in a truck pushed in line ahead of me. This only happened because they had two lanes going through the drive through which merged into one. As this truck pulled ahead of me I looked at the old lady he had with him and gave her the look like, "What the hell are you guys doing? Wait your turn!" He didn't back up so I opened the door and had one foot on the pavement because I was going to teach this guy a lesson. What stopped me was I could see myself pulling him out of his truck and kicking the hell out of him while this old lady watched the whole thing, and then me getting taken away by the cops. Now by this point I'd learned that would have been the wrong thing to do, so I changed my mind. Man, was that hard to do, but I did it. If he only knew how lucky he was that day.

My uncle was a photographer for the Canucks back in 1982 when they had that run to the Stanley Cup. In 1983 he gave us kids a Moe Lemay hockey stick, which had all the signatures from the players on it, as well as one of the goalie sticks John Garrett used during the series with the Islanders. The stick with the signatures got broken one day when one of the guys on our team at school needed a stick. We were living down the street from the high school so I told him to go to my house, and just inside the door were a bunch of sticks. I didn't realize he'd grabbed the stick with all the signatures, and he broke it during the game so it went into the garbage, but I hung onto the goalie stick for a long time. My younger brother Jason had built a games room down in his basement so I gave him the stick to hang on the wall. It was lucky that I gave it to him, because several months before I'd talked to the manager of a new pub in Maple Ridge called "Don Cherry Sports Bar & Grill," and I'd asked if he would like to hang the stick up in the bar. He said he would love to use the stick, and to drop it off when he was there. It's a good thing I didn't, because that bar burned down a few months after I gave it to my brother.

As usual, things started to get worse again with my addiction. I was sitting at home by myself watching the Stanley Cup final, and no one had called me that day to watch the game. After watching the riot I made the call for help. Three days later I was in a treatment centre in Kamloops called Sage.

Just before I left to go to Sage my Aunt gave me my Grandfather's wallet, which she'd kept all these years, and the next day I lost mine. I eventually found mine, but I think that was my Grandfather telling me he was there with me.

I had to call Laura up again to tell her that I was going back into treatment. That was one thing she never complained about, me going out of town to clean up and leaving her to look after Chevelle. I think it was because she was there herself at one time, and could relate to the addiction.

When I arrived at Sage, I was sitting in the media room where the presentations took place, and on the wall was a list of the twelve steps of NA. As I read the steps, I realized that I had already written about them in my book without knowing what they really were.

The Twelve Steps

- *"We admitted that we were powerless over our addiction, that our lives had become unmanageable."*
- *"We came to believe that a Power greater than ourselves could restore us to sanity."*
- *"We made a decision to turn our will and our lives over to the care of God as we understood Him."*
- *"We made a searching and fearless moral inventory of ourselves."*
- *"We admitted to God, to ourselves, and to another human being the exact nature of our wrongs."*
- *"We were entirely ready to have God remove all these defects of character."*
- *"We humbly asked Him to remove our shortcomings."*
- *"We made a list of all persons we had harmed, and became willing to make amends to them all."*
- *"We made direct amends to such people wherever possible, except when to do so would injure them or others*
- *"We continued to take personal inventory and when we were wrong promptly admitted it."*
- *"We sought through prayer and meditation to improve our conscious contact with God as we understood Him, praying only for knowledge of His will for us and the power to carry that out."*
- *"Having had a spiritual awakening as a result of these steps, we tried to carry this message to addicts, and to practice these principles in all our affairs.*

ACCEPTANCE

Acceptance is like shaving, it gets harder the longer you wait.

While I was in Sage, I called Laura and actually thanked her for all the hell she'd put me through, and told her that I forgave her. I had to go through everything in that relationship to understand how I was supposed to treat a woman. If I hadn't, the rest of my life would have been lonely, and when I eventually did meet my soulmate I would have thrown that out the window too. But now that's not going to happen.

I am not a marriage counsellor, but I don't need to be one because I think that I have been through enough to know the right things to do. I think that it is important to communicate with one another. If you leave your toothbrush by the sink and she wants you to put it in the drawer, then she needs to tell you it bothers her, or one day, when all these little things get to her, she's going to snap. The same goes with her. If she stops doing the things you like her to do, well you need to tell her, and she needs to do it or you're going to battle. I mean, let's face it guys, as long as we get action we're happy, so put that toothbrush in the drawer.

Whenever you think you're not getting enough in the bedroom, just think of a bull moose. A cow moose only goes into heat for a 24-hour period once a year. That's why a bull will follow that cow around for week's waiting, and will fight any other bull that wants to get in there. "Fuck off buddy, she's mine." So when you think you've got the shit end of the stick, just keep thinking that it could be worse. That moose was born without any hand's so he's the one with the shit end of the stick. Talk about blue balls.

There is no reason for us to let ourselves go, other than getting old. That just means you might have to work a little harder to try and keep the way you looked when you met.

I think it's important to bring home little gifts occasionally, just to remind ourselves how much we mean to each other, even if it's only a favourite chocolate bar. When you come home with that gift, make sure you tell your spouse you couldn't live your life without that person, and that they mean the world to you.

I think most of the time people get married for all the wrong reasons, which means it's inevitably headed for disaster. The guy is standing up there with a hard on because he is getting laid for a week straight in

Mexico on his honeymoon, and the girl is happy she finally is wearing that rock on her finger and the white dress she has always wanted, but they don't even pay any attention to the words "til death do us part." If you aren't prepared to do this, maybe it's not a good idea for you to get married.

I mean, there are problems in any marriage which can lead to divorce, and maybe that is the best answer, but separating because you argue all the time is the weak way out. If you move in with a best friend you have known your whole life, chances are within the first couple of months you'll want to slit that person's throat. Does that make him or her a bad person? No. It's not easy trying to live together; it's a battle. The question is, are you ready for the battle or not?

Oh yeah, never walk by her in the kitchen or hallway without running your hand across her back. But don't grope, the caress means more.

The second day at Sage I was up at five in the morning and went for a walk to the front of the compound to get a glimpse of Kamloops Lake. While I was standing there above the highway, a five-ton Wonder Bread truck drove by, and then I could hear this ting-ting sound coming down the road. I looked and noticed the sound was coming from a pop can rolling right down the middle of the road, not veering a bit to the left or right. Once it got to where I was standing, it spun in my direction and came to a stop. I was trying to figure out what this meant and it could be one of two things. One, it was telling me how disrespectful people are to throw cans out the window of their vehicle, or two, it was my Grandfather telling me that he was there with me. Maybe it was both.

I would play cribbage with the night-man on shift at Sage, and one night he told me a story about a friend of his. He said this friend knew someone who'd died of alcohol abuse. He told me his friend had had a dream about this guy, but it wasn't quite a dream; he said it was real. He saw him living the same life he'd lived here on earth and nothing had changed. I had already thought that if I didn't clean up and finish this book, I was going to come back here and live this life over again, or live it somewhere else until I got it.

It's just like school, where if you fail a grade you don't move forward, you do it all over again until you get it right. So all you people out there who have a problem, you need to address it or your misery will never end. You can do it, we have it in all of us, you just need to find it. I did. Remember, lesson presented until learned.

We pray to God for help, but we have to help ourselves. That's why he gave us will, because without it we wouldn't learn a thing. If he can fix what you ask him for, why is the whole world so fucked? We have to fix this mess ourselves. I prayed for sleep for months and never got it. Why? Because if I could have gotten eight hours of sleep I wouldn't have learned the hell this addiction had brought me, and I would just keep using. Right? You have to learn your lesson no matter how many times it takes you.

Life is like a game of cribbage; it seems utterly pointless in the beginning to move that peg only one hole, but in the end, it's what counts.

While up at my Mom's house trying to detox, before treatment, we watched Michael Jackson's *This Is It* video. After watching the video a song came on which I can't remember the name of, but he was talking about how he loved the earth, the plants, the trees, and so on. After watching that video I felt an attraction, or energy, coming from him that I can't describe. I think it has something to do with the fact that I like those same things, and this book I'm writing is hopefully going to change the way people think about our planet and themselves. He knows I am trying to change things for the good, so therefore he's right at my side.

So having told you this, while up at Sage, and in our group, the Michael Jackson song *Man in the Mirror* came into discussion. I went back to my room to write down in my notebook, "Man in the Mirror," so I could listen to the words at a later date, to understand what they were talking about in group. I opened my book to write the title down and there was his name, written in my book already. I had written down his name days before, but was this for a reason? I feel there are bigger things I have to accomplish in this world, and one of them is doing my part in cleaning up the environment.

We all had to make a collage while I was in Sage, and I went and grabbed a few magazines from the three boxes they had on the floor. All the magazines had horoscopes in them, and the very first one I read stated the following:

The ferocious beasts that surround you are not quite paper tiger's, they have fur, teeth and they can roar. Still, they are not alive. They are stuffed dummies playing tape-recorded noises at intervals. It's the same with the obstacles you are up against. They are fairly solid, but if you kick them, they will collapse. Be respectful, but don't be afraid of anyone or anything. Emotionally, you are stronger than the forces you are up against.

I cut this one out and used it for my collage.

We also had to write a poem or a letter to our addiction saying good-bye, and then we were to burn it in the fire pit we had out back. I wrote a poem, but I made sure I made a copy of it before I burned it. I wasn't supposed to keep it because we were saying goodbye to our addiction and that was the whole purpose of the exercise, but I wanted it to share with you:

OXY

I was out having fun and met a new friend,
His name was Oxycontin. He would be my friend til the end.
I never met someone like him, he would never leave my side,
Little did I know, it would be a hell of a ride.
He always made happy, I felt like I was 20.

We only started to argue, as soon as I turned 40.
This might sound sick and funny, I could almost call him "Honey",
Until he started to take all my bloody money.
We broke up once before, back in 2008,
But we got back together, he would teach me to hate.
I would distance myself, from everyone close,
To hang out with my friend, and then lose my house.
I had a nice car which I loved and enjoyed,
He took that car too, I was blind to the void.
It was getting so bad, I almost lost my soul,
I came back to earth with meaning and goal.
I started to write, with my friend at my side,
I got to the end, got hold of my pride.
As I was watching TV, seeing the Stanley cup riot,
I knew then I was crazy, everything all went quiet.
I picked up the phone, as this needed to end,
I packed up some clothes, said goodbye to my friend.

The day I left Sage I was heading to the mall up the road. I was there a few times during my stay, but I ended up getting lost trying to find it. I did a complete circle and ended up at the set of lights facing the treatment centre. I knew this was telling me that I wasn't ready to leave even though I had to get back because I couldn't afford (financially) to stay any longer. However, I knew emotionally I couldn't afford to leave.

Before I left, they'd told me how important it was to go to a meeting as soon as I got home. I told them that I was picking my daughter up as soon as I got into town, and that I would go to a meeting the next day. I picked my daughter up at her house and Laura answered the door, so right away I felt anxiety. I told my daughter that I had a lot of running around to do the next morning, so she wanted to stay at her friend's house that night instead. Now I was alone again, and I used before I even got home.

One Saturday while at work I started to have some withdrawals, and had nothing to stop them. Since the yard was slow I took the work truck and headed up the road to the clinic. I went and got a prescription for Tylenol 3's, then I went and filled the prescription and took all twenty of them. About forty-five minutes later my body was red just like I was sunburned, and my eyes were swollen. I had to book off, and told my mate that I must have eaten something bad. I was so itchy that when I got home I had to put cold towels all down my legs to stop the itching. It did get rid of the withdrawals, but that wasn't worth it. I will never do that again, stupid idiot.

On August 1, 2011, I stopped at the full serve gas station. I got out and asked where the water was, and the jockey pointed to a cooler next to the building. As he was putting gas into my car I walked over and started to talk to him. He was telling me how tired he was because he was working two jobs. He drove a dump truck through the day and pumped gas at night. I asked why the two jobs, and he told me his best friend was getting married. I asked if he was paying for the wedding, and he said no, but they were are going on a three-week cruise and it was costing him and his girlfriend $7,000 each. He was the groom's best man, but he was paying for his vacation all on his own, so he had to come up with $14,000 for the trip, plus spending money for when they were on the boat. This guy had started his second job back in April, and the wedding wasn't until the next August. Do you see what he was doing for his friend? Getting a second job for eighteen months so he could be there for his friend. Now, I know what you're thinking: Why did the groom pick a trip for three weeks knowing that it would be very expensive, and that his best man needed to work a year and a half just to be there for him? I do think that's a little ignorant unless he plans on paying for everyone, but, oh well, it's not my wedding. The point I am trying to get across is what that one guy was willing to do for his best friend, and that's what friends are made of. Good for you buddy. ENJOY.

It was the first week in September, and when I picked up Chevelle from school on the Friday she wanted to go to a game store in the Zellers mall to see if they had a game she wanted. She had told me that she'd had a Kool-Aid stand set up outside her house the day before in hopes of making enough money to buy this game that she wanted. Once we were at the store she found the game. She had a purse with her that I had never seen before, and told me that she had about $15 in it from sales at the Kool-Aid stand. The game was $30 and she had $15 in change. As she put her purse on the counter to see if she had enough money, it was breaking me apart to tell her I didn't have the rest of the money to give her for the game because I was broke. But I wasn't broke, I just needed the money I had in my pocket to get myself a pill for that day. So here is my little girl bringing her purse to the mall because she wanted to feel like a big girl, and to see the disappointed look on her face when I told her I didn't have the money to help her get the game. You know, we are supposed to reward our children for doing something good, but instead I was being selfish and thinking more about myself than my own daughter. You would think that would make a guy think enough is enough, and it was time to quit, but that didn't happen, not until later.

Chevelle doesn't like the fact that I live in an apartment where they don't allow pets. I did promise her that I hope I could eventually move to a place where she can keep a horse. It's a promise that I plan to keep.

My older brother always thinks he has it tougher than anyone. One day at work he came up to me and said, "Three weeks." He was going to the hospital so they could run some tests on him because they couldn't find out what was wrong with him, and by joking about three weeks he meant they might tell him he had three weeks to live. I said to him that it could be worse, and he said "Yeah, it could be four weeks." We both had a good laugh over that one, but you just have to pick up your socks and carry on whatever the case may be.

I was at work one day, and I started to laugh because I was thinking of the times I would dance like Linus on the Peanuts Christmas special when I was drunk. That night my brother came over to my apartment with this little Charlie Brown tree that he'd found at a joke shop. Once I'd put it together it played that same song I would dance to… just like the Christmas special. It's weird how things happen like that, considering he had never been to my place before.

I was on the phone with my Mother December 17th and, jokingly told her that I'd had enough, and I was standing on the Port Mann bridge. We both started to laugh, and then I told her that, given my luck, when I jumped, there would be a tug boat towing a barge full of feathers passing under. Just a couple of weeks ago I was talking to Allan on the phone and he jokingly told me he was ready to kill himself. I told him not to ask me for advice about how to do it because I wasn't that good at it. It's pretty bad that I was telling him the truth.

A girl that I was in treatment with caught her seven-year-old boy playing the game *Grand Theft Auto*. When she told me that there were hookers in the game, and how to play it, I just about shit myself. What kind of a government do we have that allows this shit on the shelf for sale? Kids nowadays want to be just like the guy in the game. You never see a kid mowing somebody's lawn anymore, nor do you see them jumping a ramp with their bikes. Instead we have all the retired people starting businesses, cutting lawns. That's crazy.

If these game companies want to make games, make games like *Mother Earth* and *Addiction*. *Mother Earth* could be about picking up garbage and planting trees, and helping to clean up the environment for points, while *Addiction* –for the older kids – would be about seeing what drugs and alcohol can do to you. Show them a family falling apart because the Dad is a drunk and loses his job and friends. Show them ending up in the street. The kids could get points for putting them in treatment, and if they don't sign on every day, the guy relapses and they lose points. Even show what cocaine does, heroin and every other drug, so it will scare the hell out of them. Then they will understand before it's too late.

I would like to see all the gangs in North America play basketball, and put a tournament together so they can all learn to play together. If we don't learn to forgive and forget, we might as well bury our head between our legs and kiss our ass goodbye because that is where we are going to end up. They would learn more about themselves in that tournament than they have in their whole lives. It is important that you make your kids learn how to earn an honest dollar, because if you don't, the first opportunity they have for easy money (illegal or not), they're more likely to take that road. There are 130 gangs in B.C. alone, what about the rest of the world? If you just put your kids downstairs in the basement playing video games until they graduate, what the hell are they going to learn?

I would also like to see a charity golf tournament, the Garage Sale Open. They could have someone go around to garage sales and buy up the old golf sets. You only get one small bucket of balls to warm up with, and then it's off to the races. Let's see what they shoot then. If it ever happens, I would love to play with John Daly.

I thought that it would be cool if Metallica made a CD called "Nursery Rhymes" dedicated to the children's hospital, and sing songs like Humpty Dumpty, Little Miss Muffit, Jack and Jill etc. I bet it would be number one on the charts.

I remember one weekend when they came to Vancouver, I rented a five-ton moving van, put my furniture in the back, and about 20 of us road downtown and partied in the back. Now they have limo buses.

One of my favourite songs is *Crazy Train* by Ozzy Osborne. I always listened to the song, but not the lyrics, but then I discovered he says, "Maybe it's not too late, to learn how to love and forget how to hate… You got to listen to my words." This song is about thirty years old and we still don't listen. Also, *When We Stand Together* by Nickelback. Most of us watch the video and nod our heads in agreement but do nothing to help.

Here's an example of how lazy we are: you can actually get a remote control for your car stereo. Really? Is it that much work to lift your arm and push the button?

I think that if you look at prisoners in a different way, you might be able to see what I see. There are so many people locked up in prison, that when they get out they will never have the chance to pay back society. So many people are in prison for such little crimes that when they finally get out, how are they going to be able to find work? If they can't find work, what do you think their only option is? CRIME. Even though some have committed horrible crimes, some of them feel remorse for what they did and they never get a second chance.

Why doesn't the government start up a program for them to get a trade ticket when released? Maybe a company called KON Construction. Teach them how to build houses, bridges, schools, hospitals etc. KON Construction can now do all the building for the government. The government would save money by not having them locked up, and it would have its own construction company building everything for them, and would give the ex-prisoners jobs. Have the chosen ones finish their time with a chip that is implanted in their bodies somewhere so the government knows where they are, every step they take, and if they make one bad move, back to prison they go.

Now I know that the world's economy is having some trouble, and the people who aren't in prison are having a hard enough time looking for work, but it's just a thought, maybe for a later date. Can't people see that some of these prisoners could do more good outside, going to schools to talk to kids to teach them wrong from right? This would be better than keeping them locked up, not doing anyone any good, and costing the government a fortune. Maybe this is the government's lesson. Stop ruining their souls.

I don't think doing time for a crime makes you pay for what you did. Only when someone feels remorse for what they did have they finally paid the price, for now they have learned their lesson.

Just another crazy incident to tell you about that happened at work on January 25, 2012 before I wrap this thing up. I was working out in the trainyard and my apprentice saw something unusual under this semi-trailer. He told me to back up, he got out of the truck and went to get it. This thing looked like a bomb because it had two canisters taped together, and wires hanging out the top. He was shaking the device up and down telling me that he didn't think anything was inside, so I told him to throw it in the back of the truck. We did our work and headed back to the lunch room for coffee. At 3 p.m. I said to the guys sitting at the lunch table that the kid and I had found this thing that looked like a bomb. One of the guy's said, "Bring it in." I went and got it out of the back of the truck, and when I walked into the lunch room I was swinging it around by the wires. There were a few looks of concern I can tell you, so I brought it into the health and safety office to show them.

With surprised looks on their faces, they asked me what the hell it was? I said, "I don't know, it looks like a bomb." They immediately told me to go put it outside by the tracks out of the way, and called the rail police. The car foreman was called, and he evacuated all of us to the shop. Everyone was saying, "Magri, couldn't you have waited until 3:50 p.m. before you brought that thing in?" We were off at 4 p.m. What it turned out to be was a device the maintenance department used for checking signals, and I guess it fell out of one of their trucks. The shop foreman was pretty shaken up because I put the bomb outside right in the very spot where we are supposed to meet if there is an emergency. Work was going to take a statement from me, but I went and signed an "Admittance of Guilt" form and got a warning. Lesson learned. Don't swing bombs around in the lunch room.

The "bomb."

I used every day after I got out of Sage, other than a couple of days when I couldn't find any pills, right up til January 6, 2012. My new clean day, my day to keep. There are demons and devils here on Earth, and I have fought them all. Several demons have come to fight me, and the second to last time they came I told them to bring some friends with them next time. Well did they ever. They brought their whole army, and finally, after twelve years, I've won the war. I beat them up so bad there is no way they are going to come back. It took me forty-two years to cage up the monster, but he is always there in case I need him, because I wear the key to the lock around my neck.

I'm clean and still crazy, but I wish you all the best.

EVERYTHING HAPPENS FOR A REASON

Sometimes people come into your life and you just know they're meant to be there. They serve some sort of purpose. Maybe to teach you a lesson, or help you figure out who you are, or who you want to become. You never know who these people may be; your roommate, your neighbour, a long lost friend, a lover, or even a complete stranger. Someone who, when you lock eyes with them, you know that very moment that they will affect your life in some profound way. Sometimes, things happen to you, and at the time they seem horrible, painful and unfair, but upon reflection you realize that without overcoming those obstacles you would never have realized your potential strength, willpower and heart.

Everything happens for a reason; nothing happens by chance, or by means of good or bad luck. Illness, injury, love, lost moments, true greatness and sheer stupidity all occur to test the limits of the soul. Without these small tests, whether they are events, illnesses or relationships, life would be like a smooth-paved, straight, flat road to nowhere; safe and comfortable, but dull and utterly pointless.

The people you meet who affect your life – your successes and downfalls – are the ones that create who you are; even the bad experiences can be learned from. Inevitably those lessons are the hardest, and probably the most important ones. If someone hurts you, betrays you, or breaks your heart, forgive them for they have helped you to learn about trust, and the importance of being cautious about who you open your heart to. If someone loves you, you love them back unconditionally, not only because they love you, but because they are teaching you to love. They're opening your heart and eyes to things you would have never seen or felt without them.

Make every day count, appreciate every moment and take from it everything you possibly can, for you may never be able to experience it again.

Talk to people you have never talked to before and actually listen, let yourself fall in love, break free and set your sights high.

You can make of your life anything you wish.

Create your own life, and then go out and live it.

I wish you all the best in your endeavours as well as struggles in life.

Have a fighting spirit and never hesitate to get back in the struggle.

AUTHOR UNKNOWN

LESSONS I HAVE LEARNED

About Bullying

All the terror I went through in this life all started from the bullying I was subjected to. Sitting in that hole that I made in the backyard was a safe place for me, but it also made me this angry monster because of all the thoughts I would have about people harming me.

Once I learned some self-confidence the monster was released, and inside sat this huge heart. When I would lose my temper all the abuse came out tenfold, making me very angry. I get tired of seeing this bullying problem in newspapers and on the news, and still there is nothing done. Not only was I bullied, but I turned into a bully myself.

Seeing all the kids these days with their cell phones makes me sick. I think to myself how many kids are being tortured by the terrible things these kids text to one another, and all the suicide attempts that happen because of it. Every kid I see walking down the street with their head down, I wonder if it was because of some cruel text that someone sent to them, and I wonder whether they are as lonely as I was. Something has to change.

With all the problems that I had growing up, hurting people was my way of getting the attention I desperately wanted, and my way of making me feel like I was finally getting even. One thing for sure, the problems definitely shaped my character. The lessons that are good I'm keeping, and the ones that are bad I'm slowly washing away.

<u>Revenge</u>: *"To exact retribution for, or for the sake of; to inflict injury for or on account of, in order to gratify one's bitter feelings. Vengeance involves the idea of wrathful retribution, more or less just, and may arise from no personal feeling, but may be taken solely for another's wrong."*

About Being Selfish

I was even selfish while hunting. I poached, and killed an animal without playing by the rules and regulations of hunting. I know it's easy to say: "Well, who makes the rules?" But someone has to, because if there weren't any rules, there wouldn't be any animals left. I have learned to play by the rules, and if I can't do this I haven't learned a thing.

About Being A Criminal

All you twenty-year-olds out there who think crime pays – well, does it look like it does? Where do you think the phrase, "CRIME DOESN'T PAY" comes from?

I always wanted to drive a Rolls Royce and wear a Rolex watch. In spite of all the money I have had in my life, I now drive a 1986 Chrysler LeBaron, and I don't have any credit. Does that sound like crime pays to you?

If you can believe it, I'm happier now than I was when I was living that criminal life, so what does this tell you? If you like dodging bullets, and enjoy seeing your friends get shot and killed, keep doing what you're doing. That's all the advice I have for you.

About Family

There is nothing more important than family. I look back on what kind of parent I was to my stepkids, as well as to my own daughter. I never did like the house full of kids. I felt like it was taking away my time. How selfish a man I was, and if I had to do it all over again that house would always be full of kids. I look back at my own Dad and remember he never seemed to have time for me, and I was hurt because of it.

The words to the song "Cat's In The Cradle" by Harry Chapin seemed like they were written just for me, but the truth of the matter is, they apply to many parents. Looking back at my relationship with my Dad, it turns out there wasn't one, and the relationship I have with my kids is distant. And it kills me.

I was at the dentist the other day and he told me that he was too busy to play golf with his son. We all have to make time, whatever the cost, or why did we have kids in the first place? You don't want to be the cat in the cradle do you? I did a lot of damage in my relationships with my kids, and I still don't know how I can fix it. All I can say is that I can only be there for them if they come knocking, and hope to have a closer relationship with them in the future.

My daughter is only eleven and we seem to be drifting apart. All I think about is how is she going to make it in this cruel world? I love you kids more than you think, and a day doesn't go by that I don't feel remorse for the way I raised you. I should have been there for you. I'm here now.

About Relationships

Relationships have always been a tough one for me. I look back on my last one and shake my head at all the wrong things I did. I treated Laura so badly right from the start that it's no wonder she did the things she did. Every time she came close to me I would push her away, showing no affection whatsoever. I feel terrible for that, because I think she took the fall for all the mistreatment that I received in earlier relationships. I mean, I never kissed her once before leaving for work or when I would come home, not once. I pushed her away when she wanted to cuddle up to me in bed for a bit of affection, but all I wanted was to get my rocks off.

Here's a good example of how I was: One night, a partner of mine dropped by the house with some ecstasy. I took one pill and waited for it to work because he had told me it would make me all touchy-feely. Well, when one didn't do anything I took another, and then another, until I'd downed all seven of them in a two-hour period… and I still didn't want to cuddle. How sick is that, that I figured pills would enable me to show affection to my woman.

A friend told me, "A happy wife is a happy life" – and I called him a fucking little wimp and an idiot. Now I am single with nothing to my name, and he's still married and just bought himself a new truck and trailer so he can take the family camping. Who's the idiot?

The next serious relationship I get into, she can come home all excited with a plan to move to Iceland, live in an igloo and eat off the land, and I will get off the couch and tell her, "I'll go get some boxes to start packing."

Again, a day doesn't go by when I don't look back on how I was, and realize how sorry I feel now. We were two different people, and the relationship wouldn't have worked anyway, but that was hardly a reason to treat her like a piece of shit. I am not going to take all the blame here, because it takes two to tango, and right from the start she knew I wasn't affectionate. She kept looking for something I couldn't provide, but that doesn't mean I couldn't have tried to be a decent human being.

In the present situation, Laura's influence has certainly affected the relationship I have with my daughter, and that's another tragedy.

I still don't have closure from the break-up, only because I keep thinking to myself how different things would have been had I just been a more caring man. At least if I'd been that man and it hadn't worked out, I wouldn't have these squirrels of regret racing in my head. I still hang onto those resentments to this day.

About Dating After Addiction

With all that I learned in that relationship, I have to admit I'm a bit afraid to try out the new me. There have been a few girls interested since I got myself clean, but the chemistry isn't there. The new me says it's not fair to date a girl when there isn't any chemistry just to get a piece of tail.

Besides, it isn't a good idea to date in your first year of recovery anyway, and now I can see why. That's all you need, to find someone good in the sack who then dumps your ass, because the first thing you'll do is making a run to whatever it was that fixed your pain before, be it drugs or alcohol. Now you know why God gave you two hands and allowed the invention of hand cream. Probably too much information, eh?

When the counselor in the treatment centre told me that I wasn't allowed to date for the first year, I asked him, "What am I supposed to do, go home and beat it like it owes me money? Like that's going to happen!" Well, I have been clean for eight months and haven't been laid for over a year. I guess he was right. I see other couples holding hands, and see that they are happy, and that's what I want. I don't think I will ever be that super affectionate guy, it's just not in me, but I will try my best. I have to… and want to.

About Anger Management

I am trying to learn to keep my mouth shut about things that don't really matter. For instance, it used to piss me off when I would hold the door open for someone and they wouldn't say thank you. You see, you're opening that door for your own sense of having done something polite and helpful, and if they can't be bothered to be polite in return, well, that's their problem. In other words, don't do something for someone if you are expecting something back… it rarely pays off.

One thing I learned in anger management was, if you act in anger nothing good comes from it. Keep your cool. This has been one of the hardest lessons of all for me. I'm not going to lie to you now, my blood still boils about things like the way this world is run, with so many wrong decisions. Man does that piss me off. But I guess it's more the frustration about the whole thing that gets me going. I mean you can barely see the mountains anymore for the pollution, and we want to put another pipeline in. That oil company can take that pipeline and shove it right up their ass.

The following is a quote by writer Jessie Worobey:

Human nature is a funny thing. People can let go of the hope that a loved one will recover from a terminal disease. But, they never lose hope that they will win the jackpot.

About Detoxification and Kicking Addiction

The first step in recovery is admitting you are powerless over our addiction. I really didn't have a hard time with this… I knew I was a mess, but the problem with me trying to get help was that I really didn't care about life anymore. My boss called me into the office one day because I was missing a lot of time and losing weight. I sat down and he asked me what was going on. I started to ball my eyes out, and told him that I was really messed up on these painkillers. He told me that I had better get some help before the company made me go get help. I left work early and called up Family Assistance.

First, I had to go to detox, and then I was scheduled to go into treatment after that. While I was in detox I had to see the doctor. I asked him when I would receive my medication and he told me soon. I walked out and headed to the TV room, to wait for my meds. After waiting about an hour and a half they finally gave me my meds, and I thought to myself, "If this is how things roll here, I'm out of here."

I mean, why did the doctor wait so long to give me my meds when I was just starting to go into withdrawal? The counselor asked me to just wait a little longer until the meds started to kick in, but I said, "Nope, I'm out of here." For Christ's sake, I almost killed myself falling asleep at the wheel on the way home. I just wasn't ready to pack things in yet, I needed to torture myself a little further.

The councillor at the detox centre called my Mom and said that I had left, and now my family was getting worried about me. You get so selfish when you're an addict; you don't give a fuck about anybody but yourself. Like I said earlier, I eventually went to two treatment centres before I finally got it, but over the last four years I've put my family and friends through hell, and I couldn't be the father I only dreamed about being.

The hell I went through myself with the withdrawals was a sight to see. They don't tell you on TV, so I will tell you how it happens. The withdrawals start with body cramps, sweats, diarrhea, runny nose, depression and, worst of all, insomnia. The first time I tried to quit I was on the floor for four days, rolling around with cramps, and my legs vibrating so bad I couldn't sit still. After four days of that, I didn't sleep for six weeks. My doctor gave me sleep medication that would knock out a horse, but I was still awake and driving around at one in the morning. I caved, and would do the same thing over and over, trying to quit.

The first treatment centre I attended, I went in after another six weeks of no sleep. I eventually could sleep through the night, but when I woke up it felt like I'd only had ten minutes of rest. This is happening because your brain is poisoned from the drugs, and it is working overtime trying to mend the damage so your natural opiates can start to work again. It has been almost twelve months clean for me now, and I still don't sleep very well.

The hell that I have experienced through this recovery process has given me the most important tool to use. It's called, "Play the tape." This means that you look at your life as a tape featuring the hell that you went through. Whenever the thought of using again comes to mind, I play the tape. I'm never going down that road again. Lesson learned.

I have a lot to learn about recovery, I'm just getting started. I chose to go to Alcoholics Anonymous meetings only because more sobriety seems to be there in those rooms. I still don't understand why there is NA and AA, when addiction is addiction. If they put both together as one, the message would be a lot stronger because the rooms would be much bigger. You don't win a war with five soldiers.

One guy in my meetings offered to go over the Big Book of Alcoholics Anonymous with me, and do all the steps because I'd only done the first three steps in treatment, and I feel I haven't finished the program. He tells me it will stop all the squirrels in my head.

Not only did this addiction almost take my life, it sure knew how to take all my money. Now I sit bankrupt, and I have to learn how to make a living off a pay cheque. That's okay, because the greed for money just about killed me, and I sure have a lot less worries. But trying to get off the drugs and that wealthy lifestyle was hard, especially when I quit them both at the same time.

It is amazing how you notice nature when you are clean. It's like having earplugs in for seven years, and when you remove them you realize how things really sound. Being sick for the last twelve years, I forgot how beautiful nature really is. The smell of the pollen in the spring from the cottonwood trees is amazing. We have these trees at my work, and I actually went up to one of them, crushed the small pods on the branches, and stood there smelling my hands.

Just to notice the raindrops in the puddles, and to see the ripples, is amazing. To watch the leaves fall from the trees, or how clouds form in the sky is something remarkable. We are so SELFISH in our greedy world that we don't even pay any attention to how beautiful our planet really is, and how disrespectful we are in ruining it with greed.

On the previous page is a picture that was painted on the side of one of the rail cars at work; it shows what we will be wearing one day. SCARY.

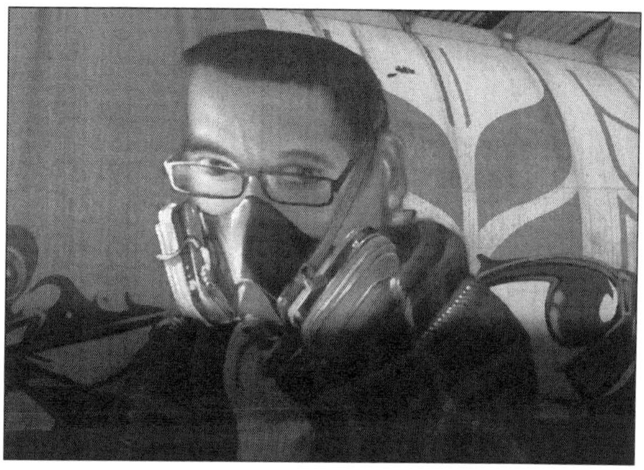

Art on a railway car

One thing is for sure, it took everything I had to open that door to the treatment centre. When I opened the door so much happened in my head at that moment. A huge part of my ego had fallen, and I realized I was no different from all the addicts I used to call names, but I also felt like a failure. For the longest time I'd thought there was nothing in the world that could ever bring me to my knees besides a bank manager.

This feeling only stuck around for about a day until I started to get comfortable in a place I didn't trust. After the second day I knew I had made the right decision. It takes a lot of courage to open that door, but once you do, it's a huge relief. For a person with any addiction it is such an accomplishment. You are finally realizing you can't do it yourself. There are people who have done it themselves, but the problem with that is they don't have the tools to fight off the demons when they come fighting back.

Here are a few quotes I heard in meetings, but the one about the trout is mine.

• *Not going to NA or AA meetings is like being a trout that has not seen a worm on a hook for a couple of years – as soon as he sees one, he takes it, and now he is hooked again.*

• *Never look back at your dark past. That's why the windshield is so big in your car, and the rear view mirror is so small.*

• *Oxycontin gave me the wings to fly, and later it took away the sky.*

• *It's funny how a dog is smarter than us, because if you feed a dog something and it pukes, it won't take it again, but we sure will.*

• *Addiction is like making love to an 800-pound gorilla, it will tear you apart and only let you go when it wants to.*

• *They always say to take one day at a time, because if you don't it's like having one foot on yesterday and the other foot on tomorrow, which means you're pissing all over today.*

I think the reason why we addicts are always chasing that comfort feeling is because we are trying to fill a void – maybe something that happened when you were young, or in the recent past. I would look at other addicts before as crack heads or drunks, but now I realize that I am no different.

In 1900 the Germans invented OxyCodone. By 1912 they'd realized how addictive it really was, so this bullshit about doctors needing to be educated on how addictive it is is a crock of shit. If a doctor doesn't know this, he/she shouldn't be one. It's the doctors that need to be punished. I heard that the company that makes this drug made seven billion dollars last year by getting rich ruining peoples' lives. When is this ever going to stop?

About Starting Over

After all that I have been through, and having been pegged by people a certain way for so long, everybody seems to look at me differently today. So many people know everything about my past relationships and drug problems that it makes me feel like I am in prison. I feel embarrassed. I know so many people that, wherever I go, I run into somebody who knows me, and the first thing they ask is, "Are you staying out of trouble?"

I have done a lot of damage living here, and while I have mended many fences I know I need to leave and start a new life somewhere else. Pitt Meadows will always be that very special place in my heart. Of all the places in the world, I came here to learn all these lessons. I grew up in this special place

October used to be my favorite time of year, with all the leaves changing colour and the itch to go hunting growing strong. Now, when that time of year comes, I feel anxiety, because when I used to go hunting while in that long relationship with Laura, I would always come home to a cold household. Being away for a week in the bush gave me a lot of time to think about how wrong our relationship was, and what I was going to do to try to fix it once I got back, but it never happened. I always hoped that I could come home to Laura and find that she wanted the change as well. All I came home to was guilt written all over her face. I don't know what it is going to take to feel excited again for the fall season, but hopefully the Big Book (AA/NA text) will help.

When I was that popular person with the phone ringing off the hook, I would think to myself, "Is this ever going to end? Is my life ever going to be at a slower pace?" Now my phone never rings. I sometimes think to myself, "Was living that crazy life worth it?" I now drive around at night by myself and think, just like I did in that hole in the back yard.

It is lonely for me now because I just don't think I am ready for a relationship and, with my life having turned around, it gets pretty quiet. My life now is so full of hurt and emptiness I don't know what to do next. I was out driving around one night, and was talking to my Grandpa (my guardian angel), and I said to him, "I sure would rather be up there with you, than be here in this tarnished world." I then quickly changed my tune and said; "How selfish could I be if I made that decision and left this world behind, without doing my part to help turn it around?"

About Trying To Make Sense of My Past

I think what made this book happen was a visit to a psychic. I'd already figured out that I was supposed to write this book, but having her tell me that I had to finish it gave me the strength to do so. Thanks Debbie.

I started writing this book in September of 2010 while going through the whole process of addiction and recovery. You should have read the first few drafts. The first draft I called everybody names because I was isolating myself, and hating the world and everyone in it. After the first few drafts, I finally realized that the problem was me, so I started to write differently. After fourteen drafts my task is finally complete, and now I have to find some happiness. I feel like I have been torn apart by a hurricane, and now the only thing I have left is debris.

Today people see the new me and they might think I'm this happy guy because, when they are around me, I always make them laugh. The truth of the matter is, they don't even know me. The sad guy on the cover, that's who I really am.

Being the crazy person I was, and having an addiction, I was left out of many get-togethers that some people had. With all the humor that I brought to the workplace, the advice I would give the guys on how to fix their homes, and the help that I would offer, it's sad to say I was only ever invited to a few of their parties. This one guy always invited me to his annual barbeque, but because he lived way over in North Vancouver (an hour away) I never did attend. But he always asked me. Thanks, Eric.

I was going to a Canucks game with my brother one night, as he had a box suite one year that he shared with a bunch of guys. As we approached the arena I ran into Eric going to the game himself. I asked him if he would like to come up to the box suite, and his eyes lit up, and he said, "I would love to." That night he had the best seat in the house. That's what friends are made of.

With regard to the psychic, by listening to everything she told me it gave me a belief that there is a power greater than ourselves. When she told me about some of my past lives I had a sense of relief because now I knew why I was the way I was. After my hour of reading was up, and I was walking out the door, the psychic asked if she could hug me. Now, because she asked my permission for this, I realized she doesn't just hug anybody, so why me? Is it because she knows of all the hardships I went through, or is it because I have bigger things to accomplish? I didn't ask. You have to figure these things out for yourself; after all, it is why we are here, isn't it?

After Debbie told me about a few of my past lives, I can almost see what I would have been like.

I can see myself during my time in the criminal underground, running in and out of establishments making deals, selling stolen items and wearing one of those newsboy hats pulled down over my eyes. I was always on the move and didn't attend many functions, only the ones that I had to attend to show my respect. I feel I didn't live very long. Look at this life. This one was harder. It had to be because I didn't learn my lesson the last time.

When I was a slave, involved in building the pyramids, I can also see them handing me some water, and me telling the supervisor to give it to someone else who needed it more than me. I can then see the supervisors giving me a little more respect for doing this, as my boss does for me today.

As a gladiator, I can see myself standing at the entrance to the arena of the Coliseum, and the place going nuts cheering for me. No different from when people would come outside from the night clubs to watch me fight and cheer me on, like they did the night at Rogers arena during that basketball game. I've known many guys over the years who liked to fight as well, but they would always get their asses kicked. I did lose a few times, but only because I made a few mistakes… like being too drunk. I'm not trying to blow my ego out of proportion here, but I can see myself being the attraction they all waited for.

About Letting People Help You

I sure learned that you need to give people a second chance, or as many as it takes, for them to figure themselves out. My place of employment is such a huge example of this. There was nowhere else in the world I could have worked where they would have put up with me all these years. In my opinion, my boss was put here to protect me through my journey, so I would have a career and an income when it was all over.

You tell me different given that just a short time ago I hurt my back at work, and my phone rang. It was my boss. He asked if I was all right and then said, "Don't you be taking those pills." If he didn't give a shit about me that phone wouldn't have rung. I will be around for you buddy, whenever you need me, til the day I die… or until you croak, whichever comes first. Ha ha.

It took my grade three teacher a full year of working with me before I could put a line through my mistakes and rewrite the word instead of pulling the page out and re-writing the whole thing. Life, at times, gets very frustrating for me because I'm a perfectionist. It's because people don't give a shit about how they do things. They say things like, "Good enough." If you say this, you know you could do better, so why the hell didn't you take the time to do things right. I don't know how many times I've shown up for work and torn apart something the last guy tried to fix, mainly because I had to rebuild it all because he didn't give a shit what it looked like. I love to try to figure out what the problem is and come up with the proper solution. I take it as a challenge, and when I figure it out it's a huge accomplishment for me. So take the time and do things right the first time.

When I mention to people I went to see this psychic in town, quite often they know who I am talking about. I was in treatment and met someone who went to school with her, and he said that Debbie has an amazing gift, and is so right about everything. People line up in the rain just to book a time to see her, and sometimes it is many months later before they can get in, so what does that tell you about her gift?

Throughout this book I refer to the people in heaven as a collective "they". It has been said by some psychics that when you die, it is like a celebration for the first three weeks, then you apparently go in front of a board and this is where you see your past lives. You are then told what you learned and didn't learn. Then it is up to you to decide when the time is right for you to come back and learn more lessons. It has also been said that it normally takes 80-120 years to come back. I obviously returned way before that time, more like sixty years for me. I was born in 1968, and I apparently worked in the criminal underground at the turn of the century so I returned quite quickly. I don't know why.

If I had written this book five years ago, I would have dedicated the book to a few people and told the rest of you to go fuck yourself, but now that I finally know what life is about, I dedicate this book to the world. We're in this mess together.

There is one thing for sure, if it wasn't for my Mom helping me with this book I don't think it would have been possible. She has so much patience, and she is probably the only one who would have put up with me. We definitely had our battles over this thing, but any fights were definitely because of me. I like things done yesterday, and I like things done a certain way, and it is almost a miracle I finished this. Thankfully, my Mom is organized and patient. She had to photocopy everything and file it to keep me on track, but because that slowed things down, it would drive me nuts. I'm good at a lot of things, but not paperwork. Luckily she has always been there for me. Love you Mom. I love my Dad as well, and I hate the feeling that he is almost dead to me, but I can't change him; he has to change himself.

About Expressing Yourself

The venerable Bede, who died in 735 A.D., was the most knowledgeable man of his day. Learning, teaching, and writing, he said, had always been his keenest joys. What he learned of Rome, probably from German pilgrims, convinced him that the gigantic arena must be the symbol of Rome's strength and greatness, bound up not only with the future of Rome, but with the whole of human history.

A poem was translated 1,000 years later, and this is what it said:

While stands the Coliseum, Rome shall stand,
When falls the Coliseum, Rome shall fall,
And when Rome falls, the world.

I didn't know that my grandfather was a poet until I told my aunt that I had written two poems myself. It was then she told me that he was quite a poet himself. This one I wrote in the treatment centre in Vancouver, October 2008.

MY LIFE

I was always in trouble, right from the start,
I did poorly in school, as I wasn't that smart.
I got bugged and bullied; I thought it was all right,
My Dad always told me, it was okay that I fight.
At eighteen years old, using booze and cocaine,
I thought I was normal but purely insane.
Later in life the charges would come,
I ended up in jail, it wasn't much fun.
I realized my life was a site to be seen,
I started all over and tried to stay clean.

Then one day, as I was out having fun,
I had an idea to take a pill from a friend.
I knew this was wrong, as it started to rain,
But who really cares, it took care of the pain.
It made me feel that I was young again,
But little did I know it would bring me more shame.
As the years started to pass, one by one,
I lost touch with myself and everyone.
I tried to quit, but it was really too hard,
I said, what the hell, I might as well go hard.
I convinced myself, what could it hurt,
It can only do damage to my liver and heart.
I tried to read to my beautiful daughter,
But she smacked me in the face,
all she wanted was her father.
As I laid in the tub, shaking and crying,
I asked myself if it's time to start caring.
The seek for help was far in the distance,
But I took control with pain and persistence.
I looked for a friend that I desperately needed,
He took my hand and said let's get started.
Here I am with the help that I need,
I have my life back with no need for greed.

About Taking Responsibility For Your Actions

If you look up the seven deadly sins, there is actually an eighth. It is called acedia. Which means: "spiritual laziness" and "listless, not caring" – a sin all on its own. I believe that some people are put here to get rich, and then turn around and help other people. That's their lesson. In order to learn their lesson they have to get rid of all their greed before they can move on. If you don't do this maybe you will experience your next life in a poor country so you will understand how they feel – finding food at the dump and drinking out of a ditch... that's if you can find one. Which of the following sins do you need to work on?

THE SEVEN DEADLY SINS.

Lust • Gluttony • Greed • Sloth
• Wrath • Envy • Pride

Bob Wilson, co- founder of AA wrote this,

> *"The inspiration of power, wealth, and prestige are tearing this world apart as never before."*

ABOUT STRANGE COINCIDENCES (BUT THERE ARE NO COINCIDENCES)

Here is something you should check out. One day at work, I Googled my name. There were two other Scott Magris who came up, one in California and the other in New York. The one that lives in New York is a musician, and he has a song called *Bullycide*. What are the chances of that, a guy with the same name as me writing a song about being bullied in school. Check it out.

ABOUT BEING HONEST

I don't think I have to tell you at this point that I have learned to be honest. Look at what I wrote.

THE TWO WOLVES

One evening an old Cherokee told his grandson about a battle that goes on inside all people.

He said, my son, the battle is between two "wolves "inside us all.

one's evil.

It is anger, envy, jealousy, sorrow, regret, greed, arrogance, self-pity, guilt, resentment, inferiority, lies, false pride, superiority, and ego.

the other is good.

It is joy, peace, love, hope, serenity, humility, kindness, benevolence, empathy, generosity, truth, compassion, and faith.

The grandson thought about it for a minute and then asked his grandfather which wolf wins? The old Cherokee simply replied, the one you feed.

The following was written in the book, *GO AHEAD* by R.L. Duke Tirschel

SURVIVAL

Every morning when that sun comes up, a rabbit wakes up

and knows it must run faster than the fastest fox or it will be killed.

Every morning when the sun comes up a fox wakes up

and knows it must run faster than the slowest rabbit or it will starve.

It doesn't matter if you are a fox or a rabbit...

when the sun comes up in the morning, you better be running.

A quote from Darrren Stanoffsky, friend and co-worker:

"Those who have nothing would be happy with something. Those who have something are not happy unless they have everything."

Albert Einstein: *"The only source of knowledge is experience."*

You know that saying people use, "You're going to hell." Well I hate to tell you, but you're already here... but that's only because we've made it that way. There might be another hell out there, but I hope not because this one's enough.

It's interesting that whenever some people have a near-death experience, they say they have seen the light. You don't ever hear anyone say they saw little red men and flames, do you? Hell to me is just a place of challenges. If you were from another galaxy and went to see a travel agent because you were thinking of taking your family on a trip to planet Earth, and you wanted to know a little bit about it, this is what she would tell you. "That planet is full of crime, drug and alcohol addiction, killings, war, greed, and everyone has about 250 toxins in their body. There's hate, disrespect, dishonesty, and the pollution is so bad that they're slowly choking themselves from the greed for oil."

Be honest, would you come here for a visit? I think not. What does that tell us? I think oil was here for us to find, but it got totally out of control and now our test is to turn things around. We can't change the world until we change ourselves. Nothing changes if nothing changes. And it starts with being honest about ourselves and what we're doing.

They say money makes the world go around, but in fact it's ruining it. If you kick the snot out of your friend all week and then ask him to help you move on the weekend, do you think he will show up? I doubt it. We kick the snot out of mother nature and the environment every week, but when we go camping for the weekend it's there for us. That's a pretty good friend if you ask me.

One thing is for sure I learned to respect the environment and Mother Nature. I know driving around at night just to think isn't helping the environment, but in a way it is. I think of ways to fix it while I'm driving. The best time to do this is at dawn or dusk. Find a road somewhere were there is little traffic and listen to music like Fleetwood Mac, Bob Seger and the song "Redemption day" by Sheryl Crow. Drive with your window down just enough that the wind blows past your ear. When each song ends, and has that pause before the next one plays, it will feel like a breath of fresh air you don't get anymore. While this is all happening look at the smog against the mountains and think about any wrongs you are doing in your life, what you do for money, family, love, and everything I have just written to you about, and see if you can come up with any changes you need to make. I want you to try this by yourself, give me this at least.

We all have to learn to live through hell before we can live in heaven.

We all have spiritual guidance through our journey, but sometimes we are too strong to accept it. It is then that we will learn our toughest lessons of all. Sometimes we get back on track, and sometimes we don't; it is those lessons we have to come back and learn until we get them right. If we keep helping the ones who don't want to help themselves, they will never learn.

WE ALL HAVE HISTORY

My counsellor Ramona asked me if she could do a report on my life, and I agreed. The following are some of the findings she saw in me, word for word.

Scott grew up in the emotionally cool atmosphere of the Magri household. He was an industrious child, and very helpful to his mother around the house, being naturally tidy and responsible. He was generally obedient, but on occasions mischievous, even rebellious. His natural consideration of others, and his easy-going sense of humour, made him a good friend once he had learned to trust. Scott tried to please others, but it was [his brother] Jason who was the most successful at pleasing and making friends with easy charm. Scott was somewhat of a worrier, sensitive and easily hurt by unkind comments, when he could sulk; at those moments, his temper came through and he learned to defend himself in fights early. He could be persistent, even stubborn, when he felt he was right. Scott was self-reliant and independent, with high standards of right and wrong, often causing him to be critical of himself more than others do.

Scott enjoyed good physical health during childhood, with a perfect physique that served him well. However, his lazy eye (resulting in nicknames such as four-eyes, Magpie and others) and his ADHD resulted in a rambunctious academic career. He had no expectations of himself, and lived one day at a time.

In grade six, Scott was sexually assaulted by the uncle of a childhood friend, which thankfully, did not appear to leave behind any long-lasting effects.

Scott only had two close friends, but that was all that he needed; he was not small-minded or envious of others. He knew he did not fit in because of his glasses and poor grades in school, but refused to change himself in order to meet anybody else's expectations, and accepted that his hyperactivity was often difficult for others to be around. When his classmates bullied him, he withdrew to forts he constructed so he would have a safe place to think.

Came the momentous day when his father encouraged him to take up karate, and he found he excelled at martial arts, turning his whole life around. Scott learned that he could get attention through fighting, and could avenge himself too. In a short time, he had gone from a sad, somewhat isolated young man, to one who would scrap if even mildly provoked; his solution had become a problem because now he was always in fights.

Scott's father retired as a railroad manager after working many years. In his own mind he loved his children, but was unable to express his feelings openly. To Scott's perception he was emotionally unavailable, a cold, hard man who was not easy to live with. Try as he might, Scott couldn't please him, or even feel acceptable in his eyes, leaving Scott feeling that he did not belong. From him, Scott learned to stick up for himself, and to hide his inner sensitivity behind a high and well-defended wall.

SOME FINAL THOUGHTS

The following is Ramona's summation of how I look at the world.

- When I feel I don't belong, I feel "less than" and unacceptable. Helpless? Unlovable?
- I have to do something special in order to feel that I belong/am acceptable.
- When I am acknowledged, I feel as if I belong; it feels good but doesn't happen enough.
- Only when everyone is smiling are things all right.
- The world is an uncertain place where innocent people can get hurt.
- Even when I have finally struggled to the top, I can easily lose my place.
- The consequences of losing my place can be bloody.
- Men are not always trustworthy to do the right thing.
- Women have to pick up the pieces and make sure that things get done properly.
- While I feel pain deeply, it is safer to keep it to myself. [No pain response]
- I can look to women to defend/protect me; when they approve of me, I feel accepted.
- My actions must be well thought out before I can act.
- I am not afraid to act in haste, if needs be, but sometimes the ending can be unexpected and unpleasant.
- I have the confidence to depend on myself/my skills in a pinch.
- When threatened, I can return the aggression and beat them at their own game.
- Sometimes, when I have a lot on my plate, I can be overwhelmed by too many things demanding my attention, at the same time.

- Once I feel accepted, I can tolerate a lot of bad behaviour.
- Final Goal: To find my place in the world by leaving it a better place. I am not afraid to see that wrongs are righted and mistakes are fixed, no matter the cost.

TO MY DAUGHTER

I hope that you are old enough to understand when you have read this, because I know this book will be damaging for you to read sweetheart, but you have to understand that your Dad was here to do this task. He was also supposed to learn these lessons. It was important that I lived this life, and I hope that you can understand for I love you. I will always be here for you. Love Dad.

7857240R00187

Made in the USA
San Bernardino, CA
20 January 2014